INTERNATIONAL LAW

Making Human Dignity Central to International Human Rights Law

INTERNATIONAL LAW

Making Human Dignity Central to International Human Rights Law

A Critical Legal Argument

MATTHEW McMANUS

UNIVERSITY OF WALES PRESS
2019

www.uwp.co.uk

British Library CIP Data
A catalogue record for this book is available from the British Library.

ISBN 978-1-78683-464-5
eISBN 978-1-78683-465-2

Typeset by Marie Doherty
Printed by CPI Antony Rowe, Melksham

Dedicated to the Memory of Connor O'Callaghan
With Love and Friendship

Series Preface

We are delighted to introduce the first title in the University of Wales Press's *International Law* series. The series has been designed to capture dynamic and cutting-edge research in international law, with a strong focus on legal theory. It is supported by a distinguished Editorial Board, comprised of leading international law academics from around the world.

Matthew McManus's *Making Human Dignity Central to International Human Rights Law* draws on a rich intellectual history to put forward a compelling argument. This book develops a unique theory of the concept of dignity, which it then applies to international human rights law. In so doing, it analyses legal and moral philosophy, critical legal studies, and key practical concerns in international human rights law. The author does not shy away from examining controversial areas of practice, nor from critically appraising the work of some of the leading authors in the field. The sophisticated debut monograph that results will no doubt leave readers keen to explore the author's future writings.

This excellent book bodes very well for the future of this series, and we look forward to receiving many excellent proposals from scholars with an interest in theory and international law.

Professor Diane Marie Amann
University of Georgia
Professor Yvonne McDermott
Swansea University

June 2019

Contents

Acknowledgements

This book (my first) has roots that go back quite some way. The initial argument about human dignity and law has its roots in my doctoral thesis, which I began to work on seriously when I was in my mid-twenties. Having now hit the age of thirty, it has become clearer to me how many people are actually involved in supporting, guiding and criticizing an author before the text even goes to print. This disposition might have surprised my younger self, who spent a healthy chunk of his time sitting on his room-mate's couch, largely determined to ignore the world outside as much as possible. That is a rather odd attitude to take for someone concerned about human rights and law, which are inherently social phenomena of tremendous concern to millions around the globe. I hope that these acknowledgements can make up for such youthful apathy.

First, I need to thank those who guided my academic career from the start, and abetted me in the weird task of moving from undergraduate to professor via a thesis. This includes my high school teachers, Margie Barkley and Cameron Jones; and my undergraduate teachers at Carleton University, Dr Amy Bartholomew and Dr Ratna Rueban Balasubramaniam. I thank the Canadian Council of International Law for supporting my early interest in the subject. Special thanks are due to Dr Trevor Purvis, who supervised my undergraduate project and who remains a good friend and mentor to this day. Thank you to Kathleen at the National University of Ireland for her ongoing mentorship. Given my almost six years at York University, it is almost impossible to pin down who warrants gratitude. I thank the administrators and faculty of the Socio-Legal Programme there for their support and guidance – especially Dr Annie Bunting, who first encouraged me to go to York; Dr Nalini Persram, for guidance and kindness; Dena Demos, for her mentorship; and Dr Jay Goulding, for many interesting conversations (and not a few free drinks). I also thank my colleagues in the graduate programme – especially Mariful Alam, Ali Malik, Daniel Zenga and Emily Lockhart – for many fond memories. I thank my colleagues Christopher Satoor, Dylan DeJong, Erik Tate and Victor Hainagiu for even more good memories, and Paul Barnes for looking over early versions of this work. I thank the staff of *New Jurist* magazine, *Merion West*, *The McGill International Review*, *Entretextos* and the *Journal of Human Rights* for publishing early versions of these arguments that made their way into the manuscript. Where there is overlap between these earlier pieces and the manuscript, it has been reprinted with permission. A special thank-you goes to my supervisor, Dr Lesley Jacobs, for many years of patient guidance and assistance: I learnt a great deal from her. I thank my committee members, Dr Willem Maas and Dr Allan Hutchinson, and everyone else who looked at earlier iterations of the dissertation; Dr Yvonne McDermott Rees for her early assistance in having my manuscript proposal reviewed; and the staff working with the Committee for International Justice and Accountability who were my colleagues during the early proposal process. I thank you Plan Canada, Aden Earthworks, Chapters and many other employers for helping me to keep a roof over my head. I thank countless students at York University; Tec de Monterrey, who helped me to hone my ideas through years of teaching and is owed a great deal of gratitude for offering me my first academic position teaching politics and international relations; and our Director, Dr Juan Cruz.

Of course, the personal debts of an author are always more complex and difficult to define, but I would like to thank: Andrew Thorndyke, Shefali Sarna, Justin Unsworth, Taewook Kim, Stacey Freeman, Jeffrey Farncombe, James Bowden, Brendan Nickels, Tristan Bradley, Nolan Belleville, Sam Jowett, William Norman, Agnes-Barr Klouman, Lee Doucet, Rav Excel, Victor DeLaleu, Florian Plista, Carrie Duplessis, Lorne Williams, Nicholas Young, Landon Mattesz, Borna Radnik, Sara and Sparky. I also thank David Hollands for years of friendship and collaboration. I have surely missed out some people, so will simply express my gratitude to all my friends and associates who are not listed here. My thanks and much love to my fiancé, Marion Trejo, and, of course, to my family, without whom I would never have completed this work. This includes all the many (and growing) McLeods and McManuses out there: my grandmother Patsy; Meaghan and Matt; Emily and Chris and Finnegan; Adam and Kayla; my mother; and my father, who continues to read my work and comment on the poor grammar. Finally, I thank Connor O'Callaghan, to whom this book is dedicated and who, while I was preparing its final draft, passed away – far too young – in a tragic accident. His passing impacted all those who loved him, and he will be dearly missed.

1

Overview of the Project

Introduction

> In a world of democracies, in a world where the great projects that have set humanity on fire are the projects of the emancipation of individuals from entrenched social division and hierarchy; in such a world individuals must never be puppets or prisoners of the societies or cultures into which they have been born. *Roberto Unger*

In recent years, there has been an explosion of writing on the topic of human dignity, across a plethora of different academic disciplines. Philosophers such as George Kateb have argued that dignity is an 'existential' value of basic importance to the identity of all human beings. Legal theorists such as Jeremy Waldron and Ronald Dworkin have pondered dignity's role relative to the divide between legality and normativity. Judges such as Aaron Barak have gone further and have argued that human dignity is the basic value, or 'mother right' underpinning all law. Christian theologians argue that all human beings possess a fundamental dignity that flows directly from God to man. Less positively, bioethicists and scientists such as Ruth Macklin and Stephen Pinker have looked upon dignity with scepticism, arguing that it is a 'useless' – and even dangerous – concept that imposes mystical boundaries on scientific analysis. Political scientists such as Michael Rosen have questioned whether human dignity actually helps us to settle any fundamental disagreements about how we should be governed. And while they have often been happy to invoke the value of dignity as such, many postcolonial scholars have been eager to strip dignity of its all-too Western, and often Christian, associations.

Despite this explosion of interest, one group has devoted very little – if any – attention to human dignity: critical legal scholars. One would be hard pressed to name any major critical legal theorist who has devoted any significant attention to analysing human dignity. When they have done, it has been almost always with an exclusively critical intent, often stereotypically drawing on stock 'radical' reasoning about how such bourgeois notions can only ever be implicated in a system of control and power. This is often considered part of the broader critique of liberal rights and their affiliated concepts that has been carried on by left-wing critics since at least the time of Marx's essay 'On the Jewish Question', and finds modern-day expression in the work of Duncan Kennedy, Costas Douzinas, Pierre Schlag and others. To many of these authors, human dignity, at least in its liberal formulation, is inextricably tied up in vulgar liberal conceptions of the self and of law, and would need significant reformulation if it were to be of any use to a deeper emancipatory project.[1] But their notable silence about the concept leads one to assume that they think that that is highly unlikely.

Such inattention to human dignity is echoed in the relative disinterest that many critical legal scholars show towards international law, which itself is echoed in the novel discipline of socio-legal studies, as pointed out by Eve Darian-Smith in her *Laws and Societies in Global Contexts: Contemporary Approaches*.[2] Many critical legal and socio-legal scholars emerged from Anglo-American law schools, and their choice of legal topics invariably reflects this. To give just one example, almost none of the founders of critical legal scholarship – including Kennedy, Unger, Schlag and Gabel – has devoted a significant monograph to international law. Most of their focus has been on issues in legal philosophy and American law, including a seemingly unending stream of commentary on originalism versus linguistic indeterminacy and legal pragmatism. This is unusual, to say the least, given the uniquely philosophical problems posed by international law for the traditional positivistic accounts of legality that remain the popular targets of many critical legal scholars.

These observations about critical legal theory are meant to indicate the significant gap that exists in the literature, which my book is intended to fill. I will link international law and critical legal theory through an egalitarian conception of human dignity and an affiliated set of rights. What makes my project unique is how I will try to link human dignity to a broader critical legal project that looks at law as it is, with considerable scepticism and an eye for improvement. Like other critical legal scholars, I believe that modern law is prone to reinforcing – or at least turning a blind eye to – inequities that a just society would seek to rectify. This is unacceptable, and necessitates a deep criticism of the status quo. However, I also believe that any critical project must ultimately have some moral ambition at its heart if it is to resonate and persist into the future. Here, I echo Peter Gabel's inspirational call for critical legal studies to rediscover what he claims is its spiritual orientation:

> Within the critical legal studies movement that was itself an expression of this upsurge in awareness, we were confronted by a 'legal order' and hierarchical institutions that supported this order that seemed to allow no room whatsoever for the sense of love, hope, and transcendence that we felt ineffably all around us. On the contrary, it seemed to be an enormous, spiritually dead thought-machine that produced and reproduced both hierarchies and rules that made the world of the war, and racial hatred, and sexual repression, and environmental destruction appear entirely normal and inevitable. And this disjunction between our dawning, idealistic awareness and the professional settings in which we found ourselves as young adults led us to throw ourselves into trying to (a) take apart the fixity of, and (b) reveal the meaning of what everywhere surrounded us.[3]

Gabel's plea comes at a unique time in critical legal scholarship. With the collapse of Marxist[4] narratives and meta-narratives in the late 1980s, progressive scholars were left without a grand narrative that simultaneously offered critical tools and a vision of what the emancipated future would look like. As put by Lyotard:

> In contemporary society and culture – post-industrial society, post-modern culture – the question of the legitimation of knowledge is formulated in different terms. The grand narrative has lost its credibility, regardless of what mode of unification it uses, regardless of whether it is a speculative narrative or a narrative of emancipation.[5]

The academic reaction to this declining belief in grand narratives,[6] prompted by both theoretical and historical developments, has been a retreat into various forms of epistemic and normative scepticism. The tendency on the part of critical legal scholars is to engage exclusively in 'trashing' calcified orders that perpetuate inequalities and marginalization, while offering in return very little that is constructive. Some of this might be due to a given critical legal scholar's disposition, and some to an over-eager embrace of postmodern scepticism. These are indeed important developments, and I will discuss them at some length. But, important as they are, I do not think that it is ultimately possible or helpful to engage exclusively in critical scholarship if one does not have some normative vision of what should replace a given legal order constitutive of the broader social status quo.

Fortunately, we are not bereft of intellectual resources with which to construct such a normative vision. From the critical legal standpoint, the philosopher Roberto Unger has provided by far the most comprehensive and far-reaching theoretical alternative to the status quo. Indeed, his work now stretches far beyond the confines of law, to encompass politics, social theory, psychology and even cosmology. My book draws tremendous inspiration from Unger, while attempting to go beyond him in applying Ungerian insights to international human rights law. However, it should not be understood as a dogmatic piece that applies a given theoretical framework wholesale on a new topic. I think that Unger is mistaken on several important normative and philosophical points. More importantly, I find his solutions to certain problems rather obscure and often too idealized. One of the orientations of my project is to anchor Unger's insights into a more robust and grounded normative vision. The weight of this ambition is carried primarily by my conception of human dignity.

Theoretical Orientation of the Project: the Importance of Amplifying Human Dignity

In Chapters 2 and 3, I will sketch out the theoretical orientation of my project. Chapter 2 will focus primarily on discussing the extensive literature that has recently emerged on the topic of human dignity. It is also where I will discuss the links with critical legal studies most extensively, and demonstrate why I think critical legal studies needs to be animated by a more robust normative vision. Chapter 3 will be the most theoretically significant chapter, since it is where I will present and argue for the adoption of my own – competing – conception of human dignity.

Chapter 2 discusses various conceptions of human dignity, before concluding with why I think that it can be extremely useful for critical legal studies. Dignity remains a theoretically well-contested topic, with some authors claiming that its philosophical ambiguity renders it a fairly useless[7] part of our moral vocabulary.[8] Some have even argued that a focus on dignity contributes to the rise of unwanted social conservatism in morally sensitive fields such as bioethics.[9] This is due in part to the long association of dignity with many Roman Catholic theories, the proponents of which have associated dignity with a human being's status as a divine creation.[10] Even authors more inclined to take a Kantian position[11] on dignity remain sceptical that it means something substantially different than autonomy or freedom as understood by classical liberals.

While there is a great deal to be said for many of these conceptions – and I will clarify where my own conception draws upon them – I believe that none has adequately exhausted the conceptual potential of dignity for normative purposes. This is in part because human dignity has all too often been employed for political reasons, to justify conservative or underambitious political positions that do not do justice to its normative potential. Many critical and socio-legal scholars remain sceptical of any normative concept the roots of which go back to a widely disdained source. But I also think that a key reason for dignity remaining an unpopular concept for so many critical legal scholars is that it has been theoretically misunderstood as an inherent quality rather than what I would call a continuum that can be amplified or diminished. This has bucked the transformative potential of dignity as a normative concept. All too often, it is conceptually aligned with the status quo. Since dignity is associated with inherent qualities that are either ascribed to human beings by God or that exist within us due to the *a priori* human capacity for agency, the conclusion is that social and legal institutions can play no role in diminishing or amplifying human dignity. Dignity is simply a brute fact (or not, if one is a sceptic). I feel that this is deeply unhelpful and limits the radical potential of dignity as a normative conception.

This is where the motivation to link human dignity to critical legal literature comes in. As mentioned earlier, all too often, critical legal studies has lacked a normative vision to complement its deconstructive propensities. This has also limited its transformative potential. I believe that a sufficiently robust conception of human dignity can fulfil this important function. Such a conception would be one that challenges us as human beings, and especially as lawmakers, to engender a moral vision of the world in which substantial injustices would be rectified. As I shall point out later, in a world where power and wealth are as unequally distributed as they are in ours, it seems disingenuous to claim that the dignity of all human beings is equally respected and amplified. One of the motivations for attaching a conception of human dignity to the critical legal literature is to rectify this problem, by both demonstrating how social and political institutions can amplify dignity, and clarifying why and how they still fall far short of this. In this way, human dignity provides a role analogous to that of political theory in the work of Rawls. The conception is meant as an ideal against which normatively to check the functioning of actually existent social and political institutions through attempting to reach a reflective equilibrium between theory and practice.

Chapter 3 will present the key theoretical and philosophical arguments for adopting my conception of human dignity. I will sketch out the links between human dignity, agency and self-authorship that I think make the conception unique. While there are some important analytical distinctions between those concepts, they should be understood as operating in a complex and positive dialectic, with dignity as the synthesizing term.

The theoretical orientation of my project can be seen as synthesizing certain liberal arguments about the good of self-authorship with the critical legal philosophy of Roberto Unger and the capabilities approach to agency[12] of Amartya Sen. I do this by developing a theoretical architecture that links the three in my conception of human dignity. I argue that human dignity flows from an individual agent's capacity for self-authorship, as defined by the set of expressive capabilities[13] that they possess. The overall thrust of my project will apply this theoretical architecture to demonstrate how it can aid and develop our understanding of international human rights law by making the amplification of human dignity its fundamental orientation.[14]

In my conception, dignity operates on a continuum rather than as a kind of transcendental or social status – as one finds in the work of Kant[15] and latter-day liberals such as Jeremy Waldron.[16] I argue that the level of dignity that individuals enjoy is dependent on the extent to which they are capable of acting as authors of their own lives by engaging in what Unger calls 'context transcending' acts of agency.[17] Such acts define the individual by enabling them to redefine the world around them. This can be as simple as engaging one's practical reasoning in everyday life so as to make moral judgments, and as complex as overcoming the false necessity of hierarchical state institutions to establish more egalitarian institutions in their place.

This conception of dignity as a capacity for self-authorship defined by context-transcending acts of agency is the theoretical core of my project. It is also where the critical legal association with Roberto Unger is clearest.[18] Following Unger, I emphatically reject the classical liberal conception of agency and seek to replace it with one that is far more robust and centred around an individual's capacity for dignified self-authorship. However, I try to go beyond Unger[19] through the work of Amartya Sen.[20] Specifically, my project will emphasize that the extent of an individual's dignity is dependent on how capable they are of context transcendence through deploying what I call their set of 'expressive capabilities'.[21]

Expressive capabilities refer to individual human 'functionings' that are the empirical pre-condition for dignified self-authorship.[22] In the literature, they have been closely linked to what people can do and who they are.[23] Expressive capabilities are those through which a person defines himself or herself by redefining the world around them. To use Unger's terminology, expressive capabilities are the set of an individual's 'context transcending' powers.[24] While it may be related, it is important to distinguish the set of expressive capabilities from some totalizing basis for agency such as Kantian will.[25] Expressive capabilities exist only potentially; the set of expressive capabilities that a person enjoys is determined by both their intrinsic capabilities and, most importantly for our purposes, the empirical social-historical contexts in which they live.[26] The more expansive the set of expressive capabilities that an individual enjoys, the more they are capable of engaging in acts of dignified self-authorship that transform the world around them.[27] The goal of a just social ordering would be to amplify all individuals' expressive capabilities to the greatest extent possible, so that they can lead dignified lives. Chapter 3 will conclude with a presentation of a critical legal model of two twinned rights, which I take to be necessary for the amplification of human dignity. I argue that two more concrete, but still largely abstract, rights would flow from making human dignity the fundamental orientation of international human rights law. The first is a right for all citizens to be democratic co-authors of their governing social institutions and the coercive rules that flow from these. The second is a right of all citizens to enjoy equal sets of expressive capabilities except where inequalities flow from the citizens' morally significant choices.[28]

The decision to distinguish two distinct rights was deliberate, and at least partly inspired by Thomas Nagel, who made a similar argument in his book *Equality and Partiality*.[29] I maintain that the first right (to democratic authorship) precedes the second. Individuals should have the opportunity, in a democratic context, to choose whether they wish to ensure an egalitarianism of human capabilities. Choice is important to my conception of how to realize human dignity. This is because my conception is fundamentally democratic at both theoretical and practical levels. It rests upon the claim that legitimacy is minimally bestowed by consent and increases to the degree that subjects become authors of social and political institutions, and the coercive rules that flow from them.

The link between the two foundational rights – the right to democratic authorship and that to equality of human capabilities – is that both are intended as what Seyla Benhabib calls 'jurisgenerative legal tools'[30] to be used to amplify an individual's set of expressive capabilities and so realize the dignity-oriented account of human flourishing. As I have mentioned, expressive capabilities are those that enable individuals to transcend socio-historical boundaries and assume responsibility for their subjectivity. This is what enables people to lead a life of dignified self-authorship. Only in this way would their status as morally individual subjects be respected. Therefore the first step to respecting and amplifying expressive capabilities is to democratize political and legal institutions. After this, one can make the more challenging argument for establishing the agency-enhancing[31] right to a full equality of expressive capabilities.[32]

Realizing the twinned rights to democratic authorship and an equality of expressive capabilities constitutes an ideal for which, I argue, all social institutions should strive. A just system of international human rights law would seek to respect and amplify human dignity, and so realize the twinned rights that are necessary for this task. I believe that it could do so along two corresponding dimensions, which would enable us to reconceive and direct international human rights law in a novel way.

Application I: Making Human Dignity Central to International Human Rights Law

This is where the link to international human rights law becomes clearer. As discussed above, my conception of human dignity draws heavily on the critical legal literature, and in particular the work of Roberto Unger. It is designed to provide a normative vision that has often been lacking in the critical legal literature. But rather than follow most critical legal scholars in focusing (by this point, to excess), on domestic and largely Western legal systems as the exemplar of legality, with all its contradictions and inequities, I have decided to focus on international human rights law. Chapters 4 and 5 will therefore demonstrate how my conception of human dignity can be applied through international human rights law, in ways that are both constructive and transformative. Chapter 4 will primarily establish the theoretical link between my conception of human dignity and international human rights law. Chapter 5 will conclude this work by applying the now completed theoretical architecture to a bevy of case studies – in particular, arguing for the broad expansion of our understanding of economic rights. It will also be the largest and most technical chapter. Progressive legal practitioners who are primarily interested in the 'cash value' of my conception of dignity might therefore be advised to skip directly to that chapter.

Chapter 4 will sketch out the theoretical links between international human rights law and human dignity. My approach will be primarily along the lines of a normative critique and reconstruction of international human rights law in the way suggested by my conception of human dignity. The locus of this will be taking the realization and amplification of human dignity to be the fundamental orientation, or 'mother right',[33] of international human rights law.[34] If dignity is understood in the way in which I have framed it – defined by an individual's capacity for self-authorship as determined by their set of expressive capabilities – it suggests moral reasons to move well beyond the classical liberal approach to international human rights law, which still dominates[35] the field.

Application II: Reconceiving and Redirecting International Human Rights Law

The first part of Chapter 4 will be taken up by discussing the normative project of making human dignity central to international human rights law. The second part will be a discussion of how this would entail reconceiving and redirecting international human rights law along the lines demanded by human dignity. This would lead to developments along the dimensions stipulated by the two rights argued for in Chapter 3.

First, I argue for radicalizing the Kantian argument that states have moral and legal obligations to maintain the 'rightful condition' for the flourishing of human dignity in order to retain sovereignty.[36] This would mean that states that fail to respect the dignity of their citizens would gradually cede their sovereign claims to authority[37] over the citizenry.[38] Since my model stresses that dignity is about more than just the classical liberal approach of avoiding infringements of negative rights, the scope of actions that might constitute an infringement of their moral and legal obligations should consequently be broadened. Allowing individuals needlessly to suffer from harms such as famine, or failing adequately to care for their economic needs when the required resources are available, might constitute an infringement of a state's moral and legal obligations to respect and amplify expressive capabilities where possible and necessary.[39] To believe that little can be done to prevent what is in fact an avoidable catastrophe is to cede too much power to the 'false-necessity' of a global order that is oriented around state sovereignty.[40] In such situations, international human rights law, and the organizations that uphold it, might be entitled to intervene to prevent extraordinary infringements of the dignity of citizens.[41] They operate as what I call a 'steering mechanism' towards the realization of the rightful condition.

Secondly, I argue for broadening the obligations that states have towards non-citizens.[42] Guaranteeing the standard package of classical liberal rights is not sufficient to respect and amplify the dignity of all individuals. If all individuals are to lead lives of dignified self-authorship they must also enjoy a considerable degree of economic and social flourishing.[43] It is the only way in which they could truly have a robust set of expressive capabilities. This means that, if international human rights law aims to protect and amplify human dignity, it must therefore engender a more just[44] distribution of goods and resources.[45] This might involve significant transfers of wealth and power from developed to developing countries.[46] Here, international human rights law – allied with international economic law[47] – could play an important role in enforcement, distribution and administration.

If we took these steps, it would take us a long way towards making the amplification of human dignity the fundamental orientation of international human rights law. In Chapters 5 and 6, I will unpack how this could be realized more practically through the concrete jurisprudence of the international legal system.

Application III: Amplifying Human Dignity in Practice

Chapters 5 and 6 will conclude the substantive sections of this work with an extensive look at international human rights law jurisprudence, and how it can and has worked to amplify human dignity. Here, I will follow critical legal theorists in looking at the law with qualified scepticism, while also trying to demonstrate where and how it could be useful if reconceived and oriented in the right normative direction. I will argue that many prominent cases demonstrate how international human rights law has amplified human dignity in practice. This is particularly true in cases that deal with the rights of individuals to democratic authorship of the social and political institutions that govern them. My overall goal is to demonstrate how international law is already operating, in part, to transform notions of sovereignty by requiring states to maintain the 'rightful condition' in order to retain authority.

The most important cases dealing with the right to democratic authorship, and thereby taking the most important step towards retaining Kantian legitimacy, are those dealing with the right to vote. Voting rights are important, since my conception of human dignity emphasizes the relationship between an individual's capacity for self-authorship and his power to change the socio-historical contexts within which he operates. Such rights are important in this respect, though they do not exhaust what should be the set of an individual's expressive capabilities. Two of the decisions at which I intend to look in order to ground my analysis are *Aziz* and *Hirst*. In *Aziz*, the European Court of Human Rights (ECtHR) ruled that Cyprus could not limit the voting rights of the Turkish minority. In the *Hirst* decision, the ECtHR ruled that the United Kingdom (UK) was not allowed to disenfranchise prisoners. In both cases, the court ruled that the Government's arguments (based on the sovereign right of states to do as they wish) were invalid. I will argue that the ECtHR was moving towards developing an argument based on a state's obligation to maintain the 'rightful condition' of full democratic participation if it wishes to retain all the prerogatives of sovereignty. Naturally, I intend to endorse this move and use it to show that international law can play a positive role (albeit a qualified one, since the UK rejected the decision) in enhancing human dignity.

But voting rights are far from sufficient for ensuring that individuals enjoy rights to democratic authorship. Also crucial, especially today, is including minorities and marginalized peoples in social and legal processes that impact their interests. Here, international law has also played an important role in the past. To demonstrate this, I will focus on examining the *Riza v Bulgaria* decision, which dealt with the voting rights of expatriates who primarily belonged to the marginalized Islamic community in Bulgaria.

These cases suggest how international human rights law can be used to amplify human dignity by upholding the right to democratic authorship for the individual. They also assist efforts to develop the norms required for states to retain Kantian legitimacy by establishing the 'rightful conditions' for its citizens to exercise democratic authorship.

In Chapter 7, I will analyse how international human rights law must also be reoriented along the lines stipulated by the second right: to bring about an equality of human capabilities. This chapter will be more speculative in nature, since both the positive law and the jurisprudence on these issues are considerably thinner, and more critical, since economic rights tend to be given far less emphasis than civil and political rights in the jurisprudence.

Discussing how international law can amplify dignity through realising the economic and social rights of citizens will be a trickier argument, since little of the jurisprudence on the issue has stuck. Therefore, I will rely more on treaty law and principled argument to develop a normative case on why we *should* take these rights far more seriously, including making them enforceable against states and individuals. However, I will draw on the reasoning of the Committee on Economic, Social and Cultural rights to argue that some major decisions abet a more active approach to such rights. Some pertinent ECtHR decisions include *Moldovan II*, which concerned living conditions, and *DH v Czech Republic*, which concerned the right to an education. There are also some domestic decisions that provide useful guidance. South African jurisprudence offers a good example. In *Government of South Africa and Others v Grootboom*, the Constitutional Court ruled that the state is obliged to look after the well-being of its citizens. While the earlier *Soobramoney* decision revealed some of the limitations of this approach, I still think that it is a salient example. It shows law being used to push the state to establish more actively the rightful condition for the amplification of human dignity. My argument will be that international human rights law can play a more active role in both framing contemporary liberal constitutions in a more egalitarian way by emphasising this robust account of dignity, and by penalising those who do not work to realize it. Unfortunately, states have a considerable way to go to realize this project fully, which demonstrates the continuing need for a critical approach to law as it is.

Finally, Chapter 6 will conclude this work on a constructive note, by examining how to reorient international human rights law by offering some normative arguments on the economic obligations of states towards non-citizens. I will argue that developed states have significant moral obligations to ameliorate the plight of the world's most disadvantaged peoples, and that international human rights law should reflect these by requiring states to redistribute wealth and power in a more egalitarian way. Here there are very few concrete cases to which one can point, so I will take steps in this direction by extrapolating how these obligations could be realized in legal practice by looking at the precedents set in refugee law and the laws surrounding stateless people.

PART I

Theorizing the relationship between human dignity and international human rights law

2

Dignity's Contentious History

Human Dignity: Origins and Orientation

> Different comprehensive doctrines provide different accounts of human dignity. These accounts are sufficiently convergent, though, that they allow human dignity to serve as an 'accepted principle of shared morality' ... And for those who for whatever reason do not want to push deeper, it does function as an axiom of Ur-principle.[1]

References to human dignity abound in contemporary political and legal culture. So widely is dignity invoked that it can be tremendously difficult to pin down a definition that would be acceptable to all. When it is invoked on the one hand to honour the immortal soul bestowed upon all God's creatures, and then the next minute to venerate the existential status of human subjects in a Godless world, one can sometimes sympathize with Steven Pinker's claim that it is simply a 'useless' concept that should be canned in favour of a more analytically rigorous one such as liberty.[2] But, as we shall see, the history of the concept of dignity suggests that it is less rigid than might seem at first glance. More importantly, dignity often seems to play an important normative role that is distinct from other concepts in standard moral discourses. This suggests that it assumes certain discursive responsibilities that other normative concepts might find difficult to bear.

The modern term 'dignity' arose in the thirteenth century from the Latin *dignitas*, which referred to the 'worthiness' of individuals. This was often given a specifically Christian cast, sometimes pertaining to a human being's value in the eyes of God as his creation, and at other times pertaining to the moral imperative that all human beings should emulate the inherent dignity of God and higher beings. This conception quickly found currency among the other monotheistic faiths, and references to the dignity or worthiness of humans flowing from their status as God's most blessed creation can be found in Islamic and Judaic texts. The strong association of dignity with such religious beliefs persists to the present day.[3]

Some commentators, such as Rosen,[4] might argue that this gives human dignity a specifically scholastic tinge that explains its long association with certain variations of conservative thought down to the present day. But I think that this overstates both the conservatism of Christianity specifically, and of religion broadly, with regard to the normative emphasis that is placed on human dignity. Indeed, many tended to deploy human dignity in a humanistic manner to blur or mitigate the distance between the unlimited creative power of God and the more limited, but still tremendous, creative powers enjoyed by his creation. The latter emphasis persisted down through the fifteenth century and finds its canonical expression in the work of Pico Della Mirandola, whose 'Oration on Human Dignity' has been called the manifesto of the Renaissance. Mirandola describes human beings' relationship to God in a positive manner; albeit often granting great – even idolatrous – weight to the ambitions of the former. Imagining a dialogue between God and Adam, Mirandola has God exclaim:

> We have given you, O Adam, no visage proper to yourself, nor endowment properly your own, in order that whatever place, whatever form, whatever gifts you may, with premeditation, select, these same you may have and possess through your own judgement and decision. The nature of all other creatures is defined and restricted within laws which we have laid down; you, by contrast, impeded by no such restrictions, may, by your own free will, to whose custody We have assigned you, trace for yourself the lineaments of your own nature. I have placed you at the very center of the world, so that from that vantage point you may with greater ease glance

> round about you on all that the world contains. We have made you a creature neither of heaven nor of earth, neither mortal nor immortal, in order that you may, as the free and proud shaper of your own being, fashion yourself in the form you may prefer. It will be in your power to descend to the lower, brutish forms of life; you will be able, through your own decision, to rise again to the superior orders whose life is divine.[5]

There is little that is reactionary or conservative in this articulation of human beings, their dignity, and their relationship to God. Indeed, Mirandola's God almost seems in awe of his own quasi-divine creation. These proto-Blakean sentiments come out more overtly later. In a statement of some elegance, Mirandola calls on human beings to emulate the dignity of God and higher-order angels in the creation of the novel, and asks:

> But what is the purpose of all this? That we may understand – since we have been born into this condition of being what we choose to be – that we ought to be sure above all else that it may never be said against us that, born to a high position, we failed to appreciate it, but fell instead to the estate of brutes and uncomprehending beasts of burden; and that the saying of Aspah the Prophet, 'You are all Gods and sons of the Most High,' might rather be true; and finally that we may not, through abuse of the generosity of a most indulgent Father, pervert the free option which he has given us from a saving to a damning gift. Let a certain saving ambition invade our souls so that, impatient of mediocrity, we pant after the highest things and (since, if we will, we can) bend all our efforts to their attainment. Let us disdain things of earth, hold as little worth even the astral orders and, putting behind us all the things of this world, hasten to that court beyond the world, closest to the most exalted Godhead. There, as the sacred mysteries tell us, the Seraphim, Cherubim and Thrones occupy the first places; but, unable to yield to them, and impatient of any second place, let us emulate their dignity and glory. And, if we will it, we shall be inferior to them in nothing.[6]

So, from the origins of its formal explication, dignity was understood as more than simply one or another moral characteristic of human beings. For Mirandola, dignity emerges as a consequence of humanity's divinely ceded power correctly to interpret and to transform the world. This is no doubt inspiring, even if it is occasionally overenthusiastic and, of course, specifically attached to a very distinct ontotheological tradition.

However, Mirandola's pioneering oration does demonstrate one of the considerable problems that would beset dignity down through the centuries: its conceptual ambiguity. While earlier religious thinkers deployed dignity to denote a human being's status before God, Mirandola subtly shifted the discourse to make their creative powers its central characteristic. These dramatic shifts would hardly be atypical of dignity's conceptual history. References to dignity abound in religious and philosophical literature from the Renaissance onwards, but they are applied in an eclectic and occasionally even contradictory manner. It would not be too much to say that, often, authors simply deployed dignity to baptize certain features of human beings and/or institutions with the veneer of moral and philosophical grandeur. Moreover, and in contrast to its earlier deployment in the monotheistic traditions, dignity is rarely deployed in an egalitarian manner. Most accounts that reference it relate it to one's social status and wealth. Locke and Smith both reference the 'dignity' found in the office of the king and in father figures. Rousseau refers to the 'dignity' found in prosperity. Grotius, often considered the founding theorist of international law, references dignity several times in *The Rights of War and Peace*. Typically, his references are, per Locke and Smith, concerned with the dignity and honour of institutions and sovereigns.[7] David Hume's account is somewhat closer to our modern sensibilities. In his essay 'Of the Dignity or Meanness of Human Nature', Hume relates dignity to a human being's capacity to act virtuously and embody virtues. This is because acting virtuously and embodying virtues amplifies a human being's overall worthiness. Hume also notes that dignity is already a controversial topic in the philosophical literature, and often inclines authors to rhetorical excess.

> The most remarkable of this kind are the sects, founded on the different sentiments with regard to the *dignity of human nature*; which is a point that seems to have divided philosophers and poets, as well as divines, from the beginning of the world to this day. Some exalt our species to the skies, and represent man as a kind of human demigod, who derives his origin from heaven, and retains evident marks of his lineage and descent. Others insist upon the blind sides of human nature, and can discover nothing, except vanity, in which man surpasses the other animals, whom he affects so much to despise.[8]

Despite these, and countless other references, few thinkers made dignity a central concept in their moral theories. As such, it might gradually have been relegated to the backdrop of secular moral discourse had it not been for the work of Immanuel Kant.

The Kantian Conception of Human Dignity

> What is related to general human inclinations and needs has a *market price*; that which, even without presupposing such a need, conforms with a certain taste has a *fancy price*; but that which constitutes the condition under which alone something can be an end in itself has not merely a relative value, that is, a price, but an inner value, that is, *dignity* ... Morality, and humanity insofar as it is capable of morality, is that which alone has dignity.

While there remains no consensus on what 'dignity' means, by far the most important and famous conception remains the classical liberal account of it developed by Immanuel Kant.[9] This fame is well deserved, even if Kant's articulation of his conception of dignity is occasionally quite confusing. In this section, I will briefly discuss Kant's conception of human dignity. In preparation for presenting my own conception, I will also explain why I think that it is important to go beyond Kant in some important respects.

Part of the difficulty in giving an account of Kant's conception of dignity is the range of formulations found in Kant's work. Moreover, it is not always clear what theoretical role dignity is intended to play in the Kantian system. At points, Kant seems to argue that dignity flows from, and is thus conceptually subordinate to, human autonomy. In these moments he seems to be saying that autonomy is the central feature of human life, which gives us moral value generally.[10] At other points, Kant gives dignity itself a more central place. Indeed, according to some interpretations of his work, it would almost seem to warrant pride of place in the entire moral system. Unfortunately, there is no space to deal with all these conceptual difficulties here, let alone to provide a rigorous articulation of all possible formulations of his conception of dignity. Instead, after briefly discussing some of these challenges, I will focus on reconstructing Kant's conception in the strongest possible light. This will also provide a clearer contrast when discussing how my own conception of dignity contrasts with his.

Kant's most famous formulation of dignity is cited at the beginning of this chapter: human dignity is a status that places the life of human beings above all price.[11] As a rhetorical statement, this is about as good as Kant gets, and it remains a deeply moving formulation of his particular conception. However, by itself, the formulation tells us little about his overall conception, aside from the worth that he ascribes to each human life. To understand better why he ascribes us this value, we need to dig deeper into the *Groundwork to the Metaphysics of Morals*.

In this seminal work Kant developed a complex argument to the effect that all autonomous human individuals possess a free will from the standpoint of practical reason, and are therefore able to will their own independent ends. Other objects in the world, including non-human animals, do not possess this capacity. Like all purely scientific phenomena, they are governed by material causality and therefore operate according to the laws of cause and effect. Kant argues that, on occasion, human beings are prone to the bad faith belief that we are also simply material objects in the world, governed by causality. But Kant feels that this can never be proven metaphysically without lapsing into transcendental illusion, and is denied by our practical reason, which affirms the sense of ourselves as a rational being capable of willing our own ends. The moral belief that we are simply the product of our material environment is a belief in what Kant calls 'heteronomy', and is to be rejected.

There is an important reason for Kant's being keen to reject heteronomy, and all its affiliated beliefs. This is because he believes that the transcendental capacity to will our own ends is the central reason for our not being just material objects in a value-free universe. Kant makes the radical and highly innovative argument that the autonomy of individuals is the enabling condition of moral philosophy. At first glance, this might seem like a curious feature. If it were true that autonomy and freedom were the enabling conditions of morality, how could we claim that morality had any substantive content? Wouldn't all individuals simply be free to will their own ends as they saw fit – or, for that matter, not at all?

This position would certainly become more prominent in the writings of later thinkers, particularly those in the existential tradition. But Kant is unwilling or unable to take this step. He will not claim that autonomy of the self and freedom of the will leave us free to pursue any ends that we prefer. In fact, recognizing our freedom to pursue different ends is simply the first step to recognizing the rational form, substance and end of morality to which we have a duty to conform. The capacity to will our own ends is central to Kant's broader argument that practical (moral) reason demands that we submit our will to a regulative categorical imperative, which is to direct our actions in conformity with the overall and universal moral law.[12]

Kant breaks this categorical imperative into three formulations. The first is that all human beings must always act in such a way that we could accept the maxim that we order ourselves by as a universal law. Kant refers to this as the formula for a universal law of nature. It is probably the most well-known formulation of the categorical imperative, and also the most controversial. Given these controversies, I will acknowledge this formulation only briefly here. It is obvious that Kant considers it exceptionally important to his moral thought overall. However, it is not clear what direct relationship this first formulation of the categorical imperative has to Kant's account of human dignity. The clearest link is that if the first formulation truly is a universal law, it demonstrates our capacity to will ends that are objectively moral. This places us above other animals, who are purely subject to deterministic heteronomy and therefore cannot be said to act on any imperatives that are universalizable. But the core insight here is that dignity is related to autonomy and freedom from causality, which is better captured by the second formulation.

The second formulation of the imperative bears the most important relationship to dignity. It is that all individuals must always act in such a way that we treat our humanity, and that of others, not just as a means but always as an end in itself. It is our status as the only beings with the capacity to submit ourselves to moral imperatives of our own design – in effect, to will towards ends that we ourselves have chosen but which have a rational moral structure[13] – that gives human beings a dignity that places human life above all price. Price is a variable that can be measured and affiliated with an object. However, the dignity of human beings cannot be measured in this manner, if at all. It is incommensurable and absolute. As Donnelly puts it:

> Kant's key move was to distinguish two kinds of value, which correspond to two sides of human nature: dignity (Wurde, worth) understood as 'an absolute inner worth' which is the standard of distinctively human or moral value; and price, the standard of value of the material world and man's anima nature. A human being is a creature with a worth, a dignity; that is literally priceless, outside of the domain of instrumental value.[14]

Moreover, for Kant, dignity as an end in ourselves is what sets us above and, to some degree, outside the world around us, which is defined by causal relations in which objects interact with one another according to a predefined script. This Kantian argument about the relationship between autonomy and our capacity to be moral – indeed to establish the existence of morality at all – is nicely made by J. B. Schneewind.

> The power of choice enables us to decide between the call of desire and that of morality. Kant thinks that we might have it even without having the kind of practical reason we have. It would function like the Clarkean will, enabling us to choose even where the alternatives are indifferent; in other cases its choices would be determined by the relative strengths of desires and passions. The will itself is neither free nor unfree. As pure practical reason, it provides us permanently with the option of acting solely on the reason which its own legislative activity gives us. The power of choice, which enables us to opt for morality or against it, is a free power. Because we can choose, we never have to accede to desires which, though certainly part of ourselves, are caused in us by our encounters with the world outside us.[15]

This point is complex and bears more reflection as it relates to dignity. At points, Kant seems to think that this capacity to choose to will the moral law sets us above anything else in nature except other rational beings. He could justifiably be attacked from an environmentalist perspective for so elevating human beings at the expense of nature. Kant is firmly in the classical liberal tradition in his approach to the natural world. There is little sense in which nature or any non-human animals enjoy anything approaching a dignity 'beyond price'. As he put it in his 'Lectures on Ethics': 'But so far as animals are concerned, we have no direct duties. Animals … are there merely as means to an end. That end is man.'

While Kant's later works, especially the *Critique of Judgement*, develop a formidable approach to interpreting nature's beauty and *telos*, he is committed to the idea that natural objects are appropriable for the ends determined for them by man and God. But it is important to note that this is not simply some crude speciesism on Kant's part. He does not simply assert that we are different than animals and nature because we are free to choose, and therefore enjoy a dignity that sets us apart from them. Freedom and autonomy are at the locus of Kant's account of dignity but do not exhaust it. He develops a complex argument to that effect, since, for Kant, moral value stems precisely from our capacity to set ends for ourselves. Because we are capable of doing this, and in effect bringing value into the world, we cannot be treated as means to an end since it is in some respects the duty of man to ascribe all ends to the world. Without us, there would be no value. This, in effect, elevates us above all the values that we create.

As mentioned, this is centrally related to our autonomy and freedom to choose, since treating ourselves or other human beings as means to an end removes our capacity to choose, and therefore our ability to will moral ends.[16] It is, in essence, to treat a human being as a thing in the world rather than as an autonomous person who can will their own ends. For Kant, this is failure in our moral duty, and betrays both our dignity and the dignity of the one we diminish. But there is also an important egalitarian humanism to this position. Kant's conception of dignity is firmly in opposition to accounts given by Locke, Smith and others, who associate it firmly with institutional office and rank. He would also be opposed to attempts by modern thinkers, such as Waldron, to conceive of dignity as a status or rank that is ascribed to individuals or institutions as a social gesture. We are indeed supposed to treat each individual as possessing dignity because they are an end in themselves. But, for Kant, such a conception would still ascribe too much influence to the external world, and thus risk being affiliated with inegalitarian ideas if manipulated properly. The only way properly and securely to understand dignity is as belonging to everyone, low and high, from birth to death, as an *a priori* fact. Moral imperatives are to be organized around it. Perhaps more importantly for our purposes, states and social institutions are to be organized in a manner that respects dignity and its egalitarian connotations.

This is where the third formulation of the categorical imperative comes in. Kant believes that a kingdom of individuals who are ends in themselves should be established, wherein free individuals will moral laws in tandem with one another. In later works it becomes clearer that such a society would look very different from the one in which he lived, and, indeed, from our own. In later chapters, I will discuss and apply in far more detail these Kantian ideas, particularly his argument that states have an obligation to establish the 'rightful condition' for free humans to engage one another as ends.

Kant's conception of dignity has been very influential, down to impacting the decisions of major judiciaries such as Germany's.[17] It is also tremendously powerful, especially in its egalitarian and humanistic moments. However, it is far from perfect. In the next section, I will develop some criticisms of the Kantian conception and preview some of my own ideas about how dignity should be conceived.

Criticisms of the Kantian Conception

Kant's conception of human dignity is rich and provocative, and anyone attempting to develop a different one will have to engage and learn from it. But I believe that it remains marred by some serious limitations. The Kantian conception of human dignity has never been entirely satisfying due to its apparent insensitivity to socio-historical and other empirical contexts. Here, I will argue that important features of his conception can be saved from this limitation, but only at the expense of dropping some of Kant's more specific philosophical commitments.

As mentioned in the section above, one of the (apparently) defining features of Kant's conception of human dignity is his insistence that dignity is in no way dependent on external features of the world but exists *a priori* as a defining characteristic of the human subject. This is a powerful idea, finding expression in the frequent characterization of dignity in international legal documents as inalienable or intrinsic to all human beings. But the philosophical justification for such a strong position on dignity is not as powerful as its rhetorical heft might suggest. It is centrally related to the occasionally ambiguous links that Kant draws between dignity, freedom and the capacity to bring moral value into the world. There is a sense in which Kant cannot accept that external features of the world – what I call socio-historical contexts – can impact the dignity of human beings. Acknowledging this would undermine Kant's deep commitment to the idea that all human beings are absolutely free, regardless of the heteronymous features of their life. Concurrently, if socio-historical contexts impact on human freedom, it would suggest that our dignity as lawgivers who will their own ends can be not just disrespected but actually limited and qualified. This is unacceptable for Kant, both because it limits the dignity of human beings as free lawgivers, and less admirably because it might limit our capacity to hold each individual fully accountable for their actions.

There is a sense in which Kant is too radically transcendental. He seems simply to assert that all individuals possess the transcendental capacity to will their own ends, regardless of the specific details of their lives, and that is that. Whether this is true of his conception, a monologically transcendental view, while inspiring in some respects, simply seems unrealistic after a point. Moreover, there is a paradoxical sense in which the radicalness of Kant's transcendental commitments might blunt the critical edge of his philosophy as it applies in the empirical world. If it is true that all individuals possess dignity simply as an *a priori* brute fact, it can lead one to question whether and why sociohistorical contexts and powerful institutions should be rearranged to establish a freer society. If we are simply free and dignified agents, and that is that, there can be no sense in which change could either increase or diminish that freedom. This would be a remarkable position to take. It would make little sense to say that a slave toiling in the fields in eighteenth-century Virginia could not be made more fundamentally free to lead a dignified life by the elimination of slavery. Even in the Europe of Kant's time, it would seem deeply odd to claim that individuals would not be made freer by the elimination of aristocratic political and economic institutions – and the examples can multiply.

Indeed, Kant does not seem fully to believe in this extreme position.[18] His later works in political and legal philosophy are replete with calls for reform and the transformation of both the state and cosmopolitan society along lines that would better treat human beings as ends in themselves. As pointed out by Arthur Ripstein, Kant's legal and political philosophy has a fundamentally radical edge to it that is occasionally underappreciated.[19] Kant claims that for the state to claim sovereign authority over citizens, it must maintain the rightful conditions for the exercise of their freedom as dignified ends in themselves. This includes a responsibility to maintain and deepen a host of liberal institutions that would have seemed radically progressive in Kant's time, and engage in a cosmopolitan politics that seems idealistic even to this day. Kant takes this position to the extreme by concluding that, to the extent that states fail to establish this rightful condition, they cede the moral right to sovereign authority over their citizens.

To my mind, this more realistic and contextually sensitive dimension of Kant's thought demonstrates how one should go about understanding his conception of dignity. I agree with Kant that there is a fundamental link between one's freedom and human dignity. However, I think that we must follow his somewhat constricted insight that freedom – what I will later call agency – can be very much inhibited or amplified by the socio-historical contexts within which individuals live. Because of the links I, like Kant, draw between agency and dignity, it is possible for the dignity of human beings to be amplified or limited by the socio-historical contexts within which they live. We must try to make individuals more capable of agency to amplify the dignity they enjoy as authors of their own lives. Taking dignity seriously means (re)organizing socio-historical contexts in order to amplify agency to the greatest extent possible. In this respect we still have a very long way to go. Many states still engage in practices that, directly or indirectly, limit the dignity of individuals. Significant changes are needed.

Fortunately, some resources can be brought to bear in order to move societies in this direction. One of the most important of these is positive law, in which references to human dignity already abound. In the next few sections, I will trace out how human dignity came to play a role in both the domestic and international legal systems. I will also examine several further philosophical conceptions of dignity that have emerged, some of which add much to our understanding of its logic and importance.

Samuel Moyn on Dignity's Secret Catholicism

Kant's vision of a liberal–cosmopolitan world order that respected human dignity was exceptionally innovative at the beginning of the nineteenth century. Unfortunately, he paid the eternal price of being ahead of his time; many centuries would pass before anything like the Kantian vision was realized in the law, either domestically or internationally.

The romantic nineteenth century was defined by several different intellectual currents, many of them hostile to the idea of human dignity. The most prominent in opposition to the Kantian vision were undoubtedly the various nationalist movements, which tended to draw on various Herderian and Hegelian conceptions of an organic total community like the nation state. These movements were often anti-individualistic, and therefore rejected humanistic philosophies like those oriented around human dignity. And indeed, the most militant were actively hostile towards such ideas, since they served to discredit the then ascendant imperial and colonial projects through which so-called 'civilized' nations expressed their culture and power. Simultaneously, Marxism emerged as a major force deeply critical of many of these imperialistic trends. However, there is little evidence to suggest that Marx himself was particularly attracted to any specific conception of human dignity. While there is a sensitivity to the indignity of life under the most brutal forms of capitalism in *Capital* and other Marxist texts (especially his earliest works), he never appeared to have given the idea much thought.[20] It is likely that Marx would have felt that appealing to dignity would have given his 'scientific' theory an unpalatably moral dimension. This would have run counter to his general intention of developing a relatively deterministic account of why capitalism's inherent contradictions would lead to its collapse. And indeed, most of the movements birthed in Marx's name were tragically indifferent or even actively hostile to any of the individualistic connotations associated with the idea of dignity. In this respect, they differed little from the vulgar collectivist philosophies developed by the various nationalist movements.

This is not to say that substantial efforts were not made on some fronts – many of them motivated by religious, abolitionist and anti-imperialist movements. As the century moved to a close, many women's movements also made able use of the idea of dignity to demand suffrage and respect. However, while each of these movements pushed for important demands that were integral to securing dignity for traditionally marginalized groups, there was no sense in which any of them advocated for giving it any more conceptual or legal heft beyond its moral weight in pushing for a specific set of reforms. In other words, the term 'dignity' was instrumentalized to make particular demands for particular causes.

Samuel Moyn observes that the first place where dignity enters into the law is esoteric and unexpected: the 1937 Irish Constitution. Moyn argues that the founding status ascribed to the Kantian conception of dignity overstates its actual significance for legal practice. In fact, it was in Catholic countries, inspired by the Church's emphasis on the dignity of collective entities, that human dignity entered the lexicon of legal values. But while the emphasis given to dignity was individualistic, it was hardly the autonomous individualism of Kant and other liberal thinkers. Moyn claims that the Irish were specifically motivated to establish a Christian democratic society – one that would protect the individual but also had illiberal characteristics consonant with the need to uphold Catholic values. In other words, dignity as it appeared in the law originally had a conservative slant – one that may be more admirable than the postmodern conservatism of Trump and Orban that is ascendant in the current era, but hardly consistent with the emancipatory rhetoric ascribed to it by many liberals and some progressives.

> These two groups of Catholics agreed on the rejection of the modern, liberal secular republic, which they viewed as immoral and individualistic. Instead, they favored the dispersal of authority to the 'natural' social hierarchy established by God and descending through religious institutions, local communities, and patriarchal families. This agreement was perfectly obvious to contemporary witnesses, such as celebrated political theorist Michael Oakeshott, who in this era offered readers a conspectus of European political thought in which 'Catholicism' was a possible option alongside 'representative democracy', 'communism', 'fascism', and 'National Socialism'.[21]

Moyn makes the bold claim that, for most domestic constitutions, comparably universalistic but metaphysically loaded conceptions of dignity were those that made their way into law. This problematizes the traditional cosmopolitan and liberal narrative that dignity entered the law in its full Kantian glory in 1948.

> After all, for a long time, including in the 1940s, dignity was most strongly correlated with religious constitutions in general – of which the German was merely one among others – and Christian Democratic constitutions in particular. Those constitutions as much broke with 1789 as safeguarded it, let alone rehabilitated it after disaster. The Irish were the true pioneers both in the development of religious constitutionalism and in symbolizing its project through appeals to human dignity. In their 1937 constitution, they gave dignity foundational placement, as a religiously inspired root concept connected (as in the later West German case) to the subordination of the otherwise sovereign democratic polity to God, and for many to the moral constraints of his natural law.[22]

Moyn's account of this 'secret' history of dignity, characteristic of the sceptical historicism he employs in other works, is aimed at undermining neo-utopian narratives[23] wherein dignity and rights entered the world in the post-war era and will ultimately bring about the long-promised ideal society. His work is consonant with other trends in socio-legal and critical legal studies that have aimed to undermine triumphalist narratives about what law, and the normative concepts underpinning it, are actually able to accomplish in practice. I have a great deal of sympathy with many of these arguments, and will deal with them more extensively in Chapters 3 and 4. For now, I will simply say that while Moyn's claims are historically relevant, they need not prevent one from developing a novel conception of human dignity that emphasizes different normative commitments than has been the case in the past. History is not destiny; its lessons can be absorbed without becoming determinative. I see few *a priori* reasons for why dignity cannot be put to more radical uses in the law – particularly international law – than its Catholic and conservative heritage might suggest.

At least to some extent, Moyn seems to accept this. In the conclusion of his article he emphasizes the modern-day explosion of literature on dignity, highlighting recent works by Dworkin, Kateb and Benhabib among others. But Moyn does not interpret this as evidence that dignity might possess some rhetorical or conceptual value that has led to its coming to the fore. Instead, he seems to interpret dignity in a manner analogous to his earlier treatment of human rights. The fact that one can detach dignity so easily from its Catholic (and, one assumes, Kantian) associations, demonstrates its unwelcome plasticity as a moral and legal term. On Moyn's understanding, this plasticity renders it a fairly useless part of the moral and legal vocabulary. He would rather that advocates simply state their political commitments in plain terms, without relying on universalistic rhetoric and concepts.

Here, Moyn seems to echo Carl Schmitt's cynical observation that 'whoever invokes humanity wants to cheat'.[24] In other words, invoking dignity is intended to silence political disputes through the adoption of a moralistic rhetoric that shames opponents into submission, for who would want to be on the wrong side of respecting human dignity? However, I do not find this to be a tremendously compelling point. Indeed, it is not clear to me what would be entailed by simply expressing one's political commitments in plain terms, detached from certain universalistic inclinations. Perhaps what Moyn has in mind is adopting a subjectivist political grammar predicated on an emotivist meta-ethics. Given this, one would not claim that one's stated political preferences were predicated on more universal moral truths. Instead, they simply express subjective political preferences. But even cast in this way, one would not get very far. What about those who simply prefer to cast their subjective political preferences in a universalistic manner? Those who adopt a subjectivist viewpoint in morality cannot then criticize those who simply prefer to express their political preferences by using a more objective sounding set of terms. Beyond this, I think that there are compelling philosophical reasons to reject the kind of subjectivist political semantics predicated on emotivist meta-ethics that Moyn seems to have in mind – though, again, that is somewhat unclear.

Following Dworkin, I do not think the structure of practical reason lends itself to adopting the external scepticism towards political and moral truth that Moyn seems to be implying.[25] External scepticism, or the idea that there is simply no Archimedean point from which to begin assessing the truth (or not) of political and more general moral propositions, mistakes what is important about practical reason. We cannot help but commit ourselves to certain courses of action, and in determining their moral and political worth what matters is how well we can justify such actions. From the standpoint of practical reason, what is important is the commitment that we demonstrate to unpacking the internal logic of moral and political propositions by testing their integrity and efficacy through a process moving towards reflective equilibrium. Given that, there are few good reasons to avoid at least attempting to develop a more fruitful set of political concepts.

In this historical and exegetical chapter there is no space for a more extensive discussion of these philosophical issues. I present them only so as quickly to rebut the idea that there is no need to put forward universalistic political propositions predicated on moral conceptions like human dignity. But, what about dignity itself? Why deploy it in particular? Moyn's contribution does a great deal to awaken us to the different conceptions of dignity that have existed historically, but I see few reasons why its plasticity should prevent us from articulating a new conception if that can improve, however incrementally, on its predecessors. If there is one important lesson that history teaches, it is never to underestimate the possibility that novel developments might take place. And clearly, given its attraction to many different people from many different walks of life, human dignity seems to inspire such novelty, often for the good. Dignity may be a plastic concept, but that might speak to its capacity to inspire rather than just its apparent mutability.

For instance, I think that, despite the scepticism of some, the novelty value of connecting dignity to a regime of international law was exceptional. Moreover, these developments prefaced the ascendant status increasingly given to dignity, as a growing number of scholars began to recognize its emancipatory potential. It is to these developments that I now turn.

The Internationalization of Dignity

The experience and aftermath of the Second World War undoubtedly influenced current interest in human dignity. The traditional narrative concerning the war and the burgeoning of the international human rights regime is well known and does not warrant repetition here. Instead, I will simply jump into discussing where and how dignity is linked with international human rights law. Moyn and others are right to criticize the now stock narrative that a secular conception of human dignity emerged with the philosophy of Kant, only to languish until 1948. As we have seen, the story is considerably more complex than that, but there is no doubt that the current interest in dignity owes much to its canonization in international human rights law.

The conceptual link between realizing dignity and the aims of international law are very explicit in the text of many international legal codes. The Universal Declaration of Human Rights (UDHR) – itself a non-binding but wildly influential articulation of global principles – opens with the following Preamble:

> Whereas recognition of the inherent dignity and of the equal and inalienable rights of all members of the human family is the foundation of freedom, justice and peace in the world...
> whereas the peoples of the United Nations have in the Charter reaffirmed their faith in fundamental human rights, in the dignity and worth of the human person and in the equal rights of men and women and have determined to promote social progress and better standards of life in larger freedom.

References to human dignity appear twice in the Preamble. First, human dignity is acknowledged as one of the sources of 'freedom, justice, and peace in the world'. Secondly, faith in inherent dignity is associated with the 'worth' of human beings, and is a step on the road towards 'social progress' and a better life in which all enjoy 'larger freedom'.

References to dignity appear twice more in the UDHR. The first is in Article 1, where dignity is linked to the Enlightenment ideals of 'reason and conscience' that imply that all should act towards one another in a spirit of 'brotherhood':

> All human beings are born free and equal in dignity and rights. They are endowed with reason and conscience and should act towards one another in a spirit of brotherhood.

At this point, dignity is largely articulated in rather abstract and even hagiographic terms as leading to and from all good things, somehow and someway. However, the next references to human dignity, in Articles 22 and 23(3), are far more provocative. Here, the UDHR explicitly links human dignity to one's capacity to flourish in a rich social environment. This observation will be important later, when I conceptually link human dignity to what I term 'expressive capabilities'.

Article 22 reads:

> Everyone, as a member of society, has the right to social security and is entitled to realization, through national effort and international co-operation and in accordance with the organization and resources of each State, of the economic, social and cultural rights indispensable for his dignity and the free development of his personality.

Article 23(3) is even more express in drawing an explicit connection between respect for economic, social, and cultural rights and the flourishing of human dignity:

> Everyone who works has the right to just and favourable remuneration ensuring for himself and his family an existence worthy of human dignity, and supplemented, if necessary, by other means of social protection.

The last point comes very close to implying, as I did in the section above, that states have an obligation to maintain a rightful condition that involves protecting economic, social and cultural rights. This conceptual link becomes even more express in the Covenant designed to protect just those rights.

At points, the International Covenant on Civil and Political Rights (ICCPR) comes very close to declaring that amplifying human dignity is the ideal to and from which all 'daughter rights', and indeed, the authority of the United Nations itself, flow. References to dignity appear throughout the text of the Covenant. The most striking are found in the Preamble, which seems to go out of its way to outdo that of the UDHR. The reference to dignity appears immediately:

> Considering that, in accordance with the principles proclaimed in the Charter of the United Nations, recognition of the inherent dignity and of the equal and inalienable rights of all members of the human family is the foundation of freedom, justice and peace in the world,
>
> Recognizing that these rights derive from the inherent dignity of the human person.

While admirably emphatic, the language of the Preamble toys with the same tension that wracks many normative arguments that draw inspiration from human dignity: if human dignity is 'inherent', what need have people for human rights? Here, one detects echoes of Arendt's famous argument on the right to have rights, and that individuals came to recognize the need for the universal rights of man only when their enforceable civic rights were entirely stripped away.[26] In an appropriate twist, this concern seems to be verified by the text of the ICCPR itself. After emphatically stressing the importance of human dignity as the source for all human rights, references to it appear only once more in the text of Article 10, which outlines the legal rights of individuals: 'All persons deprived of their liberty shall be treated with humanity and with respect for the inherent dignity of the human person.'

The remainder of the Article does not detail what is expressly involved in paying respect to the dignity of individuals who have been arrested. It only suggests that the accused should be treated differently than the convicted, and children differently than adults.

The International Covenant on Economic, Social and Cultural Rights (ICESCR) opens with the same dignity-centric language as the ICCPR. But, unlike the latter Covenant, the emphasis on dignity does not disappear once one dives into the heart of the text. Indeed, the ICESCR makes a strikingly programmatic reference to dignity in Article 13, linking its amplification directly to a host of related goods:

> The States Parties to the present Covenant recognize the right of everyone to education. They agree that education shall be directed to the full development of the human personality and the sense of its dignity, and shall strengthen the respect for human rights and fundamental freedoms. They further agree that education shall enable all persons to participate effectively in a free society, promote understanding, tolerance and friendship among all nations and all racial, ethnic or religious groups, and further the activities of the United Nations for the maintenance of peace.

Such sections are likely to be what the drafters had in mind when they called for the 'progressive realization' of the Covenant, as opposed to the ICCPR, which contains no such qualifications. While the section is nominally about education, it links many different goods. Education is to be available to all – not just as a good in and of itself, but because it fosters the 'development of the human personality and the sense of its dignity', which in turn should 'strengthen' and further the respect that individuals have for human rights and freedom, and contribute to establishing a lasting culture of toleration and peace.

References to dignity also appear in other major international human rights documents. The most prominent and important for my purposes are the references in the European Convention on Human Rights (ECHR). In later chapters I will refer to European Union (EU) jurisprudence when trying to indicate how amplifying human dignity can be made the fundamental orientation of international human rights law.

The most striking reference in the ECHR appears in Protocol 13, concerning the protection of fundamental freedoms and the elimination of the death penalty. The language is strikingly close to that of the UDHR:

> Convinced that everyone's right to life is a basic value in a democratic society and that the abolition of the death penalty is essential for the protection of this right and for the full recognition of the inherent dignity of all human beings.

References to human dignity also appear in the Charter of Fundamental Rights of the European Union, Article 1 of which proclaims: 'Human dignity is inviolable. It must be respected and protected.'

Finally, references to human dignity appear in the European Convention for the Protection of Human Rights and Dignity of the Human Being With Regard to the Application of Biology and Medicine: Convention on Human Rights and Medicine. The Preamble states:

> Convinced of the need to respect the human being both as an individual and as a member of the human species and recognising the importance of ensuring the dignity of the human being;
>
> Conscious that the misuse of biology and medicine may lead to acts endangering human dignity;

Then, somewhat further down:

> Resolving to take such measures as are necessary to safeguard human dignity and the fundamental rights and freedoms of the individual with regard to the application of biology and medicine.

These references indicate the ascendant prominence of human dignity in international human rights law. There are also important instances in which references to human dignity have been incorporated into domestic constitutions, including those of Germany, South Africa and Switzerland. For instance, the Constitution of South Africa indicates that respect for 'human dignity, the achievement of equality and the advancement of human rights and freedoms' is one of the founding principles of the post-apartheid state. And, most notably, Article 1, paragraph 1 of the German Constitution reads: 'Human dignity is inviolable. To respect and protect it shall be the duty of all state authority.'

The increasing legalization of dignity has been matched by a growing theoretical literature on the topic, by authors such as Benhabib, Kateb, Dworkin and many others. Many of these are explicit efforts to provide philosophical and normative support to the international human rights regime. In the next and final section of this chapter, I will look at some of these efforts and assess their relative efficacy.

Providing New Theoretical Frameworks for Human Dignity

The legalization and internationalization of human dignity, combined with declining faith in Marxist-Socialist visions, have contributed to human rights and their affiliated concepts becoming the ideology of the 'last utopia' – the final shot at establishing a truly progressive state and society.[27] Not coincidentally, the last several decades have seen an explosion of theories trying to frame new conceptions of human dignity, fleshed out with a corresponding set of rights. My own project is affiliated with this trend, and I have no desire to criticize it. Instead, this last section is designed as a quick overview of some of these projects. Generally speaking, there are two major streams of thought in the recent dignity literature. These should be treated as ideal typologies rather than as firm categorizations. While dignity is a rather plastic concept, there is a limit to its flexibility. All the authors mentioned here share a large number of overlapping concerns, are often critical of the status quo, and marry their conceptions of dignity to more general normative frameworks. But the way in which they go about doing so is subtly different and bears consideration. After briefly summarizing the positions of the various authors, I will detail what I take to be the strengths and weaknesses of both respective streams. I will conclude by highlighting how my own conception of dignity draws insight from both, as filtered through a critical legal lens.

The first stream of thought in the modern theoretical literature on dignity is an individualistic one. This is often, though not exclusively, affiliated with liberal political thought and its corresponding set of rights. Authors who are representative of this stream are Ronald Dworkin[28] and George Kateb. Such authors tend to commence their analysis of dignity by looking at the roles that it plays in the normative situatedness of the individual, and then gradually shift from there to analysing how it can and should transform the individual's relationships with those around them. The goal for these authors is to cash dignity out through an affiliated account of rights that is conceived as largely immutable and set by the overarching theoretical architecture designed to prioritize individualism.

Ronald Dworkin's account of dignity is exemplary in this field. For him, dignity is central to the moral framework that he develops in *Justice for Hedgehogs*, and which he seems to imply is latent within all his voluminous works. Most of the historical antecedents to which he appeals, including Hume, Kant and Rawls, and indeed many of his philosophical opponents such as Berlin, can be neatly classified as liberals. Dworkin's conception of dignity is firmly within that tradition. He claims that respecting dignity involves realizing two social principles. The first is that each individual should enjoy self-respect and should take their lives seriously.[29] The second is that each individual should have an opportunity to live authentically, acknowledging 'special, personal responsibility for identifying what counts as success' in that individual's life though establishing a coherent narrative of unique existential value to them.[30] As interpreted – I think correctly – by Simon, these principles perform triple duties in Dworkin's moral system. They provide guidance on what one must do to live well; demonstrate the rights that individuals have against their political community; and, finally, clarify the rights that we owe to others.[31] Added together, they are intended to provide a formula for how to live well as dignified individuals.

Another account of dignity that falls into the individualist stream, but draws on different philosophical sources, is George Kateb's. Drawing on the work of continental authors such as Heidegger, Kateb argues that dignity is an existential value that is imputed to an individual by virtue of their identity. As he puts it early in his book *Human Dignity*:

> Human dignity is an existential value; value of worthiness is imputed to the identity of the person or the species. I stipulate that when the truth of identity is at stake, existence is at stake; the matter is existential. The idea of human dignity insists on recognizing the proper identity of individual or species; recognizing what a person is in relation to all other persons and what the species is in relation to all other species.[32]

Kateb's interpretation of the existential character of dignity is related to a unique existentialist interpretation of morality. Dignity serves two functions. Its directly existential function is to delineate the absolute independence and uniqueness of all individuals relative to one another. This has a conceptual independence from 'instrumental practicality' and morality. This is not to say that dignity and morality cannot be related, and that is indeed the next step that Kateb takes. But his point is to emphasize that the existential function of dignity is to make us aware that our identity exists independently of any 'suffering' or competing consequentialist concerns for which we might feel compelled to make sacrifices.[33] Naturally, this makes Kateb deeply hostile towards utilitarian doctrines.[34] Secondly, dignity's moral function is to guard the individual from unjustifiable suffering at the hands of the state. Moral dignity exists to protect the individual's uniqueness from oppression by others who might wish to use the individual as a means to an end, and is thus an offshoot of existential individuality.

Both Dworkin's and Kateb's conceptions of dignity are individualistic, because each begins his account by analysing dignity's value for and to the individual. Dworkin believes that dignity is valuable first and foremost because individuals should enjoy self-respect, and secondly because they should be capable of living authentic lives whose narratives are of ultimate value to them. The offshoot of this is that dignity defines the way in which individuals are to relate to one another, most prominently through the mediums of politics and the law. Kateb's conception of dignity, while drawing on different authors, is remarkably similar. Dignity is first and foremost an existential value. Through it we recognize our unique identity both as individuals and as a species relative to all other species in the world. The follow-on from this is the need to develop a moral account of how to protect unique individuals from unjustifiable suffering at the hands of others, most notably at the hands of political institutions and the law. Not surprisingly, both Dworkin and Kateb place immense importance on the idea of rights as metaphysically immutable and largely set. The resulting style of criticisms tends to be immanent. Since the rights affiliated with dignity are immutable and largely set, the form and practice of politics and law must reflect or synchronize with them.

The second prominent stream in the modern theoretical literature on dignity is what might be called the 'relational' stream.[35] Again, this is often, though not exclusively, embraced by various democratic and cosmopolitan thinkers such as Jürgen Habermas, Jeremy Waldron and Seyla Benhabib. Authors in the relational stream are also concerned with the normative situatedness of the individual. However, they often commence their analysis of dignity by looking at the way in which its normative imperatives should transform the social contexts in which the individual is situated. In this respect the relational stream is often more reliant on historical and socio-philosophical analysis that demonstrates how claims about dignity operate to transform the social contexts within which individuals pursue their interests and various life goals.

The ultimate conclusion of these authors is to unpack their conception of dignity through an account of rights conceived as structural pre-conditions established prior[36] to engaging in robust political discourses about the goals and interests to be pursued collectively through the establishment and functioning of collective institutions and mediums. To put that more simply, rights are respected as necessary for carrying out political processes but because the process itself is ascribed greater weight than in the individualist stream, rights are not as immutable and set: they can be reconceived and put to new work as necessary.

Jürgen Habermas's conception of dignity is perhaps the most important, given his status as among the most pre-eminent philosophers of the modern era. However, his contributions to the direct literature on dignity have been fairly minimal. The most concrete is his paper 'The Concept of Human Dignity and the Realistic Utopia of Human

Rights', in which he notes that the proliferation of references to dignity in international and constitutional law necessitates developing a more complex account of the concept's intellectual genealogy. After briefly running through this account, Habermas concludes that dignity has played a central role in mediating between facts and norms by importing universalistic mores into positive law. This was foundational to establishing the realistic utopian[37] vision of a society organized around respecting human rights.

> After two hundred years of modern constitutional history, we have a better grasp of what distinguished this development from the beginning: human dignity forms the 'portal' through which the egalitarian and universalistic substance of morality is imported into the law. The idea of human dignity is the conceptual hinge that connects the morality of equal respect for everyone with positive law and democratic lawmaking in such a way that their interplay could give rise to a political order founded upon human rights.[38]

Habermas notes that another way to conceive of dignity is to envision a gradual extension of the concrete concept of social honour from belonging to a few individuals and offices enjoying high ranks in hierarchically ordered tradition societies to include every human being.[39] Here he directly invokes the work of Jeremy Waldron, who is also keen to develop a genealogy of dignity that traces its concrete impact in modern normative and legal discourses.

Waldron is sceptical of more directly philosophical projects, such as Kant's and Dworkin's, which seek to ground human dignity in a comprehensive account of the self and morality more generally. Like Habermas, Waldron wishes to pragmatize dignity by demonstrating the use to which it is put in social discourses and the impact that this has for subjects. Waldron argues that we should understand human dignity as deriving from a gradual attempt to grant all human beings the same moral rank that was once attributed only to aristocrats. Dignity is a normative rank that raises everyone to the same level on the moral and political hierarchy, at least from a legalistic standpoint.[40] This elevation to the same moral rank coincides with entitlement to the same basic set of rights. As Waldron puts it in his *Tanner Lectures*:

> So there is my hypothesis: the modern notion of human dignity involves an upwards equalization of rank, so that we now try to accord to every human being something of the dignity, rank, and expectation of respect that was formerly accorded to nobility.[41]

Unfortunately, while Waldron's conception is helpful and innovative, he does not provide a great deal of guidance on how this shift to granting all human beings the same rank should shift our normative understanding. His conception of dignity is uncharacteristically historical rather than critical.

The same cannot be said for Seyla Benhabib, who is perhaps the most critically minded of the authors in the relational stream. She persuasively argues that the discursive shift towards recognizing universal human rights and human dignity should change our understanding of the relationship between individuals and society. This discursive shift moves us away from a positivistic approach to law that understood rights as belonging primarily to citizens by virtue of their participation in affairs of state. Instead, Benhabib claims that human dignity enables us to conceive all human beings as moral subjects who are entitled to legal protections simply by virtue of their being human. This leads her to develop two main frameworks for conceiving how a human being can be understood and amplified. The first is to look at the different democratic iterations of human rights movements emerging around the globe, and how they advocate for a diverse array of human rights that are necessary for respecting dignity.[42] The second is to look at the jurisgenerative power of traditionally marginalized groups who rally behind the concept of dignity and deploy it to demand new rights and entitlements from states.[43] This power shakes rights discourse out of a calcified positivism and opens up new avenues for expanding our understanding of the normative obligations of states, and develops ways to translate these new obligations into a more dynamic and responsive legal medium.

What unites the authors of the relational stream is their interest in eschewing the more classically transcendental mode of argument associated with the individualist stream. Authors such as Dworkin and Kateb are interested in developing conceptions of dignity that flow from a deeper account of the self and the mores that it should adopt. Consequently, their accounts are highly individualistic. By contrast, Habermas, Waldron and Benhabib[44] develop conceptions of dignity that have two prongs. The first is to treat the concept discursively – as a concept that entered the normative vocabulary of Western public spheres during a specific time in their history. Dignity subsequently entered the legal lexicon through pressure from allied movements that were concerned with equality, democracy and human rights. This leads to the second prong of the relational approach. While Habermas, Waldron and Benhabib may be sceptical about the intrinsic quality of dignity, they appreciate its rhetorical and ideological capacity to bear the weight of diverse social aspirations that seek to deepen and broaden social equality and rights. They therefore see dignity as a relational concept that mediates between an individual's moral values and the concrete demands that they make through various mediums such as law and politics. Naturally they see it as especially useful in putting forward demands via rights discourse.

There are virtues and deficiencies in both the individualist and relational streams that warrant analysis here. I will begin by discussing what I think we should take from each stream, before moving on to their deficiencies.

I believe that the primary virtue of the individualist stream is its meta-ethical heft. The strong emphasis placed by authors such as Dworkin and Kateb on the normative worth of the individual provides a clear foundation for the more general theoretical architecture that they develop to justify their moral proposals. Both authors frame this normative worth through their conceptions of human dignity. This is exceptionally helpful relative to the relational school because it provides a deeper – some might even say intrinsic – set of reasons for why dignity is important. Put very simply, it is important because human beings necessarily value their lives and wish to make something of them.[45] After this is established, one can then engage in a more systematic review of the types of reasoning required to realize this goal, which raises all the standard questions that appear in most deontological accounts of morality.

The limitation of this individualist stream is its presumption that dignity is inherent in each individual, regardless of their situatedness in the world. In this, they echo the limitations of the Kantian approach. For Dworkin, dignity has to have an intrinsic quality to it, since it is the basis for the remainder of his liberal moral theory. For Kateb, dignity is existential and prefigures morality. This is also why their mode of argument is immanent in nature. Since dignity is taken as a given, the form of reasoning affiliated with it proceeds deductively. But this leads to a major problem that goes back to Kant's own account of dignity. If it is true that dignity is inherent in each individual, one must seriously question the degree to which empirical matters, including socio-historical contexts, can ever impact upon it. This seriously limits the critical potential of the individualist stream, because it is never clear why the socio-historical contexts in which individuals live should really have any bearing on their dignity. Of course, neither Dworkin nor Kateb accepts this, and both develop strong theories about the way in which society and political institutions should be ordered. But it is never clear to me why this connection is as tight as they presume. If dignity exists in isolation from all other factors, why should it really matter in what contexts individuals live?

This problem is rectified by the relational stream of theories on human dignity. The conceptions of human dignity developed by authors such as Habermas, Waldron and Benhabib may be less romantic than Dworkin's or Kateb's. However, they are more realistic because they appreciate that dignity can be influenced by the socio-historical contexts within which individuals exist. More importantly, Habermas and Benhabib provide complex and rich frameworks that demonstrate how dignity has been mobilized by social groups to articulate concrete sets of political and legal demands. These take place within a recognizable public sphere with institutions common to many modern states and the international legal system. The relational stream therefore eschews the abstract and monologically immanent reasoning of the individualist stream in favour of more concrete and dialectical forms of criticism. This is very amenable to the critical legal approach to dignity that I will develop in Chapter 3.

The limitation of the relational stream is that it lacks the strong meta-ethical justification of dignity's value that is offered by the individualist stream. For individualists such as Dworkin and Kateb, the self and its dignity are patently what matters. The relational stream struggles to develop such a powerful meta-ethical justification because it is too context sensitive and overdetermined by empirics. Indeed, the strongest justification for these positions has been given by Habermas, who argues that quasi-transcendental imperatives present within the structure of political and moral dialogue itself imply the necessity of realizing certain democratic and egalitarian structures. However, this strikes me as unconvincing. It does not clarify for whom or to what purposes political and moral dialogue should matter, paradoxically relegating the individuals who participate in it to secondary importance in their own drama. This can be rectified only by articulating very clearly why the individuals who engage in such dialogue have some kind of value, which I believe can be captured by a more robust conception of dignity. My goal will be to present this in Chapter 3.

Critical Legal Studies and Human Dignity

The conception of dignity that I will shortly present has its roots in critical legal studies. As mentioned earlier, this might seem unusual, given that critical legal scholars were often reticent to develop constructive normative conceptions, preferring to dedicate themselves to unmasking the hidden conceits of law and legal analysis. In this short summary I will discuss both why I think this is a virtue, and why we need to move beyond critique. There is no space here to discuss completely the complex history of critical legal studies and its intellectual offshoots. Instead, I will simply briefly describe the main characteristics of the critical legal movement, before moving on to why I think some conception of dignity is a necessary normative addition to the movement.

Critical legal studies developed the epistemic positions of the American legal realists, but innovatively gave the earlier tradition a deconstructive twist. Though there is some debate about when the realist movement died down, most believe that critical legal studies emerged in the mid-1970s, with the publication of a sequence of classic texts, including Duncan Kennedy's 'Form and Substance in Private Law Adjudication'[46] and Roberto Unger's *Knowledge and Politics*. By the 1980s, it was arguably the most prominent – and certainly the most infamous – movement in legal philosophy, inspiring both passionate advocacy and derisive dismissal.[47] Despite this brief moment of ascendancy, enthusiasm for critical legal studies petered out by the end of the decade. Many left-wing scholars became unhappy with the generally Marxist perspective adopted by most critical legal scholars. They were happy to retain the overall critical outlook towards the law, but wished to examine other intersectional forms of marginalization. For these reasons, critical legal theory branched out into a broader array of interpretive lenses and disciplines, such as critical race approaches to law, socio-legal studies and so on.

Critical legal scholars differed widely in their interests and focus, often deploying deconstructive tools to examine a broad array of topics in the law. Nonetheless, most critical legal scholars held to a few central tenets. The first was some variation on the indeterminacy thesis. This is where the critical legal scholars' debt to American legal realism was most transparent. The indeterminacy thesis held that many, or most, legal questions did not actually beget an objective answer. The text of the law was riddled with ambiguities that could not be resolved through the application of the various formalist modes of analysis taught at law schools, most of which expressly or implicitly presumed the tenability of some variant of legal positivism.

This led to the next main tenet, which was the socio-historical situatedness of legal practitioners and institutions. As much or most of the law did not lend itself to an objective interpretation, this meant that legal practitioners and institutions did not actually engage in an ideologically neutral enterprise. Since law is not self-interpreting and does not beget an objective determination, this begs the question of how legal practitioners and institutions decide what the law shall be and how to apply it in any given circumstance. The answer given by most critical legal scholars is that legal practitioners and institutions resolve ambiguities by interpreting the law in line with their ideological preferences. These preferences were determined by the socio-historical situatedness of the legal practitioner in question (their economic interests, psychology, educational background, class position and so on).

Finally, there is the third major tenet, which is that law serves to marginalize weaker members of society. This is where critical legal scholars deviated most formidably. Many took a fairly orthodox Marxist line on this point. Others, such as Unger, developed more original normative conceptions to justify their opposition to the contemporary status quo. But regardless, critical legal scholars believed that since what counted as law was largely the decision of often privileged legal practitioners who emerged out of elite institutions, the law tended to serve their interests by marginalizing other groups in society. Most noticeably, this included mitigating the capacity of marginalized groups to use the law in order to advance a more progressive agenda. Law and its advocates were fundamentally a reactionary force in society. This meant that the progressives should either use it with caution as a double-edged sword, or refrain from pushing their agenda through the law wholesale.

This last point is the most crucial one for my purposes. While very few critical legal scholars have written about dignity, their position can be inferred from how most Crits (adherents of critical legal studies) approach human rights. The scepticism of most Crits towards the law and legal institutions extended to most accounts of rights and rights discourse. In his earlier work, Unger dismissed liberal rights for flowing from a fundamentally self-contradictory psychology and metaphysics.[48] This meant that they served to reinforce a fundamentally deficient form of society in which abstract individualism took the place of genuine self-authorship and democratic community building. For Costas Douzinas, human rights are a cultural fetishism that can distract from more pertinent efforts to develop a new critique of political economy and state institutions.[49] For Allan Hutchinson and Michal Mandel, rights promise a Utopian future that is never to arrive.[50] Much like characters in a work by Samuel Beckett, naïve progressives put their faith in rights discourse only to realize, time and again, that such discourse serves only to reinforce the property entitlements of the rich and powerful. Given this, it is far wiser to put one's faith in politics. These opinions are also echoed by Duncan Kennedy, who worries that appeals to right will limit our capacity to engage in Marxist and postmodern critiques of the state and marginalizing institutions. For these reasons, progressives should look upon rights and rights discourse with a fair amount of scepticism.

> Critique is always motivated. The practitioners of the critique of rights have often had mixed motives of the kind I am describing here. One motive is leftist and the other is mpm [modernism/postmodernism]. Suppose for the moment that one didn't have to worry about the leftist implications, what would be mpm motives for a critique of rights? The answer is that belief in rights and in the determinacy of rights reasoning are important parts of the overall project of bourgeois rightness, or reason, or the production of texts that will compel impersonally.[51]

There is much to admire in the critical legal examinations, including their critiques of rights discourse and affiliated conceptions such as human dignity. However, I feel that much of this goes too far. With the exception of Unger, many critical legal scholars have been largely focused on demonstrating the flaws and dangers inherent within rights discourse and its affiliated conceptions. Few of them have been willing to give constructive suggestions on what should replace it. Indeed, most Crits ultimately come down from their critical heights and concede that one should use the law to try to achieve a more egalitarian society, while always being cognizant of the dangers of using the master's tools to deconstruct his house. What this egalitarian society would look like, let alone why it is a worthwhile aspiration, is never spelled out in much concrete detail. Sadly, this has also been true of most of their intellectual descendants in various socio-legal and legal studies movements.

I do not think this tendency to engage exclusively in trashing is an adequate response to the needs of the current era. Indeed, there is a suspicious quality to attempting to evade what Rawls characterizes as the burdens of moral judgment by claiming to be engaging exclusively in a critical appraisal of law without invoking competing moral norms.[52] This approach of engaging in critique from nowhere does not strike me as authentic, or even adequate, and demonstrates a failure of imagination. It would be more accurate to characterize many of these critical legal and affiliated efforts as invoking relatively thin sets of norms oriented around achieving a more egalitarian society. But the broad contours of what this egalitarian society would and should be are rarely spelled out, and no effort is made to inspire or orient concrete and constructive action. While the task of critique is always important, it is not sufficient if the expectation is simply that deconstructing regimes of marginalization will imminently lead to the emergence of some vaguely conceived egalitarian society. This requires examining how law, including international human rights law, can be reoriented along more progressive lines.

One critical legal thinker who never fell into this tendency was Roberto Unger. Throughout his lengthy oeuvre, Unger has developed a comprehensive account of what a more egalitarian society would look like, and has connected it to an incisive critique of the contemporary legal order. In Chapter 3, I will draw on his work to sketch out my conception of human dignity and begin to spell out why I think it should be appealing to many critical legal and progressive scholars.

This chapter has reviewed some of the various conceptions of human dignity that have emerged over the centuries. Beginning with the Renaissance, it traced the deployment of dignity in early modern thought, down to the work of Immanuel Kant. After discussing and criticizing Kant's powerful conception, it looked at the more critical history of dignity developed by Samuel Moyn. It then moved towards more contemporary issues by looking at dignity's historical internationalization in international human rights law, and its subsequent resurgence in the theoretical literature.

Chapters 1 and 2 have largely been about exegetically setting the stage for presenting my own conception of dignity and unpacking how it can be amplified if made the fundamental orientation of international human rights law. It is to this more constructive task that I now turn.

3

A Critical Legal Conception of Human Dignity

The Need for a New Conception of Human Dignity

In Chapter 2, I discussed some of the major theoretical conceptions of human dignity developed throughout the concept's long and rich intellectual history. I ended by unpacking some of the salient characteristics of what I characterized as the individualist stream and the relational stream, before arguing for the necessity of developing a critical legal conception of human dignity as the basis for a more constructive project. This would retain the critical bite of that movement while also firming up its normative basis, much of which has always been fuzzy beyond appeals to now familiar left-wing tropes.

Continentally inspired left-wing legal scholars and progressives have generally spent the past several decades dealing with the collapse of Marxism by engaging in the primarily deconstructive task of undermining marginalizing discourses and power structures. Much of this draws on the brilliant and pioneering work of postmodern theorists such as Foucault, Derrida, Spivak and others. There is a great deal to be said about continuing this task of deconstructing and undermining marginalizing discourses and power structures. But I believe that what is often left behind in these tasks is any explicit argument for any given position. Oftentimes, authors engage in the task of deconstructing marginalizing discourses and power structures simply to assume the salience of their normative motivations, and moreover assume that this will be clear to anyone who interprets their work. To my mind, this has resulted in a somewhat hermetic left-wing intellectual culture, in which we have failed to make clear why deconstructing marginalizing discourses and power structures should matter to those impacted by them. More importantly, we have failed to provide clear alternative conceptions that highlight what changes should be undertaken to reorganize society along more emancipatory and egalitarian lines. Here the resources of analytical political and moral philosophy can be a great guide in buttressing critical approaches to legality. My conception of human dignity is intended to fill this gap.

The critical legal conception of human dignity – or, as I sometimes call it, 'dignified self-authorship' – presented in this chapter is designed to explicate many implicit critical legal claims about emancipation and equality, and incorporate them within a dynamic normative approach to legality. Many of the significant ideas are drawn from the work of Roberto Unger, with considerable additions developed through an analysis of the capabilities approach of Amartya Sen and Martha Nussbaum. I draw on these authors specifically because my conception holds that human dignity is deeply related to an agent's capacity to engage in self-authorship. This requires demonstrating why human dignity, agency, and self-authorship can and should be connected in the novel conception that I present. On this point, I feel that while Unger provides a usefully broad overview of a critical legal conception of agency, Sen and Nussbaum provide the theoretical resources needed to describe what robust agency would entail in far more concrete and less macro logical detail. This makes synthesizing their views a worthwhile task.

My conception of human dignity also draws on the conceptions that have come before, while attempting to go beyond them in important respects. Most of the concrete inspiration for my conception of human dignity comes from authors in the relational stream, who approach human dignity as a starting point for the critique of existent social institutions. I reject the immanent quality of many moral arguments that flow from the individualist stream of thought, which takes dignity to be inherent. This often results in a rather static form of moral reasoning, wherein political institutions and human rights are seen as necessarily taking the form that an author thinks is important to respecting the inherent dignity of human beings. I believe that dignity operates on a continuum determined by an individual's set of expressive capabilities, and that political structures should be reoriented to amplify this set wherever possible. One of the ways in which this is exemplified practically is via the model of rights that I suggest my conception of dignity begets. This set of rights is designed to enable individuals to reconceive and reconstruct political institutions and specific positive rights along lines consonant with their interests and commitments.

The model of human rights that flows from my conception of human dignity is oriented around the central idea that individuals should be made as capable as possible of transcending the socio-historical contexts that govern them. One of the most important ways in which this can be achieved is when individuals are authors of the political and legal institutions that govern them. The other is through engaging in redistributive efforts to ensure that all individuals enjoy an equal set of what I call 'expressive capabilities', except when inequalities flow from their morally significant choices. Together, these rights should operate in tandem, enabling individuals to mobilize political and legal power to transform the social contexts within which they pursue their interests and various life goals.

Dignified Self-Authorship[1]

In this section I develop a conception of dignity that is an individual's capacity for self-authorship through context transcending acts of agency. This is the theoretical core of my project. It is also where the critical-legal association with Roberto Unger is clearest.[2] Following Unger, I emphatically reject the traditional conception of dignity and seek to replace it with one that is far more robust, and centred on an individual's ability to reject and transform the false necessity of the socio-historical context within which they live.

Unger rose to prominence with the publication of *Knowledge and Politics* in 1973.[3] While he has since shifted his overarching approach in very significant ways, and both his theoretical architecture and critique of liberalism have been subjected to considerable philosophical criticism,[4] Unger's overall position has remained relatively stable. He argues that classical liberalism is based on a poor understanding of human nature, which cannot bridge the divide between the subjectivism of its individuals and liberalism's pretensions to scientificity.[5] At the same time, Unger does not believe that either the Marxist or the hyper-theory leftist alternatives have provided adequate theoretical alternatives to classical liberalism. Much of his more constructive work is aimed at providing just such an alternative: one that takes the best aspects of liberalism while overcoming its theoretical and concrete limitations.[6]

My project draws inspiration and guidance from Unger's efforts, while deviating from them in important respects. In particular, my conception of dignity draws a close link between dignity, self-authorship and agency. While each of these occupies a unique place in my theoretical architecture, it is the link between them that animates the entire conception. Respecting and amplifying dignity is taken to be the normative goal, or *telos*, that just social institutions should strive to realize for all individuals.[7] Self-authorship occurs when individuals define themselves by redefining the socio-historical contexts in which they live, including through and sometimes in opposition to social institutions. Agency is their general capacity to do this, as defined by the set of 'expressive capabilities' that an individual enjoys.

My conception can be summarized in the claim that human beings enjoy dignity when they are capable of dignified self-authorship through context transcending acts of agency. Here, self-authorship is interpreted in a very Ungerian fashion, and is deeply related to agency. Individuals are capable of dignified self-authorship to the extent that they are able to transform the world around them by transcending and shaping the socio-historical contexts they inhabit. This is a complex claim that requires some elaboration.

Unger recognized that all human beings exist as individuals embedded in specific socio-historical contexts.[8] Socio-historical contexts are the totality of external features in the world that are subject to human control and creation. Because it is conceived as a totality, the idea of a socio-historical context should be given a robust and extensional interpretation. It includes the political-economic arrangement of a society, the laws, the culture, many semantic aspects of the language, gender and ethnic relations, sexual mores and so on. One of Unger's points is that what characterizes all these external features is that they are ultimately the product of deliberate human activity, and in some cases deliberate human design.[9] For instance, it may be true that a given legal system developed in an evolutionary manner analogous to biological life in the natural world. But what distinguishes the former from the latter is that some human beings exercised their agency to beget a system of laws, while (until fairly recently) we had little control over the dynamics of human natural selection.[10]

One of the problems that Unger detects is that we often conflate socio-historical contexts with scientific necessity. Because we are influenced by all external features in the world, it can be easy to think that, as all individuals are to some extent unchangeably determined by biological laws, so too who we are is necessarily determined by the political, cultural, legal and economic arrangements particular to the socio-historical context that we inhabit. Unger calls on us to reject this 'false necessity' and recognize that all socio-historical contexts, being the product of deliberate human activity and even design, are ultimately characterized by their plasticity. We can deploy our 'context transcending' powers to reshape them according to our will and interests. Of course, being a critical legal scholar, Unger argues that we should reshape them to be considerably more egalitarian and democratic.

This is where the links between dignity, self-authorship and agency become clear. I believe that individuals can be authors of their lives to the extent that they refuse to allow their identity to be essentially determined by the socio-historical contexts that they inhabit. Here I must be careful. This is not to suggest that all individuals must continuously revolutionize the socio-historical contexts in which they live. Nor am I taking an explicitly anti-communitarian stance and arguing that individuals should reject those socio-historical contexts and their impact on identity, especially if they personally affiliate with them. But they should not feel compelled to live according to the compulsions of socio-historical contexts whose false necessity they would otherwise choose to reject given the opportunity. Being dignified authors of our lives means being generally capable of exercising our agency to transform the world around us, in co-operation with and demonstrating respect for others, in a manner that is expressive of our individual interests and commitments. This capacity for agency can be greater or lesser, depending on the total set of expressive capabilities that an individual enjoys. The more robust a set of expressive capabilities that an individual enjoys, the more generally capable of agency individuals become. And the more capable of agency they become, and the more they can exercise this capacity in line with their personal choices, the more we can say that individuals have enjoyed lives of dignified self-authorship. Whether and how they choose to alter their world becomes a matter of choice rather than being determined by arrangements and institutions in a socio-historical context.

This is where the distinguishing features of my conception of dignity become clearer. One of the motivations behind drawing on Unger is that his argument about socio-historical contexts cuts both ways. When we respect and amplify an individual's dignity, false necessity becomes malleable to the transformations determined by individuals engaged in dignified self-authorship. Where their dignity is highly constrained, socio-historical contexts can be experienced as highly determinative, and even unbearably oppressive. The goal, or *telos*, of just social institutions should be to respect and amplify dignity while curbing the external features of the socio-historical world that constrain it.

It is my position that respecting and amplifying human dignity should be a normative goal, or *telos*, of social institutions because human dignity is something that must be achieved rather than something that is simply inherent in all individuals, or ascribed to them by moral fiat.[11] Human dignity can be understood as a continuum. Some of us may enjoy a great deal of dignity: for instance, those with a very robust set of expressive capabilities that enable them to choose what form of life they wish to pursue and enact significant changes in the world. Others, such as the very poor or individuals reduced to 'bare life',[12] may enjoy little or no dignity at all.

This, I must highlight, is not at all their fault or a moral slight against them. The argument for understanding dignity as operating on a continuum is by no means intended to say that some individuals are more valuable than others – to reinvent a kind of aristocratic hierarchy of dignity, to invoke Waldron.[13] Quite the opposite: where individuals enjoy less dignity, it is the consequence of inadequate and even hostile acts or omissions by social institutions that have a responsibility to care for them.[14] This reinforces the need for a conception of dignity that directs attention towards empirical socio-historical contexts, especially responsible social institutions such as law, rather than at transcendental features such as 'good will' or well-meaning but pious declarations about inherent qualities. Socio-historical contexts should be arranged to respect and amplify dignity, and social institutions such as law can play a major role in this effort. The easiest way in which they can do so is by acting to enhance the individual's expressive capabilities, the total set of which indicates how capable they are of agency.

This final claim requires considerably more elaboration and more concrete discussion. This section operated at a fairly high level of abstraction in arguing for my specific conception of dignity and its relationship to self-authorship and agency. In the next section, I will ground the discussion by clarifying what I mean by a set of expressive capabilities, and how this is related to agency and dignified self-authorship.

Dignity and Expressive Capabilities

As mentioned, my account of expressive capabilities draws very heavily upon the work of Amartya Sen and Martha Nussbaum. However, I give their work a twist by connecting it to Unger's critical philosophy, and my own account of dignified self-authorship. Since my account discusses an individual's general capacity to transform the world in a manner expressive of their interests and commitments, I choose to identify an individual's set of capabilities as 'expressive' so as to characterize the main idea better.

This warrants some clarification. In Chapter 2, I discussed two contemporary streams of theoretical literature on human dignity, drawing special attention to the individualist stream and the relational stream. I also briefly discussed the strengths and weaknesses of both. My account of human dignity relies on expressive capabilities to mediate between these two streams. On the one hand, I have argued that human dignity is fundamentally related to self-authorship and agency. This captures the individualist idea that, to the extent possible, dignity is correlated with being able to live our own lives authentically. As I have already indicated, in the conception of human dignity that is sketched here, the total set of capabilities determines the extent to which we are able to live authentic lives of dignified self-authorship. However, I reject the idea – embraced by many individualist authors – that dignity is somehow an inherent quality enjoyed by all. Instead, I accept the claims of the relational school that dignity depends on the relations that individuals are capable of establishing in the world, and the myriad ways in which they are able to operationalize their agency to engage in dignified self-authorship. This is captured by the idea of expressive capabilities, since the total set can be negatively and positively impacted by empirical determinants. Moreover, later in this chapter I will also draw on the relational stream in maintaining that fully amplifying dignity would entail realizing two human rights that can be normatively mobilized by individuals in a variety of socio-historical contexts and for different types of reasons.

The capabilities approach to human agency outlines the universal but context-sensitive conditions required for all human beings to enjoy a dignified life. The approach takes securing the dignity of human beings as a primary aim.[15] Sen and Nussbaum integrally link dignity to an agent's choices; but agency is understood here in a rather refined way. To discuss agency concretely, we must look at the actual capacity that an individual has to make meaningful life choices.

Such a claim is more empirically oriented than one finds in a strictly Kantian approach. Sen and Nussbaum tirelessly stress that agency means little unless one looks at what choices individuals are capable of making. For them, this means looking at what individuals are capable of doing. From the perspective of the capabilities approach to human flourishing, understanding agency means passing from transcendental philosophy to the messiness of the empirical world. This is where the connection between the capabilities approach and utilitarianism is most apparent. Sen has been especially critical of utilitarians for not being adequately sensitive to the meaningful differences that exist between individuals.[16] This suggests that Kantian individualism remains the moral centre inspiring his project. Nonetheless, Sen accepts the utilitarian claim that substantiating agency is as much a matter of developing sound policy as it is of deriving the correct transcendental metaphysics.[17]

In *Inequality Re-examined*, Sen clarifies this point by referring to the capabilities that an individual possesses as determining the 'overall agency a person enjoys to pursue her well-being'.[18] He distinguishes between (i) the well-being of individuals and (ii) their agency to pursue well-being. This is a key distinction, since Sen admits that one's well-being and the agency to pursue it or not (what he calls 'agency') may in many instances conflict. He gives the example of a doctor who is willing to sacrifice her health to secure that of others, though one can think of many far less admirable examples.[19] For example, this might also involve the capability to make what seem like unhealthy choices. A Brahmin who decides to fast for religious reasons is emphatically different from an individual struggling in the midst of famine.[20] Nussbaum claims that this distinction highlights the link between the deontological and utilitarian dimensions of the capabilities approach to human flourishing. Since human flourishing entails being able to make meaningful choices through the exercise of practical reason, all individuals should have the capabilities needed to pursue their own idea of human flourishing.[21] After this threshold is met, the capabilities approach to human flourishing is agnostic on the actual functioning of people, since their flourishing or not is now seen as being dependent on their individual choices.

This is where I will conclude my fairly limited exegesis. No doubt, much more could be said. Sen and Nussbaum have developed a very powerful moral concept of agency that brings a great deal of analytical rigour to what one could broadly call the historically ambiguous idea of positive liberty. Moreover, they work to apply their conceptual frameworks to highly concrete examples that provide a great deal of guidance on how the capabilities approach can operate in practice. However, Sen and Nussbaum have often avoided developing the more critical possibilities of their project. While their underlying moral concept is quite radical, they have been strangely reticent to develop the more substantive critique of social institutions that would seem to follow from it. This may be because they feel that the capabilities approach is fundamentally liberal in its orientation towards agency, even if it expands the concerns of liberalism quite extensively. If this is the case, there should be no reason why the social institutions of a robust liberal democratic society could not adopt and implement something like the capabilities approach to human agency.

Certainly, both Sen and Nussbaum have done interesting work demonstrating how the capabilities approach can assist marginalized individuals in even the most extreme socio-historical contexts.[22] But, ultimately, I do not believe that it is a convincing reason not to unpack the critical possibilities of their project. If one pushes the more radical dimensions of the capabilities approach to their full extent, I feel that it would require considerably rethinking both the ideological contours of liberalism and the social institutions that engender liberal democracy. This is especially true if we wish to arrange social institutions to enable dignified self-authorship of the type that I discussed earlier.

This is why I develop Sen and Nussbaum's theory by linking it to Unger's philosophy. The decision to characterize capabilities as expressive is to highlight this synthesis. Expressive capabilities are those through which a person defines himself or herself by redefining the boundaries within which they exist. To use Unger's terminology, expressive capabilities are 'context transcending' powers.[23]

While similar, expressive capabilities are distinct from the Kantian will in that they exist only potentially unless they are realized and amplified in the empirical world.[24] This means that one must look at what individuals are able to do, given both their intrinsic capabilities and the empirical socio-historical contexts within which they live.

An ideal example of an expressive capability that is incredibly important, but also often undervalued in relation to agency, is an individual's capacity creatively to deploy and use a language. Noam Chomsky has done a great deal of work in demonstrating that language includes both innate and empirical features. One such feature is the biological predisposition of human children to learn a language as their brain develops throughout infancy. Some of its empirical features include the semantic meanings actually associated with the terms used in specific languages such as English. Here, Chomsky makes the revolutionary point that the transformational rules of universal grammar permit the formation of a potentially infinite number of novel semantic statements, though all the statements produced must adhere to the rules of human syntax.[25] Human beings, essentially through playing games with the semantic inheritances that they acquire as part of their languages, bring novelty into the world. In the same way, the socio-historical boundaries within which we exist can be transformed indefinitely by the application of a human being's expressive capabilities.

The 'creative aspect' of language use can be linked to our expressive capabilities as part of my more general conception of agency. Roberto Unger has already taken a pronounced step in this direction by making clear the connection between a robust conception of agency and Chomskyan linguistics. As he puts it in *The Self Awakened*:

> [T]he Capacity to produce the infinite out of the finite changes everything, shaping our conscious experience in its entirety. It gives us our power of using limited means to generate unlimited variations in language and thought, to express different contents or meaning through similar formal relations among symbols, and to convey the same contents or meaning through different series of symbols. It results in the most signal trait of our conceptual-intentional experience: our ability endlessly to revise our thoughts by bringing pressure to bear against their presuppositions: an ability we acquire only through our more basic power to generate endless variation and complication. This power in turn informs our sensational-motor experience by allowing us constantly to change the tacit stories with which we infuse our perceptions and guide our movements.[26]

Our creative capacity to use language, both as an abstract cognitive power and as a concrete entitlement that should be realized and amplified by the political and legal systems within which we exist, provides an ideal example of how this process of redefinition takes place. By employing the creative powers of language every day to bring novel semantic structures into the world, we can transcend a particular socio-historical boundary that once limited us.[27] Language use is an important example of an expressive capability, because it has both innate and empirical dimensions that clarify its relation to agency. All individuals have the capacity to enjoy a rich semantic inheritance with which they can develop a potentially infinite number of new statements that bring novelty into the world and allow them to reflect their individuality. But to do so to the fullest and richest possible extent, they need to be able to learn a language; be exposed to a wide variety of different language games through education and participation in the arts and artistic endeavours; benefit from supportive parenting and other positive adult role models and so on. This supports my argument on why individuals should have this expressive capability amplified – for instance, through the provision of a good education made available to all individuals regardless of their level of wealth and power.

My conception of dignity maintains that our capacity for agency remains only an abstract potentiality until it is substantiated by expanding the range of choices that an individual could possibly make through increasing the set of expressive capabilities that they enjoy. For example, the agency to go where one pleases would mean little to someone stranded on an island of two square kilometres. This is why the set of expressive capabilities enjoyed by individuals are so important in determining their overall capacity for engaging in dignified self-authorship. To put this another way, expressive capabilities are those that enable us to define ourselves by re-defining the socio-historical contexts within which we exist. The set of expressive capabilities that an individual enjoys is the source of their general capacity to transcend the hegemonic aura of false necessity that can be associated with socio-historical contexts.[28] As Unger nicely puts it:

> In both the European preindustrial and the Asian postindustrial situations, success, even survival, required the practice of an art of institutional dismemberment and recombination. This art constantly rearranges the two linkages repeatedly considered in this essay ... The practice of institutional dissociation and recombination shakes up and wears down a society's plan of social division and social ranking; roles and hierarchies depend for their perpetuation on the stability of particular institutions. This shaking up and wearing down represents one of the major forms taken by the imperative of self-transformation in history.[29]

Here it is worth noting Unger's insight about the relationship between transforming social institutions and the individual imperative of self-transformation – what I would call self-authorship. Pushed to its extreme, I think that taking seriously the links between dignity, self-authorship and agency, understood as resting on a set of expressive capabilities enjoyed by individuals, would mean substantially changing the social institutions characteristic of liberal democracy. Moreover, it would also mean rethinking how global social institutions operate and pushing them in more egalitarian directions.[30] There is vastly more that could and should be done, especially by those who possess the resources, to ensure that the expressive capabilities of all individuals are respected and amplified.

Why Dignified Self-Authorship is Important

One of the criticisms that could be levelled against the conception of human dignity discussed here concerns its overall meta-ethical value. Why should we take dignified self-authorship to be an important moral aspiration and, more importantly, prioritize it over other moral aspirations? Or, to put it in terms expressed by Derek Parfit, does dignity and dignified self-authorship 'matter'? The most serious way in which this objection could be formulated is by directing criticism against the individualistic meta-ethics underpinning the project. Stressing dignified self-authorship places my project firmly in the tradition of those who believe that it is the development of the 'self' that fundamentally matters. There are many who would contest this standpoint. The most powerful objections come from two traditions in moral thought. There is the utilitarian tradition, which stresses that 'what matters' is impartially maximizing overall aggregate utility. Secondly, there is communitarianism, which stresses that the individual derives a great deal of their values from the community, which is therefore entitled to certain independent valuations against the individual's interest in reform and social transformation. The utilitarian's objections are serious, because they stress that true moral impartiality would mean maximizing welfare even if that came at the expense of an individual's own aspirations. The communitarian's objections are serious, because they stress that an individual's personal development takes place only within a reasonably settled horizon of meaning, thereby making a project of context transcendence both impossible and potentially dangerous.

I will first discuss the utilitarian objection. The most powerful variant of the utilitarian objection is made by Derek Parfit. He would push against a project such as this one because the underpinning meta-ethics is inherently quite subjectivist. While we might intrinsically care about the value of our lives, he would characterize this as a psychological rather than a meta-ethical argument for adopting a given position. This can easily lead to a kind of naturalism that is very close to nihilism. Moreover, some of Parfit's objections go even deeper and suggest that a project such as mine presumes that there is a 'self' in some strong ontological sense that is the source of 'what matters'. He gives a number of different philosophical arguments against that idea that there is such a self in the strong ontological sense. This means that the development of our self-hood and its private satisfactions cannot be the foundation for a moral system. Instead, Parfit argues that we should adopt what he calls a 'triple theory', prominent features of deontological and contractarian moral theories, but is fundamentally consequentialist and therefore utilitarian at its core.[31] The core of this triple theory is the claim that we should adopt moral principles that would result in optimific consequences – would make things go best, in other words. Unfortunately, Parfit gives few concrete examples of such principles, which is odd for a three-volume work running to many thousands of pages. However, the one example that he does give is quite provocative: those beyond a certain level of affluence should always donate at least 10 per cent of their after-tax wealth to assist those with much less.

Parfit's argument against morally focusing on something like human dignity is very powerful. I cannot address his broader philosophical points at great length here – in no small part because they have many different dimensions. The most powerful is his claim that the development of the self should not be what matters, because the self in a strong sense does not exist. My most immediate objection is that the kind of soft-Platonism adopted to counter subjectivist naturalism also strikes me as unconvincing.[32] Parfit is convinced that our cognition enables us to establish certain independent moral facts that would not exist in our absence but that obtain a kind of objectivity regardless of our subjective preferences. His comparison is with the truths of mathematics: they only come into existence through human beings but then assume a kind of existence independent of our will and preferences. In some respects this might be an accurate account of meta-ethics, but it overemphasizes its objective features to say that these are entirely binding regardless of our human subjectivity. If it is true that moral facts come into the world only through our cognition, there is a sense in which it is ourselves that make them 'matter', to deploy Parfit's preferred terminology. Soft-Platonic moral facts bind because they 'matter' to someone who believes that they have good reasons to act morally.

To provide an example, consider a planet of mechanical entities who engage in rote processes requiring systematic engagement with other mechanical entities. Then consider that these processes are organized by computer programs that have enough memory to record each run-through of their process and its engagement with other mechanical entities. Rather like Parfit's deflated vision of the self, these entities seem to retain some memory of what they are doing, and engage in actions with other such entities.[33] But I do not think that we could take the extra step and say that such entities have certain moral obligations – for instance, to 'make things go best' – because though they have some form of memory, there is no psychological impetus of practical reason to make it significant for any of them whether things do indeed go best. This suggests that, at least to some extent, for moral facts to matter they must matter to some self that ascribes them value. This is obviously not a decisive objection, because it entails the presumption that such a self does indeed exist, which is what Parfit's arguments in *Reasons and Persons* and his earlier paper 'Personal Identity' tend to undermine. However, I think that there are good reasons to believe otherwise, so long as the self is reconceived in the correct way.

Those who believe that it is possible to be rational about morality, such as Parfit, must also adopt the position that it is possible reflectively to change an individual's stance on what matters, through their being presented with strong arguments and evidence about the existence of moral facts both in the abstract sense of the word and in the world of experience. In other words, it supposes that individuals have a capacity for second-order reflection on the values developed throughout their personal history. But this entails committing to at least some conception of self-hood that is strong enough to engender a second-order capacity for reflection on first-order values previously taken to be determinative of action. It suggests that the self exists at least to the extent of being a process of reflection enabling us to shift what we value and, consequently, our behaviours as they flow from these values. This is where I think Unger's ideas are of use.

For Unger, there is also no 'self' that exists in the sense of being a firm ontological entity that grounds the individual through a determinative personal history and permanently frames their personal actions. In other words, there is no ghost underpinning all our machinery. Unger encourages us instead to look at the 'self' as a pragmatic creation that is continuously developed throughout the finite period of the human organism's life. This also relates back to his metaphysical commitment to time being real, and the universe therefore being characterized by real change at the ontological level. For Unger, time's reality means that ontology is fundamentally about becoming rather than being: what is, is what changes.[34] Time is also real for the human individual, and so what the 'self' of that individual 'is' changes also in a particular sense.[35] This means that being an individual can be wearying, since it means existing as a self that is continuously being created. But Unger encourages us to regard this as a positive feature of our lives, since it enables individuals continuously to rise above the determinant circumstances of their personal history and rearrange the world in a manner more conducive to their interests. It is only through this process of transformation that we can choose both what to value, and reflectively to reassemble our values in reaction to superior forms of argumentation. In this sense, a self that is not set but one that is (continuously being) created through self-authorship is a prerequisite for the emergence of moral values. The self – or at least something like it – must precede morality.

This has ramifications for the claim that we should adopt a purely impartial approach to moral reasoning. Such an approach would look exclusively at how to maximize aggregate utility across all relevant moral subjects, which may well include both animals and even future generations of living beings who may be impacted by our actions in the present. The implication of such an impartial approach is that moral significance is exclusively ascribed to those actions that we can take, and those we refrain from taking, in order to maximize overall aggregate utility. Applied 'stringently', this could well entail ceasing to engage in any actions that are oriented around self-authorship and the pursuit of happiness, and focusing exclusively on utility maximization.[36] Few utilitarians would fully accept this position, since it would seem to fall entirely victim to Sidgwick's dilemma; at a meta-ethical level, such an absolutely impartial attitude towards morality would preclude any motivation to be moral and ultimately become self-defeating. If everyone is compelled to sacrifice themselves, no matter what, to be moral, one suspects that few of us would have any motivation to act morally.[37] But it is always questionable how far a utilitarian can accept limitations on the stringency of the principle of utility maximization and still be a utilitarian in any robust sense.

The problem of complete impartiality is one that I do not think the utilitarian can ever solve. It may be true that adopting what has sometimes been called 'the point of view of the Universe' would result in a more optimific distribution of resources. But, following critics such as Rawls, Nagel and others, I feel that such a point of view abstracts away from the actual motivations that individuals have to adopt a moral outlook. Parfit claims that moral values are akin to quasi-Platonic forms that emerge, like mathematics, with cognition but are not simply the products of constructivism or a natural evolutionary process. I suspect that this might be the case. But Parfit's subsequent emphasis on the impartiality distracts from the cognitive dimension of this point, and its deeper existential ramifications.

Kierkegaard once observed that 'truth' – at least in values – redoubles if it tries to be entirely objective, but is sustainable as a kind of subjectivity.[38] This point was also made by Heidegger, who noted that what precedes the formulation of any explicit moral code or even metaphysical doctrine is the phenomenological point that individuals 'care' about the world. 'Care' is, in a sense, the fundamental orientation that precedes value. It begins from the care that individuals have for their 'selves', and should be extended, where possible, to the world at large.[39] This might include at points adopting a gradually more impartial 'view' from the Universe. But it never ceases to be 'care', which always has an element of partiality to it since it flows outwardly from our subjectivity. Seen from this standpoint, the firmly impartial utilitarianism called for by Parfit does not seem to mesh very well with the existential orientation of individuals that is the motivational basis of morality. Morality involves formalizing the explicit connotations of the commitments implied by our care for the world. Such an understanding of morality marries itself far more easily to prioritizing dignified self-authorship, and trying to ensure that all are capable of it, than to utilitarianism.

I will now move on to discussing the second main competitor to dignified self-authorship: that offered by communitarianism. If the utilitarian attaches too little importance to the concrete values constitutive of human partiality, the communitarian attaches far too much importance to them. There is a whiff of conservatism about communitarianism, which is insufficiently radical to overcome the false necessity of what are ultimately incomplete moral doctrines that serve to engender support for inadequate political and legal institutions. It should therefore be rejected in favour of emphasizing dignified self-authorship.

Communitarians hold a complex view about the sources and motivations behind human value that leads to support for an ambiguous array of concrete moral commitments. The essential insight of the communitarian position is that moral and political theories such as utilitarianism and various comprehensive liberalisms, which are excessively rationalistic, have a deeply flawed understanding of what actually motivates individuals to hold to concrete moral commitments. According to the communitarian narrative, political and moral theorists from Kant to Rawls hold to the idea that morality should be formulated along rationalistic lines that divorce it from specific socio-historical contexts. But the communitarian objection is therefore quite a radical assault on this position. It is precisely these socio-historical contexts that provide the framework within which individuals engage in moral reasoning about not just how to pursue given ends but, importantly, which ends are worth pursuing.

This framework has two dimensions to it. The first is meta-ethical. The socio-historical contexts within which individuals exist provide the motivational basis for the adoption of a moral standpoint: the belief, if you will, that something matters. If individuals were not embedded in such socio-historical contexts, they would not form the affective attachments to others that are a prerequisite for 'caring' for their well-being and interests. One of the standard criticisms made by communitarians against impartial or rationalistic philosophies is that they are both wrong and in fact destructive. They engender support for a nihilistic standpoint wherein the atomized individual is the centre of the moral universe, gradually ebbing support for the socio-historical contexts out of which affective attachments grow. This leads to individuals adopting an increasingly immoral – or 'unvirtuous', if you will – outlook. Some commentators would go even further than this position. Following the later work of Alasdair MacIntyre, and demonstrating admirable sensitivity to the dangers of relativism, some communitarians such as Jeff Nicholas take the strong position that the capacity to reason is itself conditional upon individuals operating within certain pre-given socio-historical contexts.[40] On this outlook, the attempts of epistemic and meta-ethical foundationalists were always doomed to failure, since they looked for grounds for their viewpoints by up-ending the soil upon which they could be built. This echoes the pragmatist standpoint on epistemology and meta-ethics defended by philosophers such as Richard Rorty and Robert Brandom, to name a few.

The second aspect of this framework is more ambiguous. This is because once the communitarian establishes that all individuals inhabit a given socio-historical framework that establishes the affective attachments necessary for morality, it becomes important to examine the substantive norms that flow from each given socio-historical framework. To put it according to the typical slogan, modern individualism overemphasizes the procedural means by which people pursue ends.[41] It ignores the more substantive discussion about which ends are indeed worth pursuing. Here the communitarian says that each individual develops a hermeneutic within which they interpret the context-specific values present in the socio-historical framework(s) in which they live, and decide which ends are worth pursuing. Some may even live in several socio-historical frameworks – or 'spheres', to invoke Walzer – each with its own context-specific affective attachments and value sets.[42] Within each of these frameworks, the virtuous individual develops their own best interpretation about which ends are morally excellent, and behaves in a manner to achieve those ends. Standards of excellence are constituted by those who perform particularly well within a given socio-historical framework, demonstrating what can be achieved through the application of time and effort.

To give a representative example, baseball players evaluate the excellence of their behaviour not by the standards established by an excellent doctor, but by those of people who have achieved excellence within the athletic world. A soldier is not held to the same moral standards as a doctor, because the role that they play in a given set of socio-historical frameworks is quite different. A moral soldier will hold themselves to abiding by the rules of a just war, or *jus in bello*. However, they will not hesitate to use force and kill, since not to do so would be to refrain from achieving excellence when the use of violent force against an enemy is the end required. Meanwhile, few of us would ever think that a moral doctor could ever be engaged in activities that would entail the use of violent force against an enemy.

The foregrounding discussion of the two aspects of communitarian thought are meant to demonstrate why they would be unlikely to endorse the conception of dignified self-authorship discussed earlier. First, most non-religious communitarians would have to reject the meta-ethical argument that dignified self-authorship has any value in and of itself. Since value comes to exist substantively only within a given socio-historical context, dignity and self-authorship can obtain value only when individuals exist within a community that ascribes importance to them. Secondly, and more to the point, the communitarian would argue that while self-authorship is indeed an important goal, it is misrepresented here. They would claim that my conception of dignified self-authorship is overly individualistic, particularly in its emphasis on context-transcendence. The communitarian would claim that this once again replicates the dangerous dualism between means and ends, and therefore misunderstands what self-authorship entails. Self-authorship is not primarily a process by which individuals transcend the contexts within which they exist, but a matter of the ends that individuals take to be of value and choose to pursue. According to the communitarian, the choice of ends is determined by the socio-historical contexts within which individuals exist – the very contexts that I suggest they should transcend.

If I have conceived of this properly, the communitarian objection to my conception of dignified self-authorship is powerful and warrants discussion. I will raise two rebuttals to these objections. The first operates at the meta-ethical level, and the second deals more substantively with the different conceptions of self-authorship offered by me and by the hypothetical communitarian critic.

The communitarian argues that the socio-historical contexts within which individuals operate provides the motivational basis for their adopting the moral standpoint. Stronger communitarians, such as MacIntyre and Thompson, even argue that socio-historical contexts provide the basis for evaluating more general truth claims and are therefore foundational for the exercise of reason itself. This position echoes that of pragmatists such as Rorty and Brandom.[43] Personally, I am sympathetic to the anti-foundationalist project offered by communitarians and by pragmatists. But I think that it puts the case too strongly, and more importantly underestimates what is most radical and exciting about the 'pragmatic' outlook more generally. Following Unger, I take the anti-foundationalism of pragmatism – and, by extension, the communitarian position – to be a rejection of the idea that socio-historical contexts have any strong reason-giving authority over us, even though as descriptive matter any given socio-historical context may engender support for its particular rationalization of what is epistemically and morally authoritative. To put this another way, we might indeed say that, as a matter of fact, many individuals accept the socio-historically contextual reasons for adopting one position or another on epistemic or moral questions. But this does not mean that they should feel any strong obligation to accept these socio-historically contextual reasons beyond that these are simply the brute traditions into which they were existentially thrown. Again, following Unger, I take the pragmatic tradition to be offering a far more radical possibility. Once foundationalism is rejected, it offers individuals the chance to transform the socio-historical contexts into which they were thrown, and to fashion new ones that might be more conducive to their interests and, indeed, more useful in framing their moral outlooks in an increasingly complex postmodern world. This does not mean that they need to reject these socio-historical contexts wholesale, but they should not feel bound to respect them.

This brings me to my second rebuttal to the communitarian's more substantive objection to dignified self-authorship. This is that it replicates the modernist dualism between means and ends, and therefore cannot serve as a robust conception of self-authorship. This is because self-authorship can occur only in contexts in which individuals have strong inclinations to pursue certain ends, and therefore engage in behaviours and tasks that would enable them to embody the virtues that characterize that end. Again, without having a contextual standard upon which to judge what constitutes the end of excelling in baseball, no one could wish to be a good baseball player. This position, I believe, is entirely correct in certain respects. It is true that individuals pursue certain ends because they pre-existed them and are regarded as worth achieving. However, I again think that the communitarian overstates their position here. They take the given set of ends that exists within any socio-historical context to be exhaustive. This is where the conservative dimension of communitarianism comes in. What my conception of dignified self-authorship attempts to demonstrate is how, by transcending given socio-historical contexts and becoming authors of both their own lives and the legal and political institutions that govern them, individuals are capable of deciding which ends should be maintained as worthy of pursuit. More importantly, they can bring new ends worth pursuing into being. For instance, through the application of their linguistic expressive capabilities, individuals can establish new forms of aesthetic excellence and beauty that could not have been conceived before. This is what many marginalized communities have done – for instance, through the development of emancipatory forms of expression such as slam poetry and the more sensitive variants of hip-hop.

This brings me to my final observation about the communitarian position. There is much to value in it, including its emphasis on the wisdom of the past. However, as Whitehead observed in relation to the Ancient Greeks, fetishizing the wisdom of the past will often mean that we fail to live up to it.[44] Great civilizations, like the Greeks, were not staid and traditional. They boldly created new ways of thinking and being in the world. Nothing could be less Grecian than choosing to live as the Ancient Greeks did. The point of my project is to capture this quality and give it a directly political twist. I do not wish to suggest that individuals should simply efface the past in some act of radical liberty, echoing some existential thinkers such as Sartre. Rather, I wish them to have the capacity both to choose which ends should be retained as valuable, and to bring new ends into the world. This has a clear political dimension. One individual's worthy tradition is another person's malignant ideology. Individuals should be capable of determining whether they regard their traditions as worthy or malignant, and deciding whether they wish to retain or reject them as needed. Otherwise, tradition is just another form of unsubstantiated and illegitimate authority, operating for its own sake. This is why the model of rights associated with my conception of dignified self-authorship is crucial to understanding its value. I now turn to discussing this model of rights in considerably more detail.

A Critical Legal Model of Rights

In this section, I will link my conception of human dignity to a critical legal model of human rights. I will draw substantially on the literature surrounding what I earlier called the relational stream on human dignity.[45] This is because I believe that dignity operates on a continuum determined by an individual's set of expressive capabilities, and that political structures should be reoriented to amplify this set wherever possible. In my framework, dignity is normatively mobilized to transform the social contexts within which individuals pursue their interests and various life goals.

I reject that immanent quality of many moral arguments that flow from the stream of thought that takes dignity to be inherent. This position often results in a rather static form of moral reasoning, wherein political institutions and human rights assume the particular form the author thinks is most respective of the inherent dignity of human beings. My model of human rights is significantly more flexible, in that its central idea is that individuals themselves should largely be authors of the political institutions that govern them.

Arguably since Marx's brilliant and pioneering criticism of rights in his seminal 'On the Jewish Question',[46] many on the Left have been deeply sceptical or outright hostile towards the idea and theory of rights. This extends doubly towards social institutions oriented around the professed protection of such human rights.[47] Ironically, some of the radical critiques of rights discourse – that it is grounded in Western ideas, inevitably hegemonic, and replicates the neo-liberal subject[48] – echo points made by famous conservative icons such as Edmund Burke.[49] Burke would have agreed entirely that 'natural rights' at least served as an insidious idea that undermined the more realistic claim that rights were creatures of positive law that, in turn, historically evolved out of the accepted mores of a given culture. Some critics on the Left have noted and accepted this connection, even going so far as to link the Burkean and Marxist critiques in an innovative way.[50]

I think that this is an unfortunate development that speaks to deeper challenges in the general orientation of Leftist and critical thought over the last several decades. The collapse of grand narrative theories, such as Marxism, has engendered a strangely conservative Leftism. It either takes identity as it exists – embedded in socio-historical contexts – to be the locus of normativity, or focuses itself exclusively on so problematizing the very concepts of identity and normativity that very little conceptual space remains for constructive thinking. To the extent that there has been a constructive dimension to contemporary left-wing and critical thought, it has been focused on taking identity as it exists in socio-historical contexts and protecting it from invasive colonization by neo-liberal capitalism and other hegemonic forces. I believe that this is a worthy goal. But taking identity as it exists to be the sole locus of normativity undermines a commitment to dignified agency and context transcendence that I see as necessary for the advancement of any true critical progressive agenda. Individuals should be made capable of transcending and shaping the socio-historical contexts in which they exist. They should not just be shielded from colonization by other and more insidious external forces. In other words, we should look concretely to respect and amplify the dignity of all individuals by increasing their general capacity for dignified self-authorship.

This is where I think that rights can serve as important conceptual and political tools for realizing a more constructive agenda. This is in part because the language of rights is simultaneously popular enough both to mobilize attention and to articulate concrete demands, and semantically open enough to express the interests and commitments of many different groups in the formal pragmatics of their linguistic community. There are some who might say that the rhetoric and history of rights are too closely aligned with liberalism, but I think that this grants too much semantic determinacy to a term that in no sense 'rigidly designates'.[51] There is no reason why, even if these associations exist, the term 'rights' could not be decoupled from liberalism and put to more critical and radical purposes, such as the realization of the robust conception of human dignity fleshed out here.

Much more could be said on this point, but I will leave it aside here. Instead, I wish to conclude this chapter by sketching a preliminary 'twinned' model of foundational rights. I call them foundational because they are expressed in the broadest possible terms to be generative of more positive specific rights that could arise depending on the socio-historical contexts of claimants, and of course their interests and commitments. This approach is rather similar to the one described by Justice Aharon Barak, who characterizes human dignity itself as a 'mother right' that gives birth to various 'daughter rights'. [52] Another way of understanding these foundational rights would be to think of them as 'jurisgenerative': they operate as general principles that should engender a more concrete set of positive rights that are sensitive to empirical specificities.[53] I feel that this model, at an abstract level at least, has the principled heft and conceptual sweep to capture both the constructive and critical dimensions[54] of the conception of human dignity discussed earlier. If this twinned model of rights were realized, we would have gone a long way towards respecting and amplifying the dignity of all individuals.

I believe that two foundational twinned rights must be realized in order that human dignity can truly be respected and amplified. The first is a right for all citizens to be democratic co-authors of their governing social institutions and the coercive rules that flow from these. The democratic right is secured by the implementation of fair decision-making procedures that value each individual citizen equally as they engage in a deliberative process of conceiving and establishing the design of political and legal institutions and subsequently determining the laws that flow from these.[55] The democratic right is not secured by appeal to historical contingencies, such as culture, or to the abstract formulations that are common to many liberal theories. Individuals in a democratic framework must possess the actual capabilities required both to make their claims heard and to have them deliberated in a forum that formally accords equal value to all members regardless of the specific content of their deliberative claims. Their jurisgenerative rights to such democratic capabilities must be respected by the establishment of fair decision-making procedures that equally value each individual's opportunity to participate in the deliberative authorship of the laws that govern them.[56] This right to participation cannot be revoked by any democracy worthy of the name, though, of course, it does not mean that one's interests will always carry the day. This is the formal requirement to satisfy the dimension of democratic right. To the extent that such fair democratic procedures are implemented in practice, and are engaged in by individuals who are able to employ their expressive capabilities, the right of individuals to democratic self-authorship would be secured.

The second is the right of all citizens to enjoy equal sets of expressive capabilities except where inequalities flow from their morally significant choices.[57] This right would be realized by ensuring that each individual had the equal overall capacity to engage in dignified self-authorship except where differences result from morally significant choices. I have chosen to focus on an equality of expressive capabilities, rather than on goods or resources, for two interrelated reasons. The first, and most important, is that capabilities refer concretely to what people are actually able to choose in given contexts. What one is generally capable of doing is not something abstract (such as what one could transcendentally will), or even something contingent (such as what one would do with certain goods). The second, and related, point is that the focus on expressive capabilities treats people as individuals with context-specific needs and interests. A focus on capabilities takes into account the special circumstances of people's lives. The capabilities approach to justice seeks ways in which to achieve a fair distribution of expressive capabilities in a manner that is tailored to the unique status of each individual. For instance, it might be uniquely sensitive to the needs of individuals with substantial physical or mental disabilities, and look at what they need in order to enjoy a life of dignified self-authorship.[58] And, as mentioned before, it can look at variables such as an individual's overall capacity to use language to bring new richness into our semantic worlds.

The decision to distinguish two distinct rights was deliberate and at least partly inspired by Thomas Nagel, who made a similar argument in his book *Equality and Partiality*.[59] I maintain that the first right (to democratic authorship) precedes the second. Individuals should have the opportunity, in a democratic context, to choose whether they wish to ensure an egalitarianism of human capabilities. Choice is important to my conception of how to realize human dignity. This is because my conception is fundamentally democratic at both theoretical and practical levels. It rests upon the claim that legitimacy is minimally bestowed by consent and increases to the degree that subjects become authors of social institutions and the coercive rules that flow from them.

The link between the two foundational rights – the right to democratic authorship and that to equality of human capabilities – is that both are jurisgenerative legal tools[60] to be used to amplify an individual's total set of expressive capabilities and so realize the dignity-oriented account of human flourishing. As mentioned, expressive capabilities are those that enable individuals to transcend socio-historical boundaries and assume responsibility for their subjectivity. This is what enables people to lead a life of dignified self-authorship. Only in this way would their status as morally individual subjects be respected. Therefore, the first step to respecting and amplifying expressive capabilities is to democratize political and legal institutions. After this, one can make the more challenging argument for establishing the agency-enhancing[61] right to a full equality of expressive capabilities.[62]

There is another important respect in which the twinned rights are linked. Like other authors in the relational school, in my model, rights occupy a middle position between the morally abstract idea of amplifying human dignity and concrete instantiations of positive law. They express the overall normative orientation that a legal system should adopt in order to make human dignity central. Rights occupy this middle position so that they can be deployed by individuals in a variety of ways that would be expressive of and conducive to their self-authorship by transforming state institutions and the laws that flow from them. How this can be achieved will be explained in the next few chapters, as I look more closely at what law can do to amplify human dignity.

Some might object that my account of rights is insufficiently critical, since it still leaves substantial room for both the state and international institutions to play a large role in the lives of citizens. There are some left-wing theorists for whom leaving room for any kind of state or institutional interference is unacceptable. The strongest objections of this sort typically come from the anarchist tradition, which seeks to discredit the very idea that any state or international institutions can be justified. For my money, the strongest such anarchist objections typically draw on the radicalized Kantian claim that any process that treats individuals as a mere means, rather than ends in themselves, is ultimately immoral and cannot be justified. Since the state and international institutions invariably deploy coercion to force individuals to pursue ends that they themselves might reject in non-coercive contexts, they can therefore never be morally justified.

While this argument is interesting and important, ultimately I do not agree with its thrust. Discussing why in elaborate detail would require giving a full justification for the state, which I cannot entertain here. I will simply say that, following Nagel, I feel that most critical legal scholars are in a bind when it comes to choosing between their libertarian and egalitarian inclinations. There is a substantial temptation to believe that full freedom, such as that found in a non-state context, would be consonant with a more egalitarian distribution of capabilities, but I do not believe this to be the case. Robert Nozick discussed why in some detail in *Anarchy, State, and Utopia*.[63] Any egalitarian theory must invariably seek to establish some patterned distribution that would not necessarily accord to a distribution of capabilities that would be established if individuals were just left to interact with one another over a period of history. An egalitarian theory has to redistribute capabilities in accordance with some pre-set and fairer design, and to continue to do so even where that might interfere with the totally free economic transactions that individuals might otherwise make. Doing so, to my mind, would require a state. This is even more the case if we want to talk about expounding an egalitarian theory that accords significant distributive weight in the pattern to non-citizens.

Of course, this is not intended to provide ideological support for the most robust possible state. Protection against the undue growth and expansion of state power is provided by the first right, which stipulates that citizens must be democratic authors of the political and legal institutions that govern them, and the laws that flow from these. Once a robust democracy is engendered, egalitarians can and should begin pushing for the realization of the second right, to an equality of human capabilities. This model of rights is critical legal because it historically[64] makes central the capabilities that citizens have to transform political and legal institutions, while still strongly emphasizing the need to adopt an egalitarian pattern in the distribution of capabilities. It obtains legitimacy by creating a great deal of room for us to pursue the projects of democratization and redistributive justice.

Realizing the twinned rights to democratic authorship and to an equality of expressive capabilities constitute an ideal towards which, I argue, all social institutions should strive. A just society would seek to respect and amplify human dignity, and so realize the twinned rights that are necessary for this task. But this does not imply that there is only one way to realize the two rights. The argument for such rights stems from the existential priority that my model places on dignified self-authorship. That is to say that there are many ways in which the ideal of the twinned rights could and should be realized. This is especially true with regard to the right to an equal set of expressive capabilities. Here, democratic communities must not only choose whether my conception of equality is what they wish to realize, but decide how they might wish to achieve it.

Individuals who exist within diverse socio-historical boundaries would undoubtedly prioritize some features of my argument over others, for both principled and pragmatic reasons. Ensuring an equality of expressive capabilities would enable individuals to become authors of their own lives in a political system that respected their dignity through treating them as being of equal value. However, expressive capabilities themselves are likely to be understood in radically different ways across various cultures. While my model's emphasis on dignity and dignified self-authorship is undoubtedly individualistic, and there is a potentially infinite number of ways in which individuality might express itself, this will always take place within pre-established socio-historical contexts steered by social institutions. Individuals define the narrative of their lives in different ways, by redefining the same socio-historical contexts within which they exist.

Given this, it is extremely likely that individuals from different cultures would choose to give more weight to certain forms of expression than others and, concurrently, would choose to maximize different expressive capabilities. They may decide to prioritize fostering the more basic expressive capabilities, such as those of bodily health and agency of thought, before committing resources to fostering those that are almost or equally important but less immediately pressing. Such decisions cannot be made theoretically, even if theory might offer some hermeneutic guidance. They must be left to those who know and understand the socio-historical contexts within which they live.[65]

This chapter has ranged across a wide swathe of theoretical issues to sketch out my conception of human dignity and its affiliated twinned model of human rights. In subsequent chapters, I will begin to turn to more concrete and practical issues concerned with how to amplify human dignity in practice and to realize the model of rights in given socio-historical contexts. This poses significant challenges, and requires an examination of the political and legal structures and cultures which reinforce policies which either constrain or at the very least do little to amplify human dignity through realizing the twinned rights.

I think that if most social institutions were measured against how effectively they respected and amplified human dignity by realizing the twinned rights, they would fall considerably short of the mark. Many states deploy highly coercive social institutions that are designed to limit, or even preclude, the possibility of substantive democratic participation. This includes even developed liberal democratic states such as the USA – perhaps the most egregious modern example – where, famously, many laws are designed to undermine the participation of African-Americans and other marginalized groups in the formal political process.[66] Many of these efforts at marginalization have been worryingly successful. And while there are many respects in which the welfare of the world's poorest has improved in the past few decades, it is also clear that inequality has also ballooned, consequently transferring greater and greater powers to the world's elite.[67] Such a concentration of wealth and expressive capabilities at the expense of others is not only damaging to the dignity of individuals; it undermines the capacity of social institutions to move beyond calcified policies that benefit the well-off while precluding full participation of the marginalized.[68] This suggests that there is a very long way to go before human dignity is fully respected, and there are many critical efforts that need to be undertaken to expose the social institutions and ideologies that preclude its full realization.

This is where I think that international human rights law can play a crucial role in ensuring the amplification of human dignity. If international human rights law were reoriented around the amplification of human dignity I believe that this would substantively transform its interactions with states. Rather than being driven primarily by the interests and power politics of states, international human rights law would be responsible for ensuring that states maintain the proper conditions for the exercise of sovereignty by doing all that they could to amplify the human dignity of both their own citizens and, crucially, vulnerable individuals abroad. It is to these issues that I will turn in Chapter 4.

4

The State, International Human Rights Law and the Amplification of Human Dignity in Practice

Introduction: Critical Legal Theory, Human Rights and International Human Rights Law

> Consolidated in the second half of the twentieth century, the human rights project entered history's large pantheon of visions for human betterment. Scaled down in operation, it differed from the grand schemes of socialist equality rooted in the inexorable laws of history, from the Manichean struggles for racialist utopias, and from religious futures sanctioned by God's plans. Some analysts place human rights under the notion of progress, although the designation is difficult to reconcile with its own historical record. Rooted in struggle rather than in one universal, moral Truth, right gains can be lost. Propelled by the genocidal wars, brutalities, and the Holocaust of the mid-century, human rights principles offered alternatives to war and destruction in an agreed-on set of universal criterial for human dignity, fundamental justice, equality, and security.[1]

While there has recently been a notable shift towards taking an interest in global issues, historically, critical legal theorists have paid relatively little attention to international law or, indeed, international affairs in general. This can no doubt be explained by pointing to the foundations of the critical legal studies movement in the law schools of the United States. Despite their comparatively radical stance, critical legal theorists seemed just as prone to the national fixation peculiar to American legal thought as their less radical colleagues. Few of the major authors in critical legal theory have written extensively on international law, leading to a notably theoretical gap in the literature.[2] While there is an abundance of critical legal theory pertaining to the structure and power of the state and national law, Crits have had little to say about non-law or supra-state law and its power structures.

One of the major goals of this work is to fill this gap in a comprehensive manner, by sketching out some worthwhile paths that might be taken in the future. Adopting a critical legal approach to international human rights law, and looking at how it can be reformed along more democratic and egalitarian lines, is an important task. Doing so means normatively decoupling critical legal thought from its moorings in the critique of the state and national legal institutions, and moving a set of constructive norms affiliated with critical legal thought to centre stage. These norms, centred on the ideal of human dignity, are set out more concretely as the twinned rights to democratic self-authorship and to an equality of human capabilities. Approaching international human rights law in this manner has two implications. First, it means that I deploy critical legal theory in a constructive way to offer moral priorities that international human rights law should pursue. Secondly, it means that I retain an important role for the state, which is to serve as a vessel for redistributing expressive capabilities.

In the previous chapters, I took steps in this direction by arguing for a critical legal conception of human dignity and an affiliated model of rights. In the next several chapters, I will demonstrate how international human rights law can be conceived and used so as to make the amplification of this conception of human dignity its fundamental orientation. This first chapter will be primarily concerned with theoretically sketching out how making human dignity the fundamental orientation of international human rights law can be carried out. It will therefore operate at a relatively high level of abstraction (though not as much as Chapters 3 and 4). In Chapters 6 and 7, I will discuss how this project can be carried out in a more practical manner by looking at actual cases that pertain to the amplification of human dignity through the application of the twinned rights.

A Very Brief History of International Human Rights Law and the State

Virtually everyone who studies international human rights law quickly runs into the contrast between the Westphalian system of independent state-centric legal systems emphasizing the absolute importance of sovereignty and the new, aspirational human rights order, which is to place limitations on the exercise of sovereign power. The most familiar and rather Eurocentric narrative runs along these lines: by the end of the Thirty Years War, most European powers were exhausted and deeply frustrated by the attempts of other states to interfere in their religious practices. The temptation to do so was affiliated with the natural law tradition pioneered by Augustine, Aquinas, Vittoria and others. These authors were all held to claim that, since all individuals have a natural right to know God, it was just and correct to wage wars if necessary to defend Christianity, and in some cases even to convert the heathen.[3] This natural law understanding of the world as spatially divided between Christendom and the Others[4] – oftentimes, as Said pointed out, the Islamic 'orient'[5] – operated smoothly enough until the Reformation and the inter-Christian conflicts that it sparked. Frustration with religious war finally led to the signing of the Treaty of Westphalia in 1648, which entrenched the idea that states had the unlimited right to do as they wished within their own territorial boundaries, and should not be interfered with by other states. While this certainly did not have the effect of ending war, it did curb the propensity towards religious war, and European relations were defined by the Great Power politics for the next two and a half centuries. The new spatial regime that overtook the old binary between Christendom and its Others was between so-called Western civilization and its peripheries, and the subordinates in the colonies. These peripheral subjects retained no rights to sovereign authority that were not ceded to them by the so-called 'mother countries'.

However, the grant of absolute sovereignty eventually became problematic. As Great Power politics gave way to the massive and intensely violent ideological conflicts of the nineteenth and early twentieth centuries, many began to question whether it was genuinely wise to cede so much power to the state – the proverbial 'mortal God'. This fear was realized with the emergence of the totalitarian regimes of Hitler and Stalin, who justified the brutal murder of their own citizens by appealing to positive law and the sovereign rights of states. It is, rightly, taken as one of the great travesties of history that very little was done to curb the violent impulses of these regimes within their own borders. It was only once they began to expand outwards, bringing with them all the machinery of death, that many Westerners finally abandoned the old Westphalian consensus.

By the mid-twentieth century, the horrors of the World Wars and growing unhappiness with imperialism convinced states to begin constructing the formal legal architecture that would constrain what sovereign states were able to do within the limits specified by human rights. The formal commencement of this paradigmatic shift was with the adoption of the UDHR in 1948, outlining which rights would serve as the threshold for the retention of sovereign power. Unfortunately, while a number of binding legal conventions further entrenching these rights were adopted in the latter twentieth century, the Cold War prevented the development of any robust legal mechanisms to enforce international human rights law. This ended with the collapse of the Soviet empire in 1989, which led to a pronounced legal thaw and indeed the remarkably fast development of international legal instruments designed to punish those who committed grave atrocities against human rights. This was a considerable victory for cosmopolitanism in the modern era. Many of the institutions formed during this period remain at the forefront of much jurisprudence in international human rights law and international criminal law. They include the International Criminal Tribunal for the former Yugoslavia (ICTY), the International Criminal Tribunal for Rwanda (ICTR), and finally the International Criminal Court (ICC).

Simultaneous with the postwar formation of the United Nations, the same European states that established the Westphalian system were gradually abandoning it and coming together in a novel, European international union with its own human rights convention and court. This gave many hope that we were entering a new cosmopolitan era, which some authors famously argued constituted the 'end of history' properly understood.

Unfortunately, the rise and fall of American adventurism during the War on Terror in the early twenty-first century and its subsequent retreat into nationalist anomie under the Trump administration have put a halt to this development. Under the Bush administration, the world's most powerful state withdrew from the international order being formed – one that was, however, consistent with the United States' own Enlightenment heritage – and pursued a ruthless policy of aggressive and unilateral interventionism. This famously resulted in the near destruction of both Iraq and Afghanistan, and the ultimate descent of both countries into ongoing warfare and secretarian conflict. It also established a disconcerting precedent of unilateral interventionism and crackdowns on domestic enemies in the name of curbing the threat of 'terrorism'. To invoke only two examples: Russia justified its intervention into the Crimea through in part appealing to the United States' history of militaristic interventionism, and the Syrian regime of Bashar al Assad continues to invoke the threat of terrorism to justify extensive crackdowns on his political opponents and the use of illegal forms of force against dissent. So, barely twenty-five short years after peaking in the 1990s, international human rights law often seems as though it is on the retreat. It has been unable to curb the nationalist and fundamentalist forces that it was expected to have extinguished, indicating that the cosmopolitan moment was just that: a brief flash of idealism in the sordid history of conflict between nation states and peoples. The reasons for this failure are complex and ongoing.

At the normative level, international human rights law was never able to orient itself around a sufficiently powerful moral ideal to motivate anything more than a perfunctory loyalty. This is true at the level of theory, where much of international human rights law remains dogmatically and unimaginatively tied to a fairly shallow Kantianism. It is also true affectively, since this shallow Kantianism has never been able to inspire and motivate individuals who often remain bound to the communitarian ties provided by their national state. International human rights law remains grounded in a highly abstract set of ideals, many of which are given such diverse and conservative interpretations by individual states that even a believer in the last utopia could be forgiven for expressing cynicism.

Another reason for the failure of international law is more fundamental and relates to the practical failure of international human rights law genuinely to curb the exercise of power by channelling power to the pursuit of an aggregable normative project. At Nuremberg, Justice Robert Jackson famously claimed that the decision to hold a trial for the leading Nazi leaders was 'one of the most significant tributes that power has ever paid to reason'.[6] These inspiring words haunt the ongoing aspirations of international human rights law. It is transparently clear that the international order is still largely oriented around power – whether it be the power of states, multinational corporations, hidden networks of espionage and terror, or whatever. Power has yet to cede control to reason. At best, it has made a few perfunctory gestures. Many in the world still live in conditions in which they face gross restrictions on their civil and political rights. Just as pressingly, the dramatically unequal concentration of human capabilities concentrates wealth and power in the hands of an ever more withdrawn global elite who use their resources to ensure that dramatic reforms to the status quo will never take place. International human rights law has been largely ineffective in preventing the violation of civil and political rights, though the triumphs that it has enjoyed are noteworthy and impressive. It has also been very ineffective in engendering a more just redistribution of human capabilities. Indeed, with the exception of refugee law and the operation of a few well-meaning but sparingly funded UN aid agencies, it is difficult to see where international human rights law has meaningfully contributed to realizing the economic and social rights of global citizens.

This is an immense problem for international human rights law, since repeated failures to live up to its ideals by curbing political violence and redistributing human capabilities has led many to adopt an increasingly cynical stance towards the whole project. This is true even among educated global leaders, who should be at the forefront of pushing the project of international human rights law. Indeed, many of the most influential globalists of the era, such as Bill Gates, seem willing to bypass international human rights law and the related institutions wholesale and just fund the projects in which they are personally invested. This is a tremendous tragedy, since such a piecemeal approach undermines efforts to form a more robust and ambitious international human rights-based system that could persist and deepen over time, independent of the altruism of the 1 per cent.

This failure either to develop a sufficiently powerful normative framework or to subordinate power to it demonstrates why we need to continue theorizing and advocating on behalf of international human rights law. Specifically, we need a theoretical account of international human rights law to meet two criteria. The first is to provide a sufficiently powerful normative framework that can successfully inspire theoretical and affective loyalty. I believe that my conception of human dignity and its affiliated model of rights offers a good start in this direction. Since I have covered extensively in the last two chapters how this operates, I will not rehash my argument here. The second criterion is to demonstrate how international human rights law can successfully devolve power to marginalized people, to ensure that their dignity is amplified and to prevent a return to the cynical belief that the international arena is destined to be dominated by power politics. Millennia ago, Thucydides famously wrote that questions of right and wrong can only exist between equals: 'Right, as the world goes, is only in question between equals in power, while the strong do what they can and the weak suffer what they must.'[7]

Thucydides' quote has long been taken as a mantra for a realistic vision of politics and international affairs – ignoring, of course, that the Athenians who invoked it were ultimately brought down by their hubris and lust for power. The cosmopolitan moment offered us a brief flash of a different kind of international ordering. In the next section I will try to retrieve what is valuable in this moment, while developing a more robust and critical account of international human rights law that might be forceful enough to avoid a long slide into calcification.

Theorizing a New Relationship between International Human Rights Law and the State

I: A Reply to Schmittian Arguments

Theorizing on a new relationship between international human rights law and the state presupposes a robust account of what constitutes international human rights law and what constitutes the state.

On the first point, as mentioned in the section above, I will primarily be proposing a normative rather than a descriptive account of what constitutes international human rights law. Mine is a normative reconstruction of international human rights law that argues that its fundamental orientation should be the realization of a critical legal account of human dignity.

On the second point, on what constitutes the state, there is no space here to engage in an extensive theoretical and practical reflection on what constitutes statehood. Rather than engaging in such a complex task in a limited space, I will instead follow Habermas by adopting Carl Schmitt as a theoretical foil.[8] This is done for three reasons. The first is that, to my mind, among his contemporaries, Schmitt presents the most powerful arguments against the possibility of a sovereign state being constrained by a higher set of norms. For Schmitt, sovereignty is defined by a state deciding what constitutes right and wrong. To be limited in this capacity is to efface the state. The second reason is that Schmitt is hostile to the idea of democracy. In *Constitutional Theory*, he claims that Rousseau is fundamentally correct that the only true democracy can be one in which a general will exists that embodies the real interests of all citizens.[9] Since this cannot occur in practice, there will always be some groups that possess more political power than others, and they will use the power of the state to crack down on dissent. Finally, the third reason is exactly this last point. As a hard-edged realist, Schmitt is sceptical that the operation of power can ever be mitigated in state politics. Any political order that faces a fundamental threat to the ontological beliefs of the political theology that it seeks to uphold will always crack down on dissent, even where doing so compromises important facets of this moral order. For instance, this is the case in most liberal democracies. So, the idea of a rights-respecting state that seeks to secure the dignity of all is deeply compromised, since those who willingly accept and support the political theology protected by a state will always be legally privileged over those who merely feel obliged to accept it due to force and coercion (or not, in the case of revolutionaries).

These problems pose fundamental challenges to making the realization of human dignity the goal of a just state and using international human rights law to steer states in such a direction. Some of them can never be fully overcome. But, as I shall argue, I feel that Schmitt overstates his case in many respects. His account of politics, the state and political theology is far too totalizing. There is little room for recognizing the possibility of overcoming false necessity to establish a new form of state ordering, in particular by following Foucault in 'cutting off the head of the king' by making retention of sovereign authority subject to respecting and amplifying human dignity. My argument is that international human rights law can play a fundamental role in the last regard. I shall discuss this in more depth after further analysing the specifics of Schmitt's thought.

Schmitt's philosophical outlook can be nicely understood as being: power is never innocent, because it is always determinative and decisionist. This is why Schmitt was largely dismissive of any idealization of a robust democracy, such as the one formulated by Rousseau. Since politics will always be about deciding what and who to prioritize and not – a democracy oriented by the 'General Will' of all was something of a fantasy.[10]

The closest that one could get was a liberal representative democracy, in which coalitions of friends and enemies organized themselves into political parties and competed for public attention and legislative power. Because this is the closest that Schmitt believed one could get to a true democracy, we will mostly be examining his opinions on liberal democracy and ignoring his comments about a more robust democratic polity. Schmitt believed that a liberal democracy would always be partial, since one party would take power and enact its agenda at the expense of another, even if it claimed to represent the people as a whole. The only truly democratic feature of such a system was that elections were held, allowing other parties to take power and enact their own agenda for a time. But Schmitt was deeply sceptical about the stability of even such a liberal democracy, believing that it would also be faced with the burden of making decisions on who was to be allowed to participate politically and who not. We shall examine in some depth why he felt this way.

One of the things that Schmitt disdained about liberal democracy was its belief that there could be established a given legal order that left people free to live their lives as they wished, without state interference or control. This belief can still be seen in the work of seminal liberal theorists such as John Rawls[11] and Martha Nussbaum,[12] who remain committed to the idea of a 'political' rather than 'metaphysical' liberalism that can be legally and politically endorsed by individuals from a wide variety of philosophical perspectives. Such arguments made belief in 'liberal pluralism' and multiculturalism cognitively possible.

To Schmitt, these liberal pretensions were nonsensical for two interrelated reasons. First, Schmitt thought that liberalism's claim truly to respect difference was a sham. This reason is fundamentally related to Schmitt's more general account of how law and politics operate in both liberal and illiberal regimes. For Schmitt, ideologically, all politics is based on incompatible secularized theological concepts. In practice, this means that the fundamental concept of the political is the friend/enemy distinction.[13] Political friends are those who conform to our own political theologies, and who wish to see a state and a legal order that conform to our own outlook. Political enemies are those who hold to a different political theology that is incompatible with our own. The practice of politics is always a form of violence, whether literal or figurative, as different groups of friends and enemies attempt to overcome one another and seize control of the state.

Liberal democracies attempt to quiet politics through the operation of parliamentary democracy. They believe that by giving different groups of friends and enemies space in which to engage peacefully, as political parties in the legislature, the friend/enemy distinction on which politics is predicated can ultimately be overcome. But, for Schmitt, this is ultimately an illusion, since the daily to and fro of normal parliamentary politics shows us very little about where the real power in political societies ultimately resides. For Schmitt, there is always one sovereign body that rises above the morass of everyday politics, including in a liberal democracy. This sovereign is the person or body that 'decides the exception' – that is, they are capable of suspending the normal operation of politics as organized by law and cracking down on dissent to reaffirm a given order based on a given political theology. In other words, the Sovereign decides the exception to maintain the existential consistency and homogeneity of the body politic through the repressive power of the state.

> Every general norm demands a normal, everyday frame of life to which it can be properly applied and which is subjected to its regulations. The norm requires a homogenous medium. The effective normal situation is not a mere 'superficial presupposition' that a jurist must ignore, that situation belongs precisely to its immanent validity. There exists no norm that is applicable to chaos. For a legal order to make sense, a normal situation must exist, and he is sovereign who definitely decides whether this normal situation actually exists.[14]

This gloomy picture of liberal democracy and politics in general has a tremendously levelling effect. Schmitt is effectively saying that all politics is about groups of friends and enemies who organize themselves along fundamentally incompatible theological lines. The attempt to avoid this is an attempt simply to avoid politics. The extraordinary consequence of Schmitt's line of reasoning is to conclude that there is little that distinguishes a liberal democratic regime from a more authoritarian one. Indeed, the chief distinction is that authoritarian regimes are simply more honest about what they are doing. Liberal democrats, with their idealized conceptions of rights and respect for difference, will always be faced with two choices when truly confronted with the stark face of the 'Other' who holds to a very different political theology. They may either attempt to hold consistently to their beliefs in difference, in which case the Other might well overcome them and establish an illiberal regime, or they can deploy sovereign authority to decide that the Other is a dramatic exception to the 'normal' rule of respect for difference.

The second reason why Schmitt felt liberal democracies were fundamentally unable to manage difference in the way they claimed is related to his broader understanding of politics. Since all 'political' concepts and doctrines are fundamentally based on secularized theological concepts, the differences between them are irreconcilable. From the time of Hobbes onwards, liberalism was based on a theological belief that the individual was the ontical centre of the world, and that political power is exercised to enable individuals in the pursuit of their material interests in this world. This political theology is fundamentally at odds with the outlook of groups such as Catholics, Communists and, of course, the Nazis, who understood the world in very different terms. For Schmitt, this posed fundamental problems for the liberal claim to respect difference. To invoke Rawls as a foil, Schmitt would claim that liberals reveal their true respect for difference and the Other when they say that differences in opinion and political theology can be tolerated where they are 'reasonable'.[15] In practice, this means that acts and ideological concepts that deviate too far from liberal political theology will most often be forbidden by the state. Where the liberal state fails to crack down on such differences, it runs the existential risk of being overthrown by those who hold to different political theologies.

This concludes my account of Schmitt's criticisms of liberal democracy. From here on, I will argue for the limitations of his approach, before demonstrating how international human rights law can provide a response to many Schmittian dilemmas.[16]

Schmitt develops a very powerful account of the limitations of democracy in a liberal democratic context. His claim that the state sovereign will always be responsible for making an existential choice about which group's political theology to accept has proven salient in the past. But Schmitt is also prone to generalizing too broadly. His arguments about the state are too totalizing and too bleak. There is little room in his thinking for degrees of democratic participation. Here, his theological background perhaps influences him too much. Just as God is a figure whose rule is always absolute, so, too, does the mortal Sovereign always attempt to establish an ontologically complete body politic. This may be so in some instances. However, Schmitt fell into the trap, common to some intellectuals, of tending to venerate power even while being reflective on how it was exercised.

For Schmitt, the moment at which the sovereign decided the exception demonstrates that political power can almost always re-establish the homogeneity of the body politic. Indeed, it is inherent in the very logic of sovereignty to do so. But Schmitt ascribes this logic a false necessity. That logic of sovereignty is not immanent to law and politics, but is the product of the socio-historical contexts of late modernity in which state power was organized in this way. There is no inherent reason why state power cannot be redirected and mollified through the passage to a new set of socio-historical contexts. But there is little room for such a possibility in Schmitt's work, because he remains so enamoured by power that he cannot conceive how it might ever be limited or put to more normatively worthwhile purposes. Indeed, this myopic fascination with power at times borders on self-parody. For instance, consider the depth of Schmitt's totalizing attitude, which goes so far as to criticize Hobbes's conception of the Leviathan for leaving too much space for personal deliberation on theological matters:

> All those multifarious, countless, and indestructible reservations regarding inner vis-à-vis outer, invisible vis-à-vis visible, conviction vis-à-vis attitude, private vis-à-vis public, stillness vis-à-vis noise, esoteric vis-à-vis ordinary united themselves, without any plan or organization, into a front that did not need to exert any great effort to transform the positively understood myth of the leviathan. All the mythical forces embodied in the image of leviathan now strike back at the state that Hobbes had symbolized.[17]

One can criticize Hobbes for many things, but I would never have expected one of them would be giving the state too little power and leaving too much room for personal agency.

For Schmitt, the moment of exception demonstrates the sovereign's power because it is where it decides the exception and determines what and who remains within and what is to be excluded from the body politic. I think that this is deeply wrong. The moment of exception does not demonstrate the sovereign's strength. Rather, it demonstrates its weakness: in exceptional moments, power needs to become naked and stark in order to re-establish homogeneity. But in the moments where the bare application of power becomes apparent, the state is actually at its weakest. Schmitt believes that the state is always compelled to establish homogeneity across the body politic. By contrast, and following Laclau and Mouffe, I think that it is more productive to see the body politic as always fundamentally incomplete and in tension.[18] In moments where the theological pretensions break down – to put it in psychoanalytic terms, when there is broad recognition that the Big Other does not exist – it is necessary for hegemonic groups to turn to state power to enforce by violence what is no longer sustainable through ideology. These are precisely the moments at which violence becomes a real possibility, since violence is almost always the reaction of a castrated power complex that can no longer function simply through the operation of its disciplinary and ideological mechanisms. And so, it is exactly in these moments that international human rights law can play a fundamental role in preventing violence and establishing a more dignity-respecting and therefore just society.

II: International Human Rights Law and the Establishment of the Rightful Condition

In this section, I will normatively reconstruct the role that international human rights law should play in relation to domestic law. My argument will be that international human rights law should curb Schmittian-type propensities by making the retention of state sovereignty dependent on maintaining what Kant called the 'rightful condition'. This, I will claim, is one in which the dignity of all individuals is amplified to the extent possible because the state realizes the twinned rights to democratic authorship and equality of capabilities. But before discussing this, I will briefly run though some of the theoretical conceptions of international human rights law that have been developed over the centuries.

The special status of international law relative to its domestic counterpart has long been an issue that has perplexed legal scholars. There have been claims at both extremes – from those such as the mature Hegel, who have claimed that international law is not law at all, to those, such as Kant, who have maintained that the very right to legislate domestic law should gradually become dependent on the state's acquiescence to cosmopolitan norms.[19,20] This rich and complex intellectual history, as well as the problems raised throughout, obviously imposes a burden on any scholar who is willing to defend a normative approach to international jurisprudence. They must show not only how such a conception would be defensible with respect to domestic law, but also how it can be applied rigorously and adaptively to the unique conceptual and practical problems posed by international law.

The two most basic criticisms concerning the existence of international law have come from the traditions of descriptive and normative legal positivism. The first, exemplified by Kelsen and Hart, sees the task of legal philosophy as being to describe the law accurately without rendering moral judgements on its form or content.[21] The second, extending from Hobbes to modern conservatives such as Oakeshott, maintains that one should engage in legal philosophy clearly to demarcate the realm of law from that of freedom.[22,23] Normative legal positivists regard this as an important task, since a system of law, whatever its content, is morally valuable and should not be abandoned even in situations in which it competes with other moral values. Underpinning this conception is a fear of anarchy.

Descriptive legal positivists hesitate to dignify international law with full ontological status, because it does not appear to have many of the features that characterize a domestic legal system. Most notably, the international legal system does not have a source of sovereign authority – either a sovereign legislative body in the Austinian sense,[24] or a constitution stipulating rules of recognition *à la* Hart. This descriptive problem relates to a deeper difficulty for the descriptive positivist and, for that matter, the international realist: that the international legal system lacks sources of power with which to enforce its norms. For these reasons, many descriptive legal positivists have been hesitant to call international law 'law' to all intents and purposes.[25] This prejudice has persisted to the present day, when, in his otherwise fine book *Legality*, Scott Shapiro does not even address the question of international law when defending his neo-Hartian positivism.[26]

Normative positivists also maintain the points articulated by descriptive legal positivists, but they go deeper. They argue not only that international law does not possess the status of legality in practice, but that, on principle, it should not. Such arguments were 'a dime a dozen' during the heyday of the Bush administration. The essential argument flows from the Herderian idea of national determination, which itself rests upon deeper Hobbesian points about the nature of statehood as expressing the interests of the governed.[27] It is felt that each naturalistic 'community' should have the right to assert its unique moral conception without interference from the outside world.[28] Though this might appear to be precipitously close to cultural relativism of the most romantic sort, the normative positivist argument can be saved by giving it a further twist by criticizing international law for being undemocratic and unrepresentative. This makes it unlike liberal-democratic states, which at least have built-in mechanisms for assessing the actual interests of the people. Such is the position, for instance, of the late Robert Bork and Antonin Scalia.[29]

Ultimately, I do not think that either of these arguments is defensible. In the first case, the argument of the descriptive legal positivist leans too heavily on claims of efficacy. They believe that since it is unlikely that the international legal system can ever develop enforcement mechanisms as robust as those seen in a domestic legal system, it is therefore wrong – or at least misleading – to characterize it as law. But this claim grants too much weight to the ontology of the present, and therefore ascribes a false necessity to the contemporary socio-historical context. As we briefly glimpsed in my history of international law, the reasons for the failure of the international legal system do not stem from natural limitations. Powerful states and other hegemonic social actors have been unwilling to grant sufficient authority and resources to the international legal system to ensure that it operates effectively. An international realist might claim that this is very unlikely to change, but there is no built-in reason why it cannot. The decision of powerful states and hegemonic social actors not to grant sufficient authority and resources to the international legal system is a knock against their commitment to a more just global ordering. It does little to impugn the idea itself at a purely normative level. If it is unlikely that states and hegemonic social actors would grant international human rights law so much authority, it is not impossible. Far stranger things have happened, and we should not measure the normative value of a conception exclusively by the difficulties that may be faced in realizing it. Granting too much weight to such concerns moves very close to a strong conservative position that is antithetical to the spirit of both international human rights law and critical legal studies.

The argument of the normative legal positivist is more powerful: that, if fully realized, international law would be a fundamentally undemocratic force in the world, imposing universalizing norms on unwilling cultures. Indeed, it has been the locus not only of conservative critiques, but of many postcolonial[30] and radical Left[31] critics (who would otherwise reject all forms of positivism) as well. It is not enough, in these instances, to defend how international law operates in practice, since the theoretical question rests on its moral legitimacy under ideal conditions. If a full international legal system were fleshed out, complete with the sources of power needed to make it effective, would it be an undemocratic force in the world? A normative jurisprudence of international law must answer this pressing question if it is to be effective.[32]

Here, the approach pioneered by Ronald Dworkin becomes of qualified value. Throughout his long career, and despite having many things to say about justice in general, Dworkin had very little if anything to say about international law. I suspect that this relates to the problematic classically liberal approach to statehood that still underpins his conception of legality. This comes most to the fore when he discusses the nature of the community in *Law's Empire*, and why individuals concerned with justice should embrace an understanding of law as integrity as the best approach to narrating their unique constitutional story.

> [Internally compromised statutes] cannot be seen as flowing from any single coherent system of principle; on the contrary, they serve the incompatible aim of a rulebook community, which is to compromise convictions along lines of power. They contradict rather than confirm the commitment necessary to make a large and diverse political society a genuine rather than a bare community: the promise that law will be chosen, changed, developed, and interpreted in an overall principled way. A community of principle, faithful to that promise, can claim the authority of a genuine associative community and can therefore claim moral legitimacy – that its collective decisions are matters of obligation and not bare power – in the name of fraternity.[33]

This extraordinarily rich paragraph does not just contain a defence of law as integrity; it also indicates the limitations of Dworkin's theoretical analysis. He claims that a 'community of principle, faithful to that promise' can morally determine the content of law. In other words, he is here defending the right of a sovereign state to do as it will, so long as its actions are continuous with the basic liberal principles of law as integrity. Here, Dworkin comes very close to undertaking a Kantian inversion and claiming that states that fail to abide by the liberal principles that underpin law as integrity do not possess the moral legitimacy necessary to determine the law and that, therefore, individuals within these states would be under no moral obligation to obey their purported masters even if they must for practical reasons.[34] But Dworkin does not explain whether another form of law can be developed as a source of appeal for those subject to such wicked regimes. This strikes me as an unusual gap in his approach.

This productive limit in Dworkin's thought is a jumping-off point for discussing how to approach international law from a normative perspective. His argument that a state can claim the legitimate right to impose laws on others only to the extent that it is based on principle can be generalized to the global realm. I believe that doing so would entail adopting a Kantian position that sovereignty itself should be conditional on maintaining the 'rightful condition' for human flourishing.[35]

The normative requirements for maintaining this 'rightful condition' are jurisgenerative, in the sense that they can be codified as an international system of rights to which all states must become party and embody in their own domestic legal systems.[36] Ideally, over the course of time, the link between domestic and international law would gradually become blurred as states internalized the democratic and economic requirements for sovereignty and regarded them as integral principles underpinning their own legal systems. International law would then overlap with domestic law in a self-reinforcing manner, as states increasingly affirmed international law as a matter of principle rather than simply as a legal requirement. This would, in turn, establish a mutually legitimizing chain through which both domestic and international legal systems would validate their positions relative to one another.

The reasoning behind this last point is to mitigate the power of Schmittian-type arguments. As discussed in the section above, Schmitt has a totalizing understanding of state power. For him, the exceptional moment at which the sovereign re-establishes who and what is included within or excluded from the network of legality demonstrates the power of the state. Again, I think that it demonstrates the state's fundamental and ongoing weakness, and particularly its inability to realize normative principles that would be sufficiently attractive to enable power to operate without requiring the threat of violence to serve as the ultimate guarantor of legitimacy. In the global context that I am discussing, international law and domestic law would gradually come to overlap in their commitment to the realization of human dignity. Assuming that a sufficient number of people admire this commitment, it would mitigate the need for the exercise of state power to quash dissent. Indeed, I argue that the state's very right to do so should be seriously checked. Instead, international human rights law should increasingly determine when the violent exercise of sovereign authority is warranted – which I suspect would be in a very few and highly qualified instances.

This position raises two questions. The first is: which principles should be adopted in international law to establish a 'rightful condition' that all states must maintain in order to be considered sovereign? The second is: how rigidly must these principles be imposed? The two questions are deeply interconnected, since the first establishes a moral ideal for international law, while the second qualifies this ideal by clarifying how rigidly it should be enforced.[37]

In the first case, as one might expect, I believe that we can say that international law should codify the twinned rights to democratic authorship and equality of human capabilities. Here, one might think that the normative-positivist/postcolonial argument has bearing, since I am arguing that international law can enforce change on domestic laws. But I do not think that this is undemocratic per se, since there cannot be such a thing as democratic rights for states in and of themselves. The state, as an abstract entity, does not have a democratic right to uphold a non-democratic system unless that is what its own people have consented to.[38]

In the second case, I believe that we need to look at a number of factors to determine how rigidly the principles discussed above should be enforced. This will, in turn, require an anticipatory look at the rights to which citizens and non-citizens should be entitled. As we shall see, I believe that states do have special obligations to their citizens, which in some circumstances trump the needs of non-citizens. However, I do not believe that this is always the case. There are some circumstances in which respecting the rights of non-citizens is so important to the amplification of human dignity that the more high-end interests of citizens can be side-stepped. This includes cases in which one individual's right to private property might seriously impact our capacity to help those with the most pressing economic and social needs. In such cases, wealthy individuals should give up part of their wealth to the extent that is sufficient to make a concrete difference.

International Human Rights Law and the Twinned Rights: Bringing the Domestic and the International Together

In my model, the most important hermeneutical principle that one should adopt when interpreting international human rights law is a commitment to amplifying human dignity by realizing each citizen's expressive capabilities. Human dignity is the fundamental orientation of international human rights law and should be hermeneutically linked to subsequent and increasingly more specific moral commitments, such as those required to realize the twinned rights given specific socio-historical boundaries. This, in turn, will be further concretized through realization in the positive law and jurisprudence of states. To show how this can be carried out, what was presented before at a relatively high level of philosophical abstraction must now be translated into more juridical language.

The commitment to amplifying human dignity is open ended because it is attached to agency and self-authorship. This has legal consequences. It suggests that one cannot adopt the juridical standpoint of classical liberal legal positivism when interpreting the law. Such a standpoint presupposes that the responsibility of the state is merely to forgo interference in the private lives of citizens.[39] Amplifying human dignity requires that law do more than that. To translate that into juridical language, we might say that amplifying a human being's dignity presupposes realizing a specific set of rights.

At a more abstract level, this would mean linking human dignity to positive legal rights that realize the twinned rights to democratization and to an equality of human capabilities. Concretely, we can begin to define how this would be carried out in international and domestic human rights law. In his book *Human Dignity: The Constitutional Value and the Constitutional Right*, Justice Aharon Barak has helpfully described how such a process could be carried out as an instance of dignity being a framework 'mother right' that gives birth to a number of 'daughter rights' through a process of interpretation.[40] Through this process we move from respecting human dignity at an abstract level and come to respect it as a right with real legal value.

> A constitutional right formulated as a principle serves as a 'common roof' under which a wide variety of situations crowd together. Common to all of them is that they are expressions of the general principle that shapes the right ... Under the canopy of the constitutional framework right, constitutional rights derived from it or that radiate from it crowd together. These rights are inherently

> of a lower level of generality than the framework right … A framework right is therefore a mother right. From it are derived daughter-rights. If the daughter-rights themselves are framework rights at a lower level of generality, granddaughter-rights are to be derived from them. Other imagery expressing this concept views the mother right as a tree and the daughter-rights as branches growing from it.[41]

Another way of expressing the same point would be to see the protection of human dignity as *the* – not merely *a* – fundamental legal 'archetype'. A given socio-political community's commitment to protecting and realizing this archetypal right should frame our hermeneutic interpretation of any rights identified in various international treaties, customary law and *jus cogens* norms, as well as any attempt to establish new positive rights through establishing or updating old human rights treaties.[42] The amplification of human dignity should be the unifying ideal of international human rights law, and thus be expressed through the interpretive commitments of legal officials.

If we are committed to seeing the amplification of human dignity as an archetypal 'mother right', I believe that the first daughter rights that would flow from it would be the twinned rights identified in this work.[43] One can then further concretize what this would entail in practice, through realizing the twinned rights internationally. Realizing the twinned rights might include developing increasingly specific rights to democratic participation up to the threshold where citizens become both authors of legal and political institutions, and authors of the laws that flow from them. Ideally, democratic citizens would then express a further commitment to protecting and amplifying human dignity by embracing the second right through the widespread equalization of human capabilities. These jurisgenerative democratic and egalitarian rights would in turn serve as increasingly concrete interpretive bedrock for laws that further the process of expressing the international community's commitment to protecting and amplifying human dignity.

From the perspective of the hardened legal positivist, such spurious claims about dignity are the root of international law's problems. They regard the references to human dignity and its related goods as, at best, harmless sanctimony and, at worst, dangerously open-ended principles masquerading under the guise of hard law. But this understanding is misguided, since, as I have argued, it mistakes legal procedures and the expedient production of specific laws for the normative purpose of law itself. It can never get beyond the tautologous claim that law should be obeyed because it is law, without entirely divorcing the question of legitimacy from that of legality. But this becomes even more tenuous in the international context, in which the issue of legitimacy is perhaps the foundational legal problem, and it can be resolved only through appeal to normative principles.

If we are to have a normative jurisprudence of international law, then Article 13 of the ICESCR is a good place to start recognizing human dignity as the unifying ideal towards which international law strives:

> The States Parties to the present Covenant recognize the right of everyone to education. They agree that education shall be directed to the full development of the human personality and the sense of its dignity, and shall strengthen the respect for human rights and fundamental freedoms. They further agree that education shall enable all persons to participate effectively in a free society, promote understanding, tolerance and friendship among all nations and all racial, ethnic or religious groups, and further the activities of the United Nations for the maintenance of peace.

While Article 13 lacks the striking economy of the references found in the Preambles to the ICCPR and the ICESCR, it programmatically delineates the connections between dignity, human rights, and other human capabilities in a fairly comprehensive manner. Most importantly, it is arguably legally enforceable. States that seek to realize this ideal in their particular contexts would be said to meet the requirements for maintaining legitimate sovereignty. Those that fail to meet it would move down the continuum of legitimacy to the point at which the international community might even be justified in intervening to prevent serious infringements of the dignity of their citizens.

While it was perhaps a necessary strategic move on the part of Western states during the heyday of the Cold War, in hindsight the decision to divide the two Covenants has proven deeply unfortunate. It has led to a system in which the ICCPR is shown every respect and the ICESCR is virtually ignored, with claims that states are engaging in the 'progressive realization' of the rights within. There are many reasons for this position, which I shall discuss further later. Here I will just say that the international human rights system expressly references human dignity and, as I have tried to argue, is best understood as reflecting a commitment to its realization. Given this, we should abandon now outdated visions of human dignity as an absolute status that merely exists, and start to understand it more relationally in affiliation with agency and an overall capacity for self-authorship. In such circumstances, economic, social, and cultural rights are not the peripheral rights that they are often interpreted as being. They are also vital for truly amplifying human dignity in a meaningful way. Given this, I believe that seeking to amplify human dignity depends on realizing the expressive capabilities of individuals to define themselves by redefining the contexts within which they exist. Moreover, it is not enough to realize just a few expressive capabilities at a time while focusing potential resources on other priorities such as the national military. None of the expressive capabilities exists in isolation; as both Sen and Nussbaum stress, they are integrally connected in complex and contextually sensitive ways.[44] While this means that states may have a lot of leeway in how they choose to foster capabilities in their given socio-cultural contexts, it also means that they cannot ignore some expressive capabilities (such as those stressed by the ICESCR) and expect the others to be realized successfully. While resources are not unlimited, and states cannot be expected to do everything at once, officials must use their best efforts to foster the 'full personality' of the human person and their interrelated expressive capabilities. We must also begin to broaden our understanding of the obligations that states have towards the citizens of other states, especially along economic and social lines. On the normative model of international law developed here, rich states may well prove to have obligations to the citizens of other states, which go beyond simply preventing moral catastrophes. For example, they might have an obligation to ensure that other peoples obtain a certain quality of life before they look to improve the lot of their own peoples if the latter already enjoy a certain quality of life.

I will now discuss both of the twinned rights specifically, and how they can be realized more effectively. With regard to the first right (to democratic authorship), I believe that international human rights law can play an important role in amplifying the participation of citizens in elections. This goes beyond simply allowing a few more parties to participate in elections. International and domestic courts can – and should – substantially expand the franchise; and indeed some, such as the ECtHR, have done so. In Chapter 5, I will discuss this at considerably greater length. However, they should also do what they can to make democratic rights more meaningful. When deciding cases that are centred on democratic rights, courts should rule in a way that best amplifies the dignity of the individuals in question by enabling them to redefine the socio-historical boundaries within which they exist. Courts should also ensure that democratic rights are of equal value to the broadest possible number of citizens. In Chapter 5 I will demonstrate in considerably greater detail how this could be carried out.

I would now like to discuss in more depth the right to an equality of human capabilities. We have seen that Article 13 of the ICESCR requires states to take steps to ensure that all citizens have access to a good education. Education is not connoted in purely instrumental terms here; rather, it is explicitly linked to the 'full development of the human personality and its sense of dignity'. This might very well be taken to be a positive instance of human dignity serving as a fundamental orientation for international human rights law. This is because the right to development of an important human capability – namely, education levels – is expressly linked to an open-ended goal beyond what is articulated in the text itself. In Rawlsian language, it expresses a teleological understanding of the good: in this case, for individuals to be able to realize the fullness of their personality and enjoy a sense of dignity.[45]

Following my account, the full development of the human personality – what I have called a capacity to engage in dignified self-authorship – means a great deal more than just the capacity to assume a prescribed role in a socio-historical context. It involves the capacity critically to analyse and assess the same contexts through the application of practical reason, and more importantly to choose to reject or revise the conditions within which we exist. This is because my approach emphasizes that the concrete choices that we are able to make are more indicative of what is morally significant in our personality than any other psychological features that have emerged as the result of existential and socio-historical determinants. A state that seeks to realize the dignity of individuals must use the law actively to create opportunities for the amplification of each individual's expressive capabilities to make such concrete choices, with the realization of the right to education being but one – albeit an important one – of many such positive actions.

This might appear to be an unrealistic goal. But we have seen some states that are willing to take steps in these directions, and we should employ international human rights law as a tool to get others on board. International law can especially have an impact on rich states that have the resources to commit to this project, but have been unwilling to do so for various ideological reasons.[46] By embodying a commitment to realizing the twinned rights, international human rights law can maintain a moral prerogative to guide states towards the realization of the 'rightful condition' for both their citizens and those of other states.[47]

This last point raises an important issue with which I would like to conclude this section. I do believe that international human rights law, by challenging the legitimacy of sovereign authority where the rightful condition is not maintained, also implies a further moral and legal obligation – that states have obligations to individuals beyond their borders. As mentioned before, this is bound to be an exceptionally controversial claim, especially given my argument for an expansive set of domestic obligations. How can any state be expected to respect both its expansive obligations to citizens and accept further obligations that pertain to non-citizens in far-away countries?

The Rights of Non-Citizens

The argument that states have obligations to non-citizens is hardly novel. It has long been recognized by international refugee law, the laws of war, and other standard features of the international legal regime.[48] However, I do not believe that these obligations go nearly far enough. In this section I will make the argument that states have considerable obligations to amplify the expressive capabilities of non-citizens if they have shown adequate concern for their own citizens and have the resources to do so. The consequence of this would be that rich states would have substantial obligations to transfer wealth to the developing world.

Unfortunately, such arguments still have little practical currency. Most states feel that their primary – and often exclusive – obligations are towards their citizens (if that). There is a deep history behind this rather unsettling reasoning, on which I can only touch here. Its deepest macro logical roots lie in the Westphalian consensus that has dominated European thinking – if not action[49] – on the relationship between state and citizens since the seventeenth century. The reification of the modern sovereign state in the seventeenth century, and the immense discursive and institutional authority granted to it, was an important precondition for the ideological formation of the nation.[50] The sovereign state achieved this by controlling, inter alia, various disciplinary and biopolitical[51] mechanisms that established criteria for citizenship, fostered reproductive programmes, and erected an immense array of symbolic apparatuses. Per Schmitt, the logic of these mechanisms was deliberately exclusionary: the state constituted the identity of the nation through denying identification and rights to those deemed unworthy or 'foreign'.[52]

Not coincidently, the political and legal theory of the time adopted a similarly exclusionary logic. The theories of Hobbes, Locke and even Rousseau were oriented around the twin goals of demonstrating the legitimacy of sovereign authority by demonstrating the existence of a bilateral agreement between ruler and ruled: the famous 'social contract'. The abstraction involved in many of these contractarian theories, often criticized by the Romantics, was undercut as the nation gradually became an object of intellectual reification. Thoughtful conservatives such as Burke and a host of Romantic authors justified the authority of the state and the rights of citizens through immanent appeals to the organic and nationalist ties that linked a given people to the state structure.[53] A canonical example would be the right-Hegelian claim that the state emerges as the materialized instantiation of the spirit of a given people on their journey through history. The consequence of this was to claim that full rights belonged to national citizens because of one's affective attachments to them. Proximity to others, in both the literal and affective senses, became a precondition for thinking that they deserved rights, though, of course, what constitutes proximity is eminently contestable.

While the descriptive dimension of these immanent claims has since been highly problematized, their normative force has never eroded. Indeed, the force of these arguments persists in the work of communitarian thinkers such as Alasdair MacIntyre and Michael Walzer,[54] who stress the neo-Aristotelian claim that the affective proximity of community and tradition is what gives rise to moral sensibilities and thus to moral obligations. But there are deep problems with deploying such theories to justify the focus that states place exclusively on their citizens. While there might be some truth to the argument that we feel[55] stronger moral obligations to others based on proximity, by itself this cannot generate justifiable moral obligations. As has often been observed, throughout history, many people have felt strong obligations to wicked social orders and the legal systems that supported them that were based solely on proximity and attachment. We would not say that such people were right to act on their feelings of strong obligation, although we might sympathize with those who felt obliged to act as the state commanded.[56] In contrast, I think that we have many good reasons to assume strong obligations to help those beyond our borders. In the next few paragraphs, I will try to demonstrate why.

One of the most important and influential arguments for expanding the rights of non-citizens and indicating where states have obligations to individuals beyond their borders is found in Peter Singer's seminal 1972 article 'Famine, Affluence and Morality'.[57] The article was inspired by Bangladeshi war refugees. Beginning in March 1971, Bengali revolutionaries pushed for independence from West Pakistan, resulting in a brutal genocide that ended with the independence of Bangladesh by the year's end. The exact figures on civilian deaths are hard to come by, with estimates ranging from 300,000 to as high as 3 million. During the conflict, almost 30 million people were displaced, the majority of them Hindus. Many of these refugees had left incredibly violent situations, only to find themselves deprived of food, medical attention and shelter. Singer prefaces his article by noting that, despite the scale and depth of human need, most countries – including those of the wealthy Western world – gave very little aid proportionate to what was needed.[58] Following the utilitarian argument, he goes on to argue that 'suffering and death from lack of food, shelter, and medical care are bad'. Since they are clearly bad, if it is in our power to prevent them without sacrificing something of equal significance, we have a moral obligation to do so.

This brings us to the most famous part of Singer's article, in which he asks us to consider the following provocative thought experiment. He asks us to imagine that we are walking past a shallow pond and see a child drowning in it. We are capable of wading into the pond, although the consequence would be that our clothes might get muddy. However, Singer argues that this consequence is morally insignificant next to the very bad result of the child's drowning. Singer observes that, though the principle operating in this thought experiment seems uncontroversial, consistent application of its logic to world affairs would be very radical. First, it suggests that proximity to need has no moral bearing on what we should or should not do. The only factor that is determinative is the significance of the need itself. And, secondly, it de-individuates our moral obligations by focusing exclusively on consequences. It makes no difference whether I, or millions of people, choose to do something. What matters is that the most significant needs are met.

If taken seriously as a moral position, Singer's argument significantly transforms the way in which we would think about our obligations to individuals living in distant parts of the world. As he puts it, he effectively effaces arguments concerning proximity and individual relations.

If what matters is maximizing the happiness of all relevant moral actors in the world, then we have stringent obligations to commit our resources wherever they would do the most good.

> The outcome of this argument is that our traditional moral categories are upset. The traditional distinction between duty and charity cannot be drawn, or at least, not in the place we normally draw it. Giving money to the Bengal Relief Fund is regarded as an act of charity in our society. The bodies which collect money are known as 'charities.' These organizations see themselves in this way – if you send them a check, you will be thanked for your 'generosity.' Because giving money is regarded as an act of charity, it is not thought that there is anything wrong with not giving. The charitable man may be praised, but the man who is not charitable is not condemned. People do not feel in any way ashamed or guilty about spending money on new clothes or a new car instead of giving it to famine relief. (Indeed, the alternative does not occur to them.) This way of looking at the matter cannot be justified. When we buy new clothes not to keep ourselves warm but to look 'well-dressed' we are not providing for any important need. We would not be sacrificing anything significant if we were to continue to wear our old clothes, and give the money to famine relief. By doing so, we would be preventing another person from starving. It follows from what I have said earlier that we ought to give money away, rather than spend it on clothes which we do not need to keep us warm. To do so is not charitable, or generous. Nor is it the kind of act which philosophers and theologians have called 'supererogatory' – an act which it would be good to do, but not wrong not to do. On the contrary, we ought to give the money away, and it is wrong not to do so.[59]

Singer's argument is extremely powerful and in many respects persuasive. He admits that many such arguments might appear counterintuitive. Most people would argue that we have clear moral obligations to those proximate to us, and others that might flow from our political and legal connections to the state. However, while any actions that we take pertaining to those less proximate might be admirable, they are nonetheless not morally stringent obligations. At best, they are charity. But Singer is keen to point out that this constitutes a fundamentally arbitrary limitation on the horizon of our moral concern. Invoking the merits of the impartiality – what he will later term the 'point of view of the universe' – he observes:

> The moral point of view requires us to look beyond the interests of our own society. Previously, as I have already mentioned, this may hardly have been feasible, but it is quite feasible now. From the moral point of view, the prevention of the starvation of millions of people outside our society must be considered at least as pressing as the upholding of property norms within our society.[60]

Unfortunately, as I have already mentioned, I do not think that the adoption of such an impartial standpoint is entirely possible. Singer himself seems to admit this when he comments on the Sidgwick–Urmson line that we must have a morality that does not deviate too far from the capacities of ordinary people. Singer characterizes this as an empirical issue, since it pertains to what individuals are willing to accept as morally binding and what goes too far. He then proceeds to argue against this position by maintaining that our sense for what is morally acceptable often flows from social norms, which can be changed and subject to critique, but I do not consider this a sufficient rebuttal. As I have already mentioned in my critique of Derek Parfit's utilitarianism, there is a deeper sense in which we need to demonstrate why morality should 'matter' to people. It seems impossible to do this without appealing, at least in some respect, to their subjective embeddedness within a world of concrete human relations. Simple appeals to the quantitatively determined possibilities of doing the most good cannot overcome this gap. Indeed, Singer's own thought experiment about the drowning child implicitly appeals to typical and sentimental human attachments for much of its rhetorical and argumentative power. What is necessary therefore is to combine Singer's arguments about the moral arbitrariness of proximity with an account of our moral obligations to non-citizens, which is not so radically de-individuated.

Kant was the first to formulate a non-utilitarian justification for assisting those beyond state borders, in his seminal essay: 'Towards Perpetual Peace: A Philosophical Sketch'. He argued that with the formation of the modern nation state and technology, it became possible to register when violations of rights occurred around the globe. These acts were a violation of the unwritten laws of humankind, which of course commanded us to respect the dignity of all through the establishment of the rightful condition, and could not be tolerated:

> The peoples of the earth have now gone a good distance in forming themselves into smaller or larger communities; this has gone so far that a violation of rights in one place is now felt throughout the world. So the idea of a law of world citizenship is not a legal flight of fancy; rather, it is necessary to complete the unwritten code of civil and international law and also mankind's written laws; and so it is needed for perpetual peace. Until we can establish a law of world citizenship, we mustn't congratulate ourselves on how close we are coming to that.[61]

So, Kant argued, states – and indeed the league of states – had an obligation to respect rights of universal hospitality for all. Individuals fleeing from violations of their rights must be granted protection by other states concerned to preserve the integrity of the 'unwritten code of civil and international law' that conforms to objective morality. This is an inspiring start but , as Kant himself admitted, one that is merely a sketch. We must go considerably further to advance and improve upon Kant's position.

I argue that the normative goal of amplifying dignity necessitates rich states redistributing wealth to poor ones, for the following reason: under conditions of fairness, no person could agree that the arbitrariness of proximity should have such a determinate impact on the dignity of individuals. This flows from the obligation that states have to maintain the rightful condition to retain sovereignty. International law plays a role in ensuring that states retain this rightful condition. In the same manner, it can play a decisive role in ensuring that states meet their obligations to help the world's poor by ensuring that they redistribute wealth and co-ordinate the process of doing so.

This is a controversial claim that demands elaboration. I think that Singer is correct to claim that the arbitrariness of proximity should not have such an impact on our sense of moral obligation to the world's most destitute people. Connecting this to a non-utilitarian argument for redistribution means reformulating the difficulty of proximity in terms of its arbitrary impact on dignity, rather than simply its consequences for aggregate utility. I have already claimed that individuals within the state should enjoy an equality of expressive capabilities except where inequalities arise from their morally significant choices. It is apparent that one's place of birth, and the determinate impact that it has on life, is not a morally significant choice. It is therefore deeply unfair that an individual born in Afghanistan is likely to live a significantly less comfortable life for sixty years than an individual born in Japan who is likely to lead a significantly more comfortable life for eighty-three years. This means that, at a purely theoretical level, the inequality in expressive capabilities that engenders such differences cannot be justified if we are concerned about respecting and amplifying the dignity of all individuals.

This is simply the first step of the argument, of course. One can immediately say that, while it is true that such differences cannot be justified at a purely theoretical level, this is a different problem than that of who has a responsibility to ameliorate the arbitrary inequalities that undermine, or completely deny, people's ability to exercise their expressive capabilities to amplify their human dignity. Even if one accepts my claim at the start of this section that states should not limit their moral outlook exclusively to their citizens, it is yet another step to say that states have a specific moral obligation to help the world's poorest. One might simply say, following Kant, that one has imperfect moral duties to give charitably.[62] Or one might follow Rawls in arguing that, while states have an obligation to assist people who are suffering under an unjust political regime, this cannot extend to a redistributive policy that would involve significant transfers of resources from states and their citizens to non-citizens.[63] Both positions have proven attractive to those who advocate for non-utilitarian approaches to international relations.

A variety of arguments are made for why rich states have specific obligations to assist non-citizens in different parts of the world, and which do not draw from the Singer-type claims. There is no space here to devote attention to all iterations of such arguments, so I will focus on two of them. The first is that, given the history of colonialism and exploitation that enabled most rich countries to develop to their current status, they have compensatory obligations to assist undeveloped, developing or 'poor' countries, especially those that suffer deprivation as a direct or indirect result of their former colonial status. The second is that, given that the current distribution of goods at the individual level is largely arbitrary and infringes the dignity of the destitute living both within wealthy states and outside the developed world, states have substantial obligations to assist the world's poor.

These two arguments can be understood as mutually reinforcing or exclusive, depending on one's interpretation of historical events. If, following Fanon and other postcolonial theorists, one accepts the claim that many wealthy countries are prosperous in no small part due to their long term exploitation of the developing world, one might contend that the distribution of resources is not actually arbitrary.[64] In fact, it is the result of morally significant decisions to marginalize a substantial part of the world, with consequences that persist to the present day. This naturally gives greater weight to the significance of my second argument, since the distribution of resources is not simply arbitrary, but the consequence of moral decisions that wrongly impacted individuals. This highlights the need to rectify the current injustice in distribution. On the other hand, if one rejects the historical account – or at least is not willing to grant it the weight that I suggest – this need not impact the argumentative heft of the second argument. The arbitrariness in the distribution of resources, even if purely the consequence of nature, remains unfair and negatively impacts the dignity of many people. The second argument implies that these inequalities in resources should therefore be ameliorated by states that have the capacity to make a difference.

Following Nozick, my first argument is a historical moral one that suggests that poor countries may demand compensation from those who have taken resources from them in the historical past.[65] This argument is compelling from a critical legal standpoint because it is effectively a derivation of the claim made by Frantz Fanon in *The Wretched of the Earth*. Since the peoples in many poor and formerly colonial societies were entitled to the resources that were taken by exploitative colonizers, the current population is entitled to compensation, given that they would have – or at least might have – been better off had those resources not been taken by those who were not entitled to them. To invert this claim, since the rapid development of rich states was spurred in no small part by exploitative practices that took resources from peoples who were entitled to them, the current population owes compensation to the populations of poor countries, since the rich are better off because they appropriated resources to which they were not entitled.

There is a strong dimension to this argument, since it is concerned with rectifying deep-rooted historical injustices. On this basis, the reason that a person in Afghanistan remains poor is not simply because of natural arbitrariness. It is at least partly the result of the choices made by rich countries at some point in their history. It might be objected that this argument is unfair because it makes present-day individuals in rich countries responsible for providing compensation to individuals who were injured not directly as a consequence of their specific choices, but rather due to the actions of their predecessors over which they had no control or influence. Analogously, it might be argued that present-day individuals in poor countries were not themselves directly harmed by the actions of anyone in rich countries – though that is highly debatable. However, I do not think that either of these arguments is especially strong. Compensation for a historical injury should not be determined exclusively by looking at the direct actions of individuals; the consequences of such actions and the efforts taken to ameliorate their negative impacts is also important. If individuals in rich countries continue to benefit from an unjust exploitation of resources that occurred centuries ago, and individuals in poor countries continue to suffer – or at least not thrive to the extent that they might have done had this unjust exploitation not occurred – then the former owe it to the latter to provide compensation for past injustices.

My second argument is a more directly moral one on the basis of fairness, drawn largely from Rawlsian-type reasoning and its extension to the international arena by Thomas Pogge, Daniel Weinstock and others. It is that the arbitrariness in the distribution of expressive capabilities across the globe constitutes a great infringement of the human dignity of many people. Wealthier states have a moral obligation to redistribute resources to poorer countries in which increases in the marginal utility[66] that accrue from amplifying the expressive capabilities of their own citizens are drastically lower than amplifying those of citizens in other countries. While their primary moral obligation remains to their own citizens, drastic and arbitrary[67] inequities cannot be morally justified and should be ameliorated to a substantial degree.

Following Rawls, I argue that the most obvious way to determine how individuals would distribute resources in a manner that would respect and amplify their individual dignity is to determine what distributive scheme they would accept in conditions of full impartiality – from the point of view of the universe. These individuals would recognize themselves as being members of an international order organized along state lines. Given the focus on the state, they would grant their membership significant moral weight relative to other concerns. If my argument in earlier chapters is correct, they would see the goal of their parent state as being the amplification of each citizen's human dignity. Much of this would flow from the state's increasingly being the democratically authored creation of dignified individuals. Since individuals are the authors of the state institutions that govern them, and contribute the resources necessary for their perpetuation, they are entitled to be the primary beneficiaries of state policies. This includes having the second of the twinned rights – to an equality of human capabilities – respected, before taking significant efforts to amplify the dignity of non-citizens.

However, such impartial reasoners would also recognize that, as a general moral concept, the goal of amplifying human dignity is universal rather than simply belonging to one state or another. Moreover, I believe that while impartial individuals would give moral weight to the state's obligations to its own citizens, they would not accept that limitation beyond a given threshold. They would recognize that the arbitrariness of belonging to this state or another should not have the profoundly determinate impact on the dignity of individuals that it now does.

Given the deliberative facts discussed above, and being asked to determine which distributive scheme they would regard as morally palatable, I believe that individuals would accept a scheme in which states were obligated first to amplify dignity within their own state by ensuring that the most important expressive capabilities of their citizens were respected. This would include all the expressive capabilities and individual requirements to realize the first of the twinned rights – to democratic self-authorship – and a substantial portion of those required to realize the second – to a relative equality of expressive capabilities. However, after a certain threshold the marginal utility of maximizing citizens' expressive capabilities might be far lower than what can be achieved through transfers to poorer states. Once this threshold was reached, states would then begin to redistribute their resources to poorer countries, since that would address the arbitrariness of location by ensuring that dignity was amplified to a greater extent than would be possible on a state-centric approach.

This brings up a further problem. How would one prevent free-riding on the part of some rich states? What if a given state assumes the moral obligations that I believe they should, but others do not? I believe that there are two answers to this. The first is that, regardless of what other rich states do, one should still fulfil one's obligations. This is good in itself and would also have positive consequences for the individual beneficiaries of redistributive policies. But I think that there is a second argument that could function to ameliorate these concerns: that the greater number of states that agree to fulfil their moral obligations to assist the world's poor, the more likely it is that other states will accept the obligation as binding both intrinsically and due to the social pressure that they will face to live up to what others are doing.

Here one might appeal to the 'isolation paradox' developed by Amartya Sen for justification: certain ends that individuals may eschew in isolation might be more palatable if others are willing to contribute towards their realization to a degree consistent with each individual's relative available resources.[68] If states do have obligations towards all the individuals in the world, these obligations certainly cannot be allowed to trump each state's obligations towards its own citizens. However, it would be both possible and morally preferable if states operated together to pool their resources, relative to what is available to each, to lift many individuals out of both absolute and especially degrading relative poverty. No individual state would bear the exclusive burden of this obligation, though rich states would bear the brunt of it.[69] The goal would be to establish a global equality of human capabilities over time, with rich states gradually being required to donate less and less until a reasonable parity of conditions was established for states across the world.

This might seem like a highly idealistic aspiration[70] – and indeed it is. The neo-liberal regime – or, to use Hardt and Negri's term, the 'de-centered empire' – that currently organizes the distribution of wealth and power across the globe is deeply resistant to any attempt to redistribute resources to the world's poor even at the state level, let alone between developed and underdeveloped states.[71] The practical task of achieving a more egalitarian distribution would be immense, and warrant a very substantial and empirically oriented argument. More importantly, it would require a substantial theorization on the nature and power dynamics of the contemporary neo-liberal regime – especially given the ascendency of postmodern conservatives such as Donald Trump – which cannot be undertaken in this work. However, I do feel that the possibility of a redistributive effort such as the one that I have described is not as bleak as it might appear at first. In the following section, I will argue that international human rights law already provides many of the mechanisms that would be required.

International Human Rights Law as a Steering Mechanism for Realizing Human Dignity

As I highlighted in earlier sections, international human rights law can play an important role in establishing the rightful condition for the amplification of human dignity. This should be international human rights law's fundamental orientation. It could achieve this goal by making state sovereignty conditional on realizing the twinned rights necessary for human dignity's amplification. Finally, I discussed the obligations of states towards non-citizens, arguing that, beyond a certain threshold, wealthy states have significant moral obligations to redistribute wealth to those in need. In the final section of this chapter, I will discuss how these goals could be achieved in more practical terms. This will then be grounded in the final two substantive chapters through an extensive analysis of many of the developments in international human rights law and its jurisprudence.

The conception of 'human dignity' emerging from documents such as the UDHR, the ICCPR and the ICESCR is already sufficiently holistic for international human rights law to be oriented towards its amplification. During the Cold War, the tendency to see rights as being divided into negative and positive, and to privilege one over the other, caused considerable damage to efforts to orient the various human rights documents towards a holistic conception of human dignity. While there remains considerable pushback from states who still wish to privilege some rights over others, there is quiet but growing consensus that this is a normatively flawed approach. Part of this movement draws inspiration from the efforts of modern liberals such as Rawls, Sen and Nussbaum, who have broadened liberalism's traditional horizons by focusing on economic, social, and cultural rights. Few could now cogently argue that it is fundamental that liberal societies should focus exclusively on civil and political rights and that 'individuals must look after themselves'. Even standard liberal rights not associated with economic, social and cultural rights have been reinterpreted to demonstrate the connection between the two.

This indivisibility of rights suggests that states have been wrong to focus myopically on the realization of civil and political rights while ignoring or 'progressively realizing' economic, social and cultural rights. In interpreting them holistically, I believe that the legal documents codifying rights embody a conception of human dignity that is very close to the one that I have sketched out here. I have already discussed the references to dignity that exist in international law. Here, I argue that the indivisibility of rights suggests that they can and should be oriented centrally around amplifying human dignity through realizing the twinned rights. This is because human dignity, which serves as a mother right, gives birth to the twinned rights. These are in turn realized through the positive rights that are included in international legal documents. This connection is a hermeneutic chain stretching from the normative ideal of realizing dignity, down to the fairly abstract principles of democratic authorship and equality of capabilities expressed by the twinned rights, and concluding in the specific rights guaranteed in positive law. I characterize this as a hermeneutic chain since the more abstract rights at one end provide the normative orientation, while the positive rights concretize how to realize this orientation. Neither end should be privileged over the other. Rather, they operate in tandem through a process of coming to a reflective equilibrium. Our understanding of what is immediately necessary to the amplification of dignity changes as one looks at the specific socio-historical contexts in which international human rights law is applied. In turn, the specific positive rights of international human rights law should always be understood as part of a holistic orientation of amplifying human dignity – never as simply an individual collection of rights that can be parsed and separated according to the whims of political actors and states.

The above is the germ of my argument for a more technical and complex dignity-oriented approach to interpreting and applying international human rights law. The law should be applied to steer sovereign states towards what is specifically necessary to amplify dignity in their given socio-historical contexts. On my interpretation, international human rights law should be reconceived as a set of steering mechanisms oriented around getting states to respect the dignity of both their citizens and, where required, those abroad who truly need help. When states have done so to the extent possible, they can be said to have realized the rightful condition necessary normatively to retain sovereign legitimacy. In such circumstances, international human rights law need no longer operate to steer them in the direction of amplifying human dignity. Instead, it should respect the sovereignty of states in line with what is required by the first of the twinned rights: enabling citizens to be authors of the laws that flow from political and legal institutions subordinated to their interests.[72]

How to adopt such a dignity-oriented approach to international human rights law will be the main focus of the remainder of this work. While there remains an immense number of practical barriers to achieving this globally, in many parts of the world the legal institutions are already in place for international human rights law to steer states towards realizing the rightful condition for the amplification of human dignity. These institutions are often underfunded and not especially powerful. Often, states will simply ignore their directives. However, they provide the skeletal architectures upon which to begin assembling a more robust international legal order that would not be so driven by the interests of sovereign states and the power dynamics of postmodern capitalist empire. If we are interested in realizing a more just global polity oriented around amplifying human dignity, this skeletal architecture should be beefed up. Moreover, in some parts of the world the legal institutions needed to steer states towards realizing the rightful condition not only exist; they already possess substantial powers needed to enact real change. They can therefore serve as a model for how a more general legal order can be established to implement international human rights law.

The most notable set of legal institutions possessing the power to enact real change is those on the European continent, and especially the ECtHR. While one may quibble with many of its decisions, I believe that, overall, the ECtHR has played an important role in demonstrating that we need not cede so much power to the false necessity of the sovereign state system. Most notably, the Court has played a foundational role in protecting and expanding the franchise for many individuals who otherwise would have been denied the right to vote. Legal decisions that extend voting rights to those who did not have them before can help steer states towards the rightful condition because it is an important step towards respecting the first of the twinned rights – towards democratic self-authorship. While the Court has been less aggressive in respecting the economic, social and cultural rights of European citizens, there is no inherent reason that it could not take important steps in that direction as well. If it did so, it would serve as a model for the establishment or strengthening of other international legal institutions that can also be reoriented around amplifying human dignity by steering states under their jurisdiction towards respecting the two twinned rights.

The next two chapters will discuss these topics at greater length. Chapter 5 will discuss the possibility of realizing the first of the twinned rights, by looking at legal decisions concerning democratic rights. Chapter 6 will be more speculative and will discuss legal decisions that very tentatively move states towards respecting the second of the twinned rights. In both chapters, where the relevant legal institutions failed to amplify human dignity to the extent possible, I will discuss why and how they might be reformed or refocused to ensure more just outcomes in the future.

PART II

Realizing human dignity in the practice of international human rights law

5

Realizing Human Dignity Through Amplifying Democratic Rights

Introduction

The next two chapters will demonstrate how my argument for making human dignity the fundamental orientation of international human rights law, and how international human rights law can serve as a steering mechanism moving states towards the rightful condition, can be realized practically. I will discuss how international legal institutions, especially courts, can play – and have played – a fundamental role in steering states towards the rightful condition by realizing the twinned rights to democratic authorship and to an equality of expressive capabilities respectively. Because the twinned rights operate at a high level of moral abstraction and are to be concretized in context-sensitive ways, it would be impossible to discuss all possible ways in which they could be legitimately realized. So, instead, I will here focus on where international institutions, legal institutions and courts have played a fundamental role in realizing voting rights particularly. Voting rights are obviously integral to the realization of the first right (to democratic self-authorship). While not sufficient in itself, expanding the franchise to those individuals and groups traditionally denied voting rights would be a massive step in the right direction. Moreover, international courts have been notably successful in steering states towards great enfranchisement. Voting rights are therefore an ideal example of how the project of making human dignity the fundamental orientation of international human rights law can be carried out.

There are some who might be sharply critical of the emphasis that the next two chapters will place on courts and legal decisions. Critics on the Right might observe that I am effectively demanding that unelected judicial actors be given substantial powers to overturn the policies of sovereign states. This might seem very much at odds with the emphasis that I am placing on democratic authorship. I do not believe that this is an especially powerful argument, and I will deal with it briefly. The more salient criticisms would be from those on the Left – especially those affiliated in some way with the broadly critical and socio-legal traditions. These critics might argue that I am placing a great deal of trust in judicial actors who are very unlikely to carry out the kind of radical agenda that I am pushing for. They would argue that courts are generally prone to being reactionary institutions; at the very most, one might expect them to take a cautiously liberal approach when looking at the law. For these critics on the Left, placing such trust in courts is deeply misguided and potentially dangerous.

Critics on the Right – for instance the US National Security Advisor John Bolton, former US statesman Henry Kissinger, and Nigel Farage of the UK Independence Party, have all argued that allowing international legal institutions a substantial degree of control over the policy of a sovereign state constitutes a fundamental infringement of that state's freedom. It effectively allows unelected foreign nationals to direct a state's policy in matters vital to its security and well-being. This is often connected to the strong democratic claim that a state's people, via their elected governments, should be the ones steering state policy both internally and in foreign affairs. More strident critics also claim that international legal institutions are tainted by various left-wing ideologies and are therefore likely to inhibit the enactment of a popular conservative agenda. For critics on the Right, this is damning both in itself and, again, because it constrains conservative governments theoretically elected by a majority of a state's people to enact a right-wing agenda.[1] On this more conspiratorial line of reasoning, international legal institutions are essentially a means by which the Left bypasses a state's citizens and its domestic government, and imposes policies from a global level.[2] As John Bolton put it:

> This is not the view, however, of those who want to constrain our sovereignty. After all, if we decided what is right and wrong, they couldn't second-guess us and bend us to their views. Having failed to win this point within our political system, however, they simply retreat into international organizations, hoping they and their international leftist allies can win there what they failed to win at home.[3]

Often, these right-wing critics give their opinions a distinctively patriotic and particularist bent. This can make it somewhat challenging to distinguish their more general arguments about international law from more nationally specific claims about the restrictions that it places on one country. This is especially true with regard to the United States, which is regarded by cheerleaders such as Bolton as a global leader and fundamentally a force for good in the world. I will not address here the manifold problems with such specific claims about American hegemony. The core argument that one can discern in the work of these right-wing critics is that it is fundamentally wrong for unelected bodies such as foreign courts, with little or no connection to the politics and history of a given nation state, to change domestic and foreign policy. To these right-wing critics, international human rights law – to the extent that it can be said to exist at all – should limit itself to arbitrating fairly minor disputes such as concerns over fishing rights, vindicating the right to use co-ordinated force against the 'enemies of mankind' such as pirates.

These debates echo the more general claims made by right-wing critics about the role of courts in society, particularly in the academic and political arguments about judicial activism that (rather tiresomely) dominated North American legal discourse for decades. Occasionally these take on a somewhat abstract air, with vaguely formulated appeals to the 'people' and 'liberty' being invoked to justify maintaining the status quo.[4] Much the same is true of right-wing criticisms of international law. Critics such as Bolton, Kissinger and others claim that it is wrong for unelected globalist bodies such as international courts to infringe upon the sovereignty of governments, especially democratically elected governments.

The problem with these criticisms is that many right-wing critics see their specific domestic mechanisms, which are designed to ensure the democratic legitimacy of their government, as exhausting what is required to live up to the ideal. But in many respects the entire point of international institutions oriented along the lines that I have discussed is to steer states towards adopting more inclusive voting procedures and electoral mechanisms to ensure that the government enjoys greater democratic legitimacy. So, if the argument of critics such as Bolton is that international institutions should not infringe upon the will of a free people, thereby implying that the basis of freedom is democratic freedom, he should in some senses welcome institutions that seek to amplify that. For instance, many of the same right-wing critics who decry the influence of globalist institutions on domestic politics are also very comfortable with a democratic majority choosing to place restrictions on who can vote. But such a democracy is inherently incomplete, since it is not meeting the minimal threshold of allowing each person a chance (marginally) to participate in the constitution of the laws that will govern them through voting for representatives. This is especially true if one wishes to defend a majoritarian conception of democracy, which could only be minimally legitimate if the majority was truly established by allowing every citizen to vote.

Some right-wing critics might accept many of these claims but still argue that international institutions such as courts do not need to steer developed states, which have robust democratic and accountability mechanisms in place. Unfortunately, this is not necessarily true in all cases. The sad reality is that many developed states maintain substantial restrictions on enfranchisement that domestic judicial systems have not ameliorated. To provide just one example, in the United States, which Bolton takes as the paradigm example of a modern liberal democracy, millions of Americans have restricted or non-existent voting rights. This includes roughly 5.3 million mostly African-Americans who have been disenfranchised for mostly drug-related crimes, millions of individuals in the territories and the District of Columbia, and many more who are effectively disenfranchised through voter suppression techniques operating under the auspices of preventing voter fraud.[5] In total, this means that at least 10 million Americans are *de jure* disenfranchised – essentially, the same number of people who reside in Michigan or Georgia – and many more are *de facto* disenfranchised by policies that are designed largely to suppress minority votes. This is an immense number, which demonstrates that even states that are taken as democratic exemplars have major problems with ensuring that everyone is meaningfully able to participate in political processes. This is where international institutions such as courts can steer states in a more democratic direction to reinforce their legitimacy by establishing the rightful conditions for full and meaningful participation in the democratic process. States cannot, in good faith, appeal to democratic legitimacy to justify constraining institutions that would engender greater democracy – at least not without effectively preferring an abstract conception of democracy to its more robust realization. If democratic legitimacy is a primary political virtue, critics should welcome attempts by international courts to steer states in the direction of the rightful condition.

This brings me to my final point on right-wing criticism. Ultimately, my suspicion is that the appeals to the people and sovereignty common to critics such as Bolton have relatively little to do with concern for democracy. They are more about paranoia that international courts will constrain the capacity of powerful states such as the United States from doing what is necessary to protect their 'national interest', regardless of what most citizens in the state want. This is reflected in Bolton's fear that the International Criminal Court will be used to shame the United States for its actions, and even to prosecute American servicemen who commit war crimes:

> Another hidden agenda is making the unilateral use of United States' force harder by raising the political and military risks and costs of such action, thus making it less attractive to senior decision makers; requiring other nations (whether through the Security Council or other mechanisms) to participate in the consideration of the use of force by the United States; and locking the United States into interpretations of 'international law' rather than relying on constitutional or statutory reasoning. Since the national

> security of the United States is the ultimate responsibility of its central government, the weakening of that authority is perhaps the most definitive and most crippling paralysis of 'international law'.[6]

Since this work is not concerned directly with the laws of war, I will not discuss my position on this at length.[7] Needless to say, one can certainly detach the capacity of courts to orient states towards realizing the rightful condition domestically without constraining their capacity to act internationally. For those critics for whom any restraints on states' capacity to act internationally are fundamentally noxious, this should be enough. Those interested in a more elaborate argument may look to the extensive corresponding endnote.

This completes my comments on potential right-wing criticisms of my project. I will now move on to those presented by the Left, which, given the critical legal orientation of my project, are considerably more serious.

Critical legal scholars have generally shown a great deal of scepticism towards courts, though that has softened considerably in the past few decades. This scepticism flows organically from their general distrust of the legal system as a whole. One of the fundamental tenets of critical legal theory is that law generally operates to serve the interests of powerful groups in society, while precluding the participation and full development of the marginalized in the political and legal order. Generally, two sets of interrelated reasons are given to justify this distrust in the formal legal system. The first are institutional, and the second pertain to the officials who work in the legal system.

The most powerful institutional criticisms made by critical (and socio-legal) scholars are that very few marginalized individuals in society are able effectively to access the legal system. This is due to a myriad of intersectional reasons. The most obvious are simply the tremendous amounts of money and time that a party requires to go to court. While legal aid ameliorates some of these difficulties, it is often available to only a few individuals in society who are dealing with very specific problems and is inadequate along several metrics. Other reasons, articulated most clearly in Ewick and Silbey's classic *The Common Place of Law: Stories from Everyday Life*, are more subtle. Ewick and Silbey note how there is a tendency on the part of traditional legal scholars to deindividualize individuals who go to court. The dispositions, education and capabilities of actual individuals are all ignored as individuals are reduced to the legally salient facts of their cases. This is highly problematic, since disposition, education and overall capabilities are important in determining how one both perceives and is perceived in turn by courts. Individuals who see themselves as coming 'before the law' or operating 'against the law' may well find it exceptionally challenging to negotiate the alienating and frustrating labyrinth of legal procedures. This can incline them against pushing their cases forward, even in situations in which they might have the resources to do so and it would be to their long-term benefit.[8]

The second reason why critical legal scholars often express distrust of the legal system concerns the officials who work in it, and especially judges. Many critical legal scholars observe that judges often come from elite backgrounds, which inclines them to have political, social and class biases that orient their decisions. Moreover, they observe that training in law schools often inclines officials and judges to imbibe features of the conservative and neo-liberal ideologies that pervade the law. This further reinforces the political, social and class biases of legal officials and judges, while enabling them to mask these under the guise of neutrally applying a set of fair rules. One consequence of this is that judges and legal officials are either indifferent to, or outright ignorant of, many of the institutional reasons for marginalizing individuals being unable to access the legal system. Critical legal scholars are deeply antagonistic towards formalistic accounts of the law that venerate and honour its apparently vital social role, while ignoring its institutionalized lack of responsiveness to the most vulnerable in society. The only exception to this, of course, is when it deploys carceral mechanisms to clamp down on dissent through criminal and penal law. Moreover, critical legal scholars have deepened the legal realist claims about the indeterminacy of language and given them substantially more bite.[9] They claim that, underneath the formalistic guise of simply applying the law in a neutral way, judges are actually making political decisions that have a broad social impact. Because of their political, social and class biases, these decisions are often oriented around reinforcing the status quo and buttressing powerful and oppressive elements in society. Moreover, judges who do try to deviate from these biases are often attacked by the legal community as being excessively 'activist' – that they are deviating from their job of just neutrally applying the law. But this is a smokescreen: there is no neutral application of the law in many cases, since legal language itself is indeterminate. What these critics in the legal community are truly angry about are the substantive consequences of a decision that grants greater power to historically marginalized groups whom they feel are unworthy. The invocation of activism and a lack of neutrality is an attempt to shame progressive judges from deviating from their job to maintain the hierarchical status quo. An eloquent statement of this position is given by Allan Hutchinson of Osgoode Hall Law School:

> Behind the traditional rhetoric of principled adjudication, there is a very definite and partial political agenda. While it is understandable why such critics would prefer to occupy the neutral territory of formal constitutional technique rather than the contested turf of substantive political alignment, the effort to portray and promote a non-political mode of constitutional adjudication as being possible and desirable is a neat, but deceptive manoeuvre. When a closer look is taken at those occasions on which the critics raise the spectre of activism and those on which they do not, it will be seen that the difference is a blunt ideological one. Those decisions that do not fit their political agenda are condemned as activist and those that do fit are defended as appropriate. The constitutional line is one of their own political making. In general, those decisions which promote greater equality (for example, gay rights, aboriginal land claims, etc.) are dismissed as activist and illegitimate, whereas those which defend greater liberty (for example, election spending, male property rights, etc.) are showcased as valid exercises of judicial authority. Yet, in terms of their fit with the opaque constitutional text and the courts' activist tendencies, there is nothing to choose between them. It is only that some substantive values are preferred over others. Accordingly, the claim of 'activism' is simply

> a veiled criticism that the courts are being too progressive and making decisions that do not reflect desirable conservative values: any court that stands by and lets constitutional values be ignored or belittled is at fault.[10]

These two sets of reasons demonstrate why critical legal scholars have been so sceptical about using courts as a means of social change. Either immense institutional barriers prevent historically marginalized people from accessing courts, or they get there and find themselves facing unsympathetic or even frightened legal officials who either do not want to enact change or are concerned about the implications for their professional standing and advancement. So, the advice of critical legal scholars is to be very cautious and pessimistic about the law, while incrementally trying to enact change in the rare instances in which strategic openings appear.

Relatively few of these criticisms are applied directly to international human rights law, though the field of critical international legal theory is growing. This is in part due to the relative novelty of international law, and in part because its main actors tend to remain states. But I believe that the two rationales given above can apply in many cases to international law – perhaps exceptionally so. The state-centrism of international human rights law makes it several more levels removed from the individuals who are impacted by policies, which would make it especially open to the institutional criticism. Moreover, international courts dealing with human rights issues are often the target of frequent and occasionally justifiable criticisms, where they are not just characterized as entirely ineffective. For example, the ECtHR has been criticized for its excessive focus on civil and political rights at the expense of economic, social and cultural rights. Some have even observed that it tends to be overly conservative in its application of liberal principles to the law – for instance, through privileging nationals over non-nationals who might have especially pressing needs.[11] And, of course, the ICC has been heavily criticized for focusing almost exclusively on crimes committed by Africans. While it may be going too far to label the ICC an instrument of 'neocolonialism', this is no doubt an important criticism, especially in a world in which so many crimes are committed by leaders from developed states – most notably officials from the Bush Regime during the illegal Iraq War – and yet they go unpunished.[12]

However, none of these criticisms invalidates international human rights law as an aspirational project. Indeed, what unites critics who regard the ECtHR as being excessively committed to liberal rights and the ICC as being overly focused on crimes from one region of the world is a sense of chastened hopes and muted expectations. These leftist critics are not typically concerned with what international human rights law and criminal law do in fact, but with its doing too little or focusing its impact too narrowly. Given this, I would invite critical legal scholars to consider the possibilities for emancipation and egalitarianism that could be realized were international human rights law to be reoriented along the lines I have discussed here. One of the ways in which this could be achieved would be through undertaking a set of reforms to make the international legal system more accessible to individuals – for instance, by establishing more individual complaints mechanisms. Important efforts have already been made in this respect.[13] Another step would be to inspire state courts into granting individuals more leave to appeal to international courts, following the *Lovelace* precedent, while granting greater resources in terms of comprehensive legal aid.[14]

But the most salient reason that I believe for critical legal scholars being able to put their faith in an international human rights system oriented in this matter is that the very primitive system already in place has achieved some impressive successes. Rather than simply rehearse these in this section, for the rest of this chapter I will discuss these successes to argue why, oriented in the right way, international human rights law can be a force for democratic and egalitarian justice.

Expanding Voting Rights: *Aziz v Cyprus*

The *Aziz v Cyprus* decision is one of the first in which the ECtHR was asked to make a decision that could transform the entire political structure of a sovereign member state. The controversy was especially prominent given the politically charged and long-standing conflict between Greek and Turkish Cypriots over who would hold dominion over the island nation. As we shall see, I believe that the ECtHR ruled correctly by invoking democratic human rights to trump the claims of nationalists who wished to transform Turkish Cypriots into second-class citizens by denying them the right to vote. The ECtHR's reasoning also demonstrates how one can use the existing tools of international jurisprudence to link democratizing processes and state legitimacy in an analytically rigorous manner.[15]

Mr Aziz was born on the island of Cyprus in 1938, and by the turn of the millennium was a resident living in the capital city of Nicosia. He was a member of the very small Turkish community that resided in the non-occupied Greek section of the island. In 2001, Mr Aziz requested that the Government register him on the electoral role so that he would be eligible to vote in the upcoming parliamentary election. Unfortunately, Mr Aziz's request was denied that February. The Ministry of the Interior argued that, under section 63 of the Republic's Constitution, members of the Turkish Cypriot community were not eligible to vote for candidates in the Greek Cypriot elections. Mr Aziz took the matter to the Supreme Court of Cyprus (Supreme Court), which denied his claim immediately before the election. Citing principles of judicial restraint, the Supreme Court offered the following reasoning for its undemocratic decision.[16]

> The right to vote is directly linked to the communal checks and balances which provide for the compilation of separate electoral lists and for separate elections of the representatives of each community. The ideal of democracy – one person, one vote in the person's place of residence – does not provide any grounds for the Court to assume the power to reform the Constitution. Such competence is not vested in us, nor can the judicial authorities claim such power. This would be against the principle of the separation of powers on which the Constitution is based.[17]

Understandably dissatisfied with this ruling, Mr Aziz took his case to the ECtHR. He argued that, under the ECHR, Article 3, Protocol No 1 he was entitled to vote in the Cypriot election. The Article reads:

> The High Contracting Parties undertake to hold free elections at reasonable intervals by secret ballot, under conditions which will ensure the free expression of the opinion of the people in the choice of the legislature.[18]

Mr Aziz pointed out that, while it may have seemed necessary to divide the electorate into Greek and Turkish segments when the Republic achieved independence in the 1960s and the threat of invasion by Turkey was very real, those conditions had long since disappeared. The Turkish Communal Chamber, which had been responsible for the island's minority population, had been dissolved in 1963. The Greek Communal Chamber followed in 1965, to be replaced by a unified Parliament, in which Turks were, unjustly, not represented.[19]

For its part, the Cypriot Government argued that, while it did have an obligation to hold elections under Article 3, the EU and the ECtHR gave member states a 'wide margin of appreciation' to determine how they wished to carry this out.[20] They maintained that their unique Republican system, which allocated 30 per cent of the seats in Parliament to Turks and the remainder to Greeks, and granted each block considerable powers, was politically necessary to manage the 'delicate' situation on the island.[21] The Government maintained that, following its precedent in the earlier *Mathieu-Mohin* decision, the Court should demonstrate sensitivity to the political evolution of Cyprus's unique electoral system.[22] Finally, it pointed out that Mr Aziz had chosen to not participate in the Turkish elections, and that maintaining his constitutional status outlined in Article 62, and the status of the Turkish minority within Greek Cyprus, of which he was a member, was not particularly damaging, since only a 'very small' number of people were rendered unable to vote.[23]

The ECtHR disagreed sharply with the Government's argument. While it accepted that the young Republic had endured a difficult birth, especially after the Turkish invasion and occupation of the northern part of the island, they felt that this was no justification for denying over 1,000 Turkish Cypriots a fundamental right. This culpability was compounded since the Government was aware that this minority existed and had done little to rectify the situation. While the Court acknowledged that sovereign states possessed a great deal of discretion to determine how to organize democratic procedures, including elections, they argued that this could not extend to the wholesale denial of democratic rights to members of the community who were deemed unworthy or troublesome.[24]

> Although the Court notes that States enjoy considerable latitude to establish rules within their constitutional order governing parliamentary elections and the composition of the parliament, and that the relevant criteria may vary according to the historical and political factors peculiar to each State, these rules should not be such as to exclude some persons or groups of persons from participating in the political life of the country and, in particular, in the choice of the legislature, a right guaranteed by both the Convention and the Constitutions of all Contracting States … Consequently, the applicant, as a member of the Turkish Cypriot community living in the Government-controlled area of Cyprus, was completely deprived of any opportunity to express his opinion in the choice of the members of the House of Representatives of the country of which he is a national and where he has always lived … in the light of the above circumstances, the very essence of the applicant's right to vote, as guaranteed by Article 3 of Protocol No. 1, was impaired.[25]

Consequently, the European Court ordered the Government to amend the situation so that Mr Aziz, and members of the Turkish community in Greek Cyprus, were able to vote in the next election. They also ordered the Cypriot Government to pay Mr Aziz's legal costs.

I believe that the ECtHR's decision to deny the Government's claim was the correct one. In so doing, it upheld the broader conception of democracy articulated in the ECHR. While states have, and should be, granted a great deal of latitude in determining what socio-cultural 'conditions' are required in order to have a fair election, Article 10 makes it clear that elections are about more than just voting.[26] Elections are designed to manifest the 'free expression of the opinion of the people'. What the 'opinion of the people' actually is can be a contentious issue; but it is now likely to be beyond controversy to claim that it is not simply the opinion of the majority, let alone that of the most prominent cultural group in a state.[27]

In this situation, the Government of Cyprus chose wilfully to deny a substantial number of people the opportunity to employ their expressive capabilities by participating in an election that would have a direct effect on them. It maintained that this was justifiable given the contentious history of the state, and the fact that very few people were actually impacted by the policy. But this reasoning is spurious, since it puts expediency and politics above principle. But if a democratic form of governance truly expresses the 'opinion' of the people, it must ensure, as Mill claimed, that each individual has the opportunity to have their voice heard.[28] Or, in my language, democracy is about amplifying the human dignity of individuals and ascribing equal value to their democratic rights. This is especially pertinent where individuals face a strong likelihood of being disadvantaged due to given socio-historical boundaries, as was the case for the Turkish-speaking minority residing in Greek Cyprus.

This also speaks to the justifiable conditions placed on sovereignty by well-developed international legal instruments. In such instances, the ECHR can serve – and has served – as an instrument to realize the Kantian ideal. The Government of Cyprus used the Constitution to deny the Turkish-speaking minority the opportunity to employ their expressive capabilities during elections. In a sovereignty-oriented model of law, with its related philosophy of descriptive and/or normative legal positivism, this would be the end of the issue, regardless of the morality or immorality of the law in question. Indeed, the Government of Cyprus appears to have tacitly acknowledged this by focusing its argument not on the principles at hand, but instead on issues of expediency and effect. The European human rights system transforms this positivist framework into one in which the legitimacy of state law is dependent upon its maintaining the 'rightful condition' – in this case, by acting in a manner consistent with the principles articulated in the ECHR.[29]

This constitutes a great step forward in the realization of the cosmopolitan[30] project.[31]

What makes the European human rights system unique, and a (problematic) model for others to follow, is its unique capacity actually to enforce this dictum with some success compared with most other international human rights systems. This capacity is especially interesting, given that the ECtHR can have an impact on the behaviour of strong, as well as weaker, states. This gives the ECtHR system prominence as a model relative to, say, the ICC, which, for all the good that it has done, has a deserved reputation for focusing its prosecutorial efforts almost exclusively on criminals from the Global South. As we shall see in the next case, *Hirst v United Kingdom*, the ECtHR has been bold enough to try to transform the democratic policies of a great power. Unfortunately, as we shall see, this also speaks to the limitations that still face even the most robust international human rights systems.

Establishing the Rightful Condition for All: *Hirst v United Kingdom*

John Hirst was a UK citizen serving a discretionary life sentence for manslaughter committed in 1980. He was prevented from voting in national elections by section 3 of the Representation of the People Act 1983. Passed by the Thatcher Government, the 1983 Act had disenfranchised prisoners. Hirst brought the issue to the High Court in 2001, but his case was dismissed. He then brought the issue to the ECtHR later that year. In 2004, the Chamber of the ECtHR ruled that the 1983 Act violated Mr Hirst's Article 3 rights. Not taking the decision lying down, the UK brought the issue to the Grand Chamber, which ruled in 2005. The resulting decision was a long one for the ECtHR and drew inspiration from sources far beyond the ECHR, including the ICCPR, South African law, and Canada's *Sauvé* decision.[32]

Mr Hirst argued that the UK's insistence that it retain the law, both in principle and because changing it would involve 'radical change', was deeply misguided.[33] He pointed out that, at the time, most European countries, as well as South Africa and Canada, no longer denied prisoners the right to vote, and that the number of states that did had been dwindling. Mr Hirst maintained that this indicated a 'presumption in favour of enfranchisement, which was in harmony with the fundamental nature of democracy'.[34] While the Government maintained that being disenfranchised constituted part of his punishment, Mr Hirst argued that this rested on a fundamental misunderstanding of voting as a 'privilege' that could be given and withdrawn, rather than a right to which all were entitled regardless of circumstance.[35] He maintained that no link could be given between the aims of punishment, such as rehabilitation and deterrence, and removing his right to vote.[36] Finally, Mr Hirst argued that imposing a blanket ban that prevented prisoners from voting was 'disproportionate, arbitrary, and impaired the essence of the right'.[37]

The Government of the United Kingdom, echoing similar claims made in *Aziz*, argued that, under Article 3, the right to vote is not absolute, since the ECHR granted signatory states a 'wide margin of appreciation' in determining how to enact the democratic provisions contained in the Convention.[38] But in *Aziz* the UK deepened the argument made by the Government of Cyprus by maintaining that, unlike in *Aziz*, the law against prisoners voting was not simply the relic of a bygone era that was no longer contextually defensible. The Government pointed out that Parliament had supported the prohibition for many decades now, most recently by re-emphasizing it while passing the Representation of the People Act in 2000.[39] The UK also inverted Mr Hirst's argument by maintaining that, regardless of the general trend towards enfranchisement, the divergence seen in policy surrounding prisoners' voting rights in democratic states indicated that there was still room to argue the point.[40] Given this, it would be inappropriate for the ECtHR to overturn the considered position of a democratic state. This was further justifiable given that, while interpreting the ECHR, domestic British courts had upheld the ban.[41]

Finally, the Government made its most interesting argument. Echoing a position made as far back as Plato's *Crito*, the Government maintained that, by breaking the laws of the states, prisoners had violated the social contract. It was therefore justifiable to restrict them from participating in the affairs of the state, at least for the duration of their sentence. This was justifiable both in principle and because the Government felt that it would serve a further purpose in deterring future crimes.[42]

> The Government argued that the disqualification in this case pursued the intertwined legitimate aims of preventing crime and punishing offenders and enhancing civic responsibility and respect for the rule of law by depriving those who had breached the basic rules of society of the right to have a say in the way such rules were made for the duration of their sentence. Convicted prisoners had breached the social contract and so could be regarded as (temporarily) forfeiting the right to take part in the government of the country.[43]

The Government concluded by claiming that disenfranchisement for prisoners was a proportionate limitation, since it affected only those who committed a crime serious enough to warrant incarceration; it excluded those who committed less serious offences that subjected the perpetrator to fines, community service, suspended sentences, or detention in contempt of court.[44] Finally, it emphasized that the effect of disenfranchisement was only temporary, as the ban was removed once prisoners were set free.[45,46]

The ECtHR began its analysis of the case by admitting that the rights guaranteed by Article 3 differed in kind from those guaranteed elsewhere in the ECHR. This is because, rather than guaranteeing particular rights to individuals, it placed an onus on states to hold elections to determine the political will of the people.[47] This onus might seem to have an inverse implication; one way of interpreting it might be that states have significant leeway in how to interpret this democratic obligation to the national collective. However, the ECtHR quickly dismissed this interpretation by emphasizing the individualistic dimension of democratic procedures.

> Article 3 of Protocol No. 1 appears at first sight to differ from the other rights guaranteed in the Convention and Protocols as

> it is phrased in terms of the obligation of the High Contracting Party to hold elections which ensure the free expression of the opinion of the people rather than in terms of a particular right or freedom. However, having regard to the preparatory work to Article 3 of Protocol No. 1 and the interpretation of the provision in the context of the Convention as a whole, the Court has established that it guarantees individual rights, including the right to vote and to stand for election (see *Mathieu-Mohin and Clerfayt v. Belgium*, judgment of 2 March 1987, Series A no. 113, pp. 22–23, §§ 46–51). Indeed, it was considered that the unique phrasing was intended to give greater solemnity to the Contracting States' commitment and to emphasise that this was an area where they were required to take positive measures as opposed to merely refraining from interference (ibid., § 50).[48]

The ECtHR went on to emphasize its agreement with Mr Hirst that voting is 'not a privilege' that can be taken away.[49] It opined that, in the twenty-first century, the 'presumption in a democratic state must be in favour of inclusion' and, somewhat sardonically, pointed to the United Kingdom's own history of gradually moving from elite to universal enfranchisement.[50] While the ECtHR admitted that there was a margin in how to interpret Article 3, it remains its job to give the final interpretation in hard cases.[51] States need to satisfy the ECtHR that their particular way of running elections 'do not curtail the rights in question to such an extent as to impair their very essence and deprive them of their effectiveness; that they are imposed in pursuit of a legitimate aim; and that the means employed are not disproportionate'.[52] In particular, the ECtHR emphasized that any measures taken must not 'thwart' the free expression of the people in selecting the legislature; electoral measures 'must reflect, or not run counter to, the concern to maintain the integrity and effectiveness of an electoral procedure aimed at identifying the will of the people through universal suffrage'.[53]

With regard to the specific question of prisoners voting, the ECtHR emphasized that, even following incarceration, inmates retain all the rights guaranteed in the European Convention, save the right to liberty.[54] It maintained that any restrictions imposed on the other rights guaranteed in the Convention would have to be justified for reasons of security, in particular preventing crime and disorder, which is the aim of punishment. It therefore dismissed the claim that one could disenfranchise prisoners for socio-cultural reasons, such as the practice of enfranchisement for convicts who have offended public opinion. The restriction would have to be for more legitimate reasons in order for it to be proportionate to the damage caused to the integrity of democracy.[55]

The ECtHR went on to accept the Government's argument that restricting the voting rights of prisoners constituted a legitimate aim since it would enhance civic responsibility and respect for the rule of law. However, it concluded that the measures taken were disproportionate to what was acceptable in pursuit of this aim. It noted that the ban on voting affected 48,000 prisoners and that there was no evidence that the Government weighed the proportionality of its policy against its impact.[56] Finally, the ECtHR maintained that, while there still existed some disagreement among European states on the issue of prisoner voting, that itself could not be decisive. While states were given a wide margin to determine how to enact the right guaranteed in Article 3, this was not absolute but contingent on the approval of the ECtHR. Ultimately, the majority ruled that Mr Hirst's rights under Article 3 of the European ECHR had been violated, and ordered the legislature to change the policy and to pay the applicant's legal fees.

Despite his win, the *Hirst* decision was not uncontroversial, and prompted a number of justices to qualify their concurrence or draft dissenting opinions. I will briefly summarize these positions below, before going on to explain why I believe that they are mistaken. The most forceful dissent was prepared by Judges Wildhaber, Costa, Lorenzen, Kovler and Jebens. They pointed out, forcefully, that unlike every other right in the ECHR, the right guaranteed by Article 3 made no mention of individuals.[57] This is significant since no positive association is made between the right to vote and holding elections to determine the 'free expression of the people'. The dissenting judges found that this indicated that the right guaranteed by Article 3 was concerned with democratic procedures, rather than an individual's right to vote. While they conceded that denying prisoners the right to vote seemed to run counter to what was required by Article 3, the dissenting judges were not convinced that it impugned the 'essence' of the right.[58] Because of this, they felt that it was inappropriate for the ECtHR to deny states a wide margin for determining who gets to vote and who does not, so long as it did not do so in an arbitrary manner and did not affect the 'free expression of the people' wholesale. Here I will quote the judges at length:

> Article 3 of Protocol No. 1 cannot be considered to preclude restrictions on the right to vote that are of a general character, provided that they are not arbitrary and do not affect 'the free expression of the opinion of the people', examples being conditions concerning age, nationality, or residence ... Unlike the majority, we do not find that a general restriction on prisoners' right to vote should in principle be judged differently ... it is obviously compatible with the guarantee of the right to vote to let the legislature decide such issues in the abstract. [The] majority have concluded that a general restriction on voting for persons serving a prison sentence must be seen as falling outside any acceptable margin of appreciation, however wide that margin might be ... In our opinion, this categorical finding is difficult to reconcile with the declared intention to adhere to the Court's consistent case-law to the effect that Article 3 of Protocol No. 1 leaves a wide margin of appreciation to the Contracting States in determining their electoral system. In any event, the lack of precision in the wording of that Article and the sensitive political assessments involved call for caution. Unless restrictions impair the very essence of the right to vote or are arbitrary, national legislation on voting rights should be declared incompatible with Article 3 only if weighty reasons justify such a finding. We are unable to agree that such reasons have been adduced.[59]

The dissenting judges concluded by stressing that they were not in a position to determine whether denying prisoners the right to vote was proportionate to the Government's aims, since that was a determination best left to policymakers. They did, however, concede that disenfranchisement might be justifiable in the case of individuals who had committed very serious crimes and had been sentenced to life in prison.

The case concluded with the dissenting opinion of Judge Costa, who added a few remarks to those of his colleagues. He claimed to be in sympathy with the general aim of the majority in this case, and believed that state officials should do all they could to reintegrate prisoners into society. However, despite this moral outlook, Judge Costa decided to take a classically positivist stance in this case. He felt that it was not the ECtHR's role to make determinations about how this should be carried out, especially given the weight of jurisprudence that emphasized the latitude traditionally given to states in interpreting Article 3. Judge Costa felt that this should be respected, even if he was inclined to favour enfranchising prisoners.[60]

> the Court's case-law permits restrictions on the right to vote that are of a general character, such as conditions concerning age, nationality, or residence (provided they are not arbitrary and do not affect the free expression of the opinion of the people). With due respect, I see no convincing arguments in the majority's reasoning that could persuade me that the measure to which the applicant was subject was arbitrary, or even that it affected the free expression of the opinion of the people ... The point is that one must avoid confusing *the ideal* to be attained and which I support – which is to make every effort to bring the isolation of convicted prisoners to an end, even when they have been convicted of the most serious crimes, and to prepare for their reintegration into society and citizenship – and the *reality* of *Hirst (no. 2)*, which on the one hand theoretically asserts a wide margin of appreciation for the States as to the conditions in which a subjective right (derived from judicial interpretation!) may be exercised, but goes on to hold that there has been a violation of that right, thereby depriving the State of all margin and all means of appreciation.[61]

These powerful dissents speak to the consistent analytical quality of the ECtHR's rulings. When looking at *Hirst* as a whole, it becomes clear that the issues go beyond simply whether prisoners should have a right to vote. The case dealt with fundamental issues such as questions of sovereignty, conceptions of democracy, and the relationship between international law, positive law and morality. I will now briefly summarize why I believe that the majority made the right decision in this case, with the caveat that I will not discuss comprehensively all the issues raised by the case.

The most interesting argument raised in this case, and the one on which I will focus my attention, is the contractarian claim made by the Government of the United Kingdom: that, by breaking the law, prisoners had in effect abnegated their entitlement to vote. This contractarian ideal links directly to the Government's claim about a sovereign state's right to determine its own electoral practices without interference by outside bodies. Indeed, it echoes arguments made very early in the tradition – most notably Socrates' claims about one's filial duty to obey even an unjust law in the *Crito*, and Hobbes's monumental argument that citizens have a duty to obey the sovereign in almost everything since, after the transition from the state of nature to the civil state, one must keep to the initial covenant made.[62] Both of these arguments would tend to support the Government's claims – both that it has a right to disenfranchise prisoners and that a state should be given a wide margin to determine the form of its political practices, not to mention who gets to participate therein.

To put this in legal theoretical terms, this might be cast in the descriptive positivist framework of Judge Costa: that while the ideal may be enfranchisement, the drift of the law towards giving sovereign states a wide margin to interpret their democratic obligations is clear. Or, it can be cast more strongly in the terms of normative positivism: that, regardless of the particular moral status of any specific law, sovereign states must be given a great deal of leeway on issues as fundamental as political participation, since that is a basic condition for the maintenance of any orderly legal system. This approaches the position of the other dissenting judges, who were more willing to entertain the idea that states have a right to determine who gets to participate in elections so long as the reasoning for their determinations is not 'arbitrary'.

The deepest tension in the dissenting judges' reasoning is over the very question of political legitimacy, which is invoked directly by the Government of the United Kingdom when it references the social contract. The difficulty with this position, as I highlighted earlier in this chapter, is that it evades the very issue of concrete legitimacy by trying to lift it to a very high level of moral abstraction. While I believe that contractarian positions should be avoided in political theory, since they render the theorist rather than actual participants the final arbiter in determining legitimacy, it has its uses within that rich tradition. When invoked by concrete states, however, which have never in fact been the product of reasoners determining the form of political institutions that they wish to govern them, the social contract cannot but come across as an ideological weapon. It attempts to evade the question of the state's legitimacy to act in the way that it does, both in particular instances and generally, by appealing to a transcendent norm, or 'constitutive point', which is meant to accomplish the Midas-like task of transforming political decisions into legal ones.

But a state is not legitimated by a transcendent norm, or constitutive point. As I have argued throughout, it is legitimated by establishing and maintaining the 'rightful condition' for the amplification of human dignity. The first right that must be recognized in order to establish a 'rightful condition', in my model, is a democratic right to participate in the authorship of political and legal structures, and to determine the laws that flow from these structures. The obligation to realize the democratic right is not exhausted by the establishment of political procedures, even representative democratic political procedures, since the right is inherent, regardless of the actual status of the individuals who make up the state, including prisoners. The point of democratic procedures is to ensure the equal value of democratic rights to all – something that is bucked when a state chooses to disenfranchise prisoners. This, I take it, is the conceptual point made by the majority about the individualistic consequences of Article 3 of the ECHR.

The dissenting judges in *Hirst* erred in thinking that the ECtHR was improperly treading upon national sovereignty by declaring that the United Kingdom must grant prisoners the right to vote. The role of international human rights law is to secure the conditions that legitimate sovereign authority by steering states towards respecting the rights of all the citizens who make them up. Repellent as it may seem to some, this includes criminals and even those who commit the vilest crimes, such as Mr Hirst. While it may seem attractive, on a contractarian model, to deny them the opportunity to vote, this misunderstands the nature of legitimacy and its relationship to rights. A right should be understood not as a privilege granted by a magnanimous state to the social body that it claims to represent, but as the legal concretization of the more abstract jurisgenerative principles upon which states must act if they are to retain sovereign authority. Rights are legal tools that amplify human dignity through the realization of each individual's expressive capabilities. Denying rights to any individual does nothing to further respect for the law; it only serves to undermine the moral basis for the law by infringing the dignity of citizens. A normative jurisprudence of international law, by contrast, would seek to link my articulation of human dignity with actual law wherever possible, even where to do so would run counter to trends in the domestic legal system. This is why the majority made the right decision in *Hirst*.

Developing Democratic Institutions: *Riza and Others v Bulgaria*

Riza and Others v Bulgaria is an especially important case since it demonstrates that the court is willing to take steps to ensure that voting rights are more than simply an abstract guarantee. It orients states towards establishing institutions and procedures that are necessary for the meaningful exercise of voting rights. Moreover, it does so while protecting a minority group that has faced considerable pressure and prejudice over the past decade, making the protection of its democratic rights all the more essential.

Mr Riza and the other 101 applicants were Bulgarian nationals of Turkish origin who also belonged to the Islamic faith. During the 2009 Bulgarian election, the applicants were living in Turkey and had participated in the election through seventeen different polling stations available across the country. Mr Riza himself worked for the DPS political party. According to domestic law, Bulgarians living abroad were allowed to vote in elections, but only for parties and coalitions rather than individual candidates. The DPS violated this rule by placing Mr Riza on the battlefront as his party's candidate. The DPS won 14.4 per cent of the vote in the election, becoming Bulgaria's third-largest political party. It also won a considerable majority of the expat vote, at 61.8 per cent, most of which came from voters residing in Turkey. After a considerable and technical debate about the country's rules surrounding the allocation of seats according to its system of proportional representation, Mr Riza won a constituency and was elected to the Bulgarian National Assembly.[63]

In 2009, the President and three other parties, including the far-Right Order, Law, and Justice Party, appealed Mr Riza's victory. They claimed that substantial irregularities had occurred at the seventeen polling stations in Turkey, including that Mr Riza's name had been placed on the ballot as an individual candidate. After a period of review and assessment, the Constitutional Court determined that certain irregularities had been present in the voting process in Turkey. It decided to invalidate several of the votes obtained by the DPS, which would lead to a new allocation of seats in the National Assembly. As a result of the Constitutional Court's decision, the DPS lost the seat held by Mr Riza. The DPS and Mr Riza appealed the decision, but their claims were declared inadmissible by the court. They finally appealed the decision to the ECtHR, which heard their case in October 2015.[64]

Mr Riza and the DPS made two arguments concerning the law in Bulgaria. First, they argued that Mr Riza's not being allowed to place his name on the ballot as an active candidate was a violation of Article 3 of Protocol No 1 of the ECHR. They also argued that the Bulgarian Constitutional Court had violated the Article 14 rights of voters living in Turkey, by invalidating their votes due to irregularities. They noted that

Bulgarian domestic law provided them with no means of legally remedying their situations, which compelled them to appeal to the ECtHR.[65]

In rendering its judgment, the European Court relied heavily on the electoral guidelines produced by the European Commission for Democracy Through Law, which provided hermeneutic guidance when interpreting Article 3, Protocol No 1 of the ECHR.[66] It began its analysis by acknowledging the Government's complaint that Mr Riza should not have standing as a victim before the Court since he had violated electoral rules by putting himself forward as a single candidate. The Court noted that, since this was closely associated with the substance of the case, it would deal with both Mr Riza's standing as a victim and the broader questions raised. It then observed the arguments made by both Mr Riza and the 101 applicants, and the Bulgarian government. Most notably, the Court observed that the Government contested Mr Riza's claims that the voting rights of the applicants had been violated. The Government argued that the voting rights of the applicants were still protected. It was only their specific votes in this election that had been invalidated due to the irregularities involved. The ECtHR also acknowledged the Government's claim that its own Constitutional Court had reviewed the case thoroughly and had decided that the substance of the applicants' voting rights had not been violated. The Court then moved on to giving its own assessment.[67]

The ECtHR began by observing that Article 3 of Protocol 1 did not require states to develop any specific democratic system, such as proportional representation or majority voting. Indeed, it observed that the contracting parties to the ECHR enjoyed a 'wide margin of appreciation'[68] when it came to how to elect officials and organize their democracy. It also observed that the requirement that states ensure 'conditions which will ensure the free expression of the opinion of the people in their choice of the legislature' only entails that each citizen enjoy equal treatment during the election. It in no way suggests that all votes must carry equal electoral weight. The Court also observed that the rights protected under Article 3 were 'not absolute' and that states needed to be given a 'margin of appreciation' when applying them. However, it noted again that this appreciation for state sovereignty only went so far. It was ultimately for the Court to decide when the margin of appreciation ended.[69]

With regard to this case, the Court decided that the Government of Bulgaria was wrong to claim that the rights of Mr Riza and the 101 applicants had not been violated. It observed that claiming that the voting rights of the applicants had not been violated, just the validity of their particular votes in this election, was deeply strange. As the Court observed in paragraph 148 of the judgment:

> The active electoral right as guaranteed by Article 3 of Protocol No. 1 is not confined exclusively to the acts of choosing one's favourite candidates in the secrecy of the polling booth and slipping one's ballot paper into the box. It also involves each voter being able to see his or her vote influencing the make-up of the legislature, subject to compliance with the rules laid down in electoral legislation. To allow the contrary would be tantamount to rendering the right to vote, the election and ultimately the democratic system itself meaningless.[70]

Given this principle, it meant that the Constitutional Court had directly impacted the voting rights of 101 applicants by invalidating their votes. They also observed that this had an impact on the 'passive' democratic rights of Mr Riza since, by invalidating votes for the DPS, they had forced him out of his position as a legislative representative. This invalidated his right to stand for elected office.[71]

After observing that the democratic rights of the 101 applicants and Mr Riza had been violated, the ECtHR then went on to analyse whether these violations so struck at the heart of these rights that it could justify overturning the claims of the Bulgarian Government and the judgment of the Constitutional Court. It also analysed whether the latter judgment had been sufficiently rigorous to dismiss Mr Riza's and the 101 applicants' claims that they had been denied sufficient access to justice in Bulgaria. It observed that invalidating the votes of the 101 applicants and denying Mr Riza his position clearly had an impact on the election, and were therefore of substantial concern. It also observed that the Constitutional Court had not been especially rigorous in trying to ameliorate the problem. While it had done a reasonable job in analysing the irregularities that had taken place, it had made some mistakes and generalizations in establishing their scope and nature. Moreover, the Constitutional Court's decision simply to invalidate the votes of the 101 applicants was not consonant with ensuring that their voting rights were given robust protection. For instance, it did not decide to simply hold new elections in the electoral areas impacted. This was a serious mistake. As the ECtHR observed in paragraph 178:

> The Court bears in mind that organising fresh elections in the territory of another sovereign country, even in a small number of polling stations, is always liable to come up against major diplomatic and operational obstacles and occasion additional cost. However, it considers that the holding of new elections in the last polling station, where there was cogent circumstantial evidence that the electoral commission was responsible for irregularities in the voting procedure on election day (see paragraph 170 above) would have reconciled the legitimate aim of annulling the election results, that is to say protecting the lawfulness of the electoral procedure, with the subjective rights of the voters and candidates in the general elections. The Court observes that the judgment of the Bulgarian Constitutional Court also failed to take that factor into account.[72]

This is where the Court's judgment became especially interesting, and highly consonant with the approach that I am developing. The ECtHR ruled that the purely formal approach to democratic rights taken by the Constitutional Court was highly inadequate. It highlighted that both the active and passive democratic rights of Mr Riza and the 101 applicants had been violated by this formalistic approach, leaving them little capacity for resolving their problems in a domestic context. As it stated in paragraph 179:

> Having regard to the lacunae noted in domestic law and the lack of any possibility of organising fresh elections, the impugned

> judgment, which was based on purely formal arguments, occasioned an unjustified infringement of the 101 applicants' and Mr Riza's and the DPS' rights to take part in the general elections as voters and candidates respectively. There were therefore two separate violations of Article 3 of Protocol No. 1.[73]

Given this, the ECtHR ruled in favour of Mr Riza and the 101 applicants and ordered the Bulgarian Government financially to compensate Mr Riza and the 101 applicants for the pecuniary and non-pecuniary damage that they had suffered.

Riza v Bulgaria is an important recent case that demonstrates how international courts can play an important role in framing democratic rights in a broad manner consonant with what is required to amplify human dignity. The applicants in the *Riza* case came from a minority group that was vulnerable along several axes. First, they were not residents in Bulgaria at the time of the election, which already posed substantial difficulties for their democratic participation. This is especially true in an era in which governments are increasingly interested in cracking down on the democratic participation of individuals who do not reside within the state, and even flirting with more draconian measures such as withdrawing citizenship from certain groups who do not demonstrate sufficient loyalty.[74] Secondly, as Muslims, the applicants faced further barriers to their full participation in a largely Christian society. Not coincidentally, the Order, Law, and Justice Party, which took issue with Mr Riza's electoral victory, had demonstrated hostility towards Muslims in the past.[75] These intersectional axes make it especially important to take a non-formalistic approach to protecting the rights of such potentially vulnerable individuals. The Constitutional Court of Bulgaria was obviously unwilling to do this, preferring to toe the relatively conservative line of simply dismissing the votes of the applicants due to violations of electoral guidelines. This was a deeply flawed decision, and one that was entirely unnecessary.

Electoral guidelines are crucial for the functioning of democratic procedures, and are therefore integral to the realization of the principled right to democratic self-authorship. They guarantee the procedural fairness of elections, ensuring that each individual's vote is accorded equal political value – if not, as the ECtHR noted, equal potential to influence an electoral outcome. One can therefore sympathize with the Constitutional Court's concern to maintain the purity of these electoral procedures. But the decision simply to dismiss these votes was entirely misguided. Indeed, on the model that I am developing, it seriously impacted the dignity of the applicants and Mr Riza. The Constitutional Court essentially forgot that the point of ensuring procedural fairness is a deeply moral one: to protect the equal value of each individual's vote. This obviously cannot be achieved by simply discounting the votes of those who, through no fault of their own, were tarred by association with electoral violations. This is formalism at its worst: choosing simply to discount the individuals who are to benefit from electoral rules in order to safeguard the purity of those same rules.

Taking a dignity-oriented approach to realizing the first of the twinned rights would mean adopting a more individualistic and broad approach to the application of laws concerning democratic rights. It should certainly ensure that procedural fairness is respected, but primarily by making sure that each individual's vote is given equal value, in a manner that is consonant with their basic human dignity. The ECtHR therefore made the right decision in overturning the ruling of the Constitutional Court and shifting blame away from the individuals harmed by electoral violations. This is an especially important step to take when those individuals are members of a potentially vulnerable or minority group. In such cases these individuals might rely heavily on their right to democratic participation to help protect other rights on which majorities might wish to clamp down.

Conclusion: the Potential of International Human Rights Law to Establish the Rightful Condition Through Respecting the Right to Democratic Self-Authorship

In this chapter I have discussed how international human rights law can be conducive to the realization of the right to democratic self-authorship. I then grounded my analysis in several prominent cases pertaining to democratic rights at the European level. My point throughout has not been that one should emulate the ECtHR in all respects. Many of its decisions have been only vaguely supportive of, and at times even antithetical to, the full realization of democratic rights in countries that are signatory to the ECHR. But such situations should not lead us to outright reject international courts as a medium for significant social change, as some critical legal scholars have argued. It should not even incline us towards a quietist scepticism or strategic instrumentalism that sees using courts as a Faustian bargain, enabling us occasionally to deconstruct the master's house using the master's tools. Instead, it should awaken us to the potential of courts if they are normatively and jurisprudentially oriented in the direction of respecting and amplifying a robust conception of human dignity such as the one that I have attempted to sketch here.

However, as many will highlight, access to courts and legal justice remains a weighty problem for many marginalized individuals.[76] They face significant barriers to full or even significant access to domestic legal systems, let alone courts at the international level. Acknowledging this objection provides me with a worthwhile opportunity to discuss the 'twinned' nature of my model of rights. The first right (to democratic self-authorship) takes lexical priority over the second right (to equality of expressive capabilities), since I believe that individuals must be responsible for accepting and realizing so robust an egalitarian scheme. Saying that, by realizing the twinned rights in tandem and consecutively, one moves considerably closer to the 'rightful condition'. This is in no small part because respecting the right to an equality of expressive capabilities is fundamentally related to respecting that to democratic self-authorship. An equality of expressive capabilities would first make it far easier for individuals from all backgrounds to access courts at all levels, which, among other things, would give them a more consistent and powerful opportunity to amplify their democratic rights. But, more importantly, it would enable them to participate more robustly in a truly democratic polity as measured along a number of different metrics.

The most obvious of these would be ensuring that individuals from marginalized backgrounds have a greater capacity to participate in politics. As it stands now, we increasingly live within a society in which great expressive weight to political participation is granted to abstract actors such as corporations. Some more conservative courts, such as the Supreme Court of the United States, have done a great deal to amplify this power, such as through the infamous *Citizens United Case*. This is a terrible error. A corporation is not a person with agency, in the sense that it can deploy a set of expressive capabilities to redefine the socio-historical contexts within which it exists. It is a legal abstraction, constituted by language, and possesses agency only to the extent that the individuals who make it up are enabled, through law, to act on behalf of the legal abstraction to pursue certain interests. Because it lacks any immediate agency, any rights that a corporation possesses flow secondarily from those possessed by the dignified individuals who act on its behalf. These rights exist to amplify their dignity by enabling them to employ their expressive capabilities effectively. They do not exist to grant abstract legal entities greater capacity for political participation.

Anti-democratic decisions in domestic courts, most notably America's *Citizens United*, highlight the need to orient courts, where possible, in the right normative direction.[77] They also indicate the pressing need to amplify the expressive capabilities of individuals to serve as a countermeasure to the growing and insidious power of corporations, which exist primarily to benefit their wealthy shareholders and entrench their social power. Doing so is integral to ensuring the robust functioning of a democracy. In the next chapter, I will discuss how we can take legal steps towards the realization of a right to quality of expressive capabilities.

6

Realizing Human Dignity Through Establishing Rights to an Equality of Expressive Capabilities

Introduction: What Does a Right to an Equality of Expressive Capabilities Mean in Practice?

> How should the progress of countries and peoples be judged? What if, instead of judging countries by per capita income and its growth, we turn the question around and judge the success of nations according to how well they translate their resources into expanded freedoms: the freedom of people to be and do the things they value and to pursue meaningful lives with dignity? And if we use international human rights as the standards that define these freedoms, surely we can evaluate the success and failings of states and the progress of humanity.[1]

Realizing the second of the twinned rights, to an equality of expressive capabilities, is likely to be a far more controversial and complex problem than ensuring a right to democratic self-authorship. There are myriad reasons for this. The most obvious is that the first right is directly associated with democracy. Democratic principles may well be imperfectly realized and often a front for more insidious forms of political oppression. Indeed, with the rise of what I have elsewhere called postmodern conservatism, many of us should be deeply concerned about the stability of democratic principles.[2] Donald Trump, Viktor Orbán and other postmodern conservatives pose a substantial challenge for those of us who are committed to democracy. In many ways this demonstrates why it remains crucial to amplify and secure each individual's democratic rights against the postmodern right-wing pushback.

However, despite this very pressing challenge, the normative ideal of democracy remains widely popular across the globe. Very few political regimes are content to be open autocracies or dictatorships. Most of the ones that will admit to that are bordering on being pariah states. Even autocrats such as Russia's Vladimir Putin or Iran's Ayatollah Khamenei try to at least mask their authoritarian tendencies beneath the veneer of democratic legitimacy through holding highly rigged elections against disposable political opponents. So, the right to democratic self-authorship enjoys a great deal of uncontroversial normative currency, since only a few states such as Saudi Arabia and North Korea, would even admit that they do not make any substantial efforts to realize it.

This is not the case for the right to an equality of expressive capabilities. Tragically, the only substantial economic and social rights that are given significant care remain property rights. These remain well protected despite the fact that many individuals would receive far more benefit from the realization of different social and economic rights that would greatly amplify their total set of expressive capabilities. As Donnelly, who directly links the expansion of our conception of economic and social rights to an increase in the dignity of all, puts it:

> Finally, we can note that most critics of economic and social rights do not in fact reject all such rights. Quite the contrary, almost all accept a right to private property...Furthermore, there is no plausible theoretical ground that yields precisely this one economic right. For example, property is often defended because it provides needed resources and space for the effective exercise of liberty. A right to work, however, would seem at least as plausible a way to assure resources for every person, given what we know about the tendency of private property to be very unevenly distributed and readily alienated in most legal systems. A limited right to property can make an important contribution to a life of dignity. This single

> economic right alone, however, simply cannot provide economic security and autonomy for all. In fact, for many people-in the Western world, most people, whose principal 'property' is their labour power or skills-other economic and social rights would seem to be a better mechanism to realize economic security and autonomy. [3]

Fortunately, there seem to be some shifts in the direction of tackling these major issues. Inequality has become a major talking point worldwide, as is evidenced by the blockbuster success of Thomas Piketty's seminal text *Capital in the Twenty-First Century*.[4] Curiously, inequality appears to have grown so stark that even otherwise right-wing commentators and politicians have remarked that it is a problem (though sometimes with little sincerity). Canada's own world-famous public intellectual Jordan Peterson, famous for his criticisms of left-wing extremism and identity politics, has remarked that income inequality needs to be dealt with.[5] The University of Notre-Dame's Patrick Deneen has been sharply critical of liberalism for leading to ever-greater social and economic inequality.[6] And even Donald Trump, in a political ploy of massive dishonesty (even for him), tried to argue that the Republican 2017 tax cuts would take wealth away from the rich and benefit the poor and the middle class.[7]

Despite all this occasionally well-meaning rhetoric, very few substantive efforts have actually been undertaken to reduce inequality by any substantial margin. Political efforts have stalled or, as is the case with the Trump and Macron tax reforms,[8] actually made matters worse. These inequality-friendly reforms take place against a backdrop where low income taxes, high rates of return on income-capital, the ready availability of overseas tax shelters to shield wealth from even modest taxation, and so on ensure that inequality continues to rise, creating states in which a handful of individuals own as much as the entire bottom half of the population.[9] This has coincided with declining opportunities for wide swathes of the population, many of whom fear that they will have the honour of being the first generation in centuries to enjoy a lower standard of living than the preceding one.[10]

Given such drastic circumstances, it is no surprise – if somewhat disappointing – that many are turning to postmodern conservative autocrats who promise to alleviate the problem through implementing policies to reduce immigration and punish those undesirable ethnic groups who had the audacity already to be citizens when they came to power.

Moreover, these inequities only describe the unfair situation that exists between individuals living within a single state and other individuals across the globe. While there has been an admirable and fortunate trend towards decreasing numbers of people living in absolute poverty, there are still over 767 million individuals who live on less than $1.25 each day, constituting 10.7 per cent of the world's total population.[11] The overwhelming majority of these individuals hail from developing countries that lack the resources and capacity to rectify the situation as rapidly and expediently as is required to respect the human dignity of all. This makes it very important to look at the substantial differences that exist between different countries around the globe. These drastically vary their capacity to amplify the dignity of their citizens. Many of the existent are predicated on colonial and postcolonial histories, which, as indicated in Chapter 4, provide further reasons to try to rectify these inequalities.

As the global gap between the wealthiest individuals and the poorest has grown, so too has the gap between the wealthiest and the poorest countries. In 2016, the gross domestic product (GDP) per capita, adjusted for purchasing power parity, was strikingly divergent. The average American enjoys a GDP per capita of $57,293, placing them thirteenth in the world. The GDP per capita of the average German is $48,189, placing them nineteenth in the world. Compare that with the Democratic Republic of the Congo, in which the GDP per capita is $784. This makes Congo the second-poorest country in the world, as determined by measuring GDP per capita, behind only the Central African Republic. In war-wracked Afghanistan, which places at number 167 on the list of states, an individual can expect to enjoy a GDP per capita of $1,957. These figures are shockingly divergent along several different metrics. Most notably, all ten of the world's poorest countries are in Africa, while almost all its wealthiest states are Western or one of the petrol-rich Gulf States (the only notable exception is the city state of Singapore).[12] This has a major impact on the individuals who live in some of the world's poorest countries. In the Democratic Republic of the Congo, which has been wracked by war as well as extreme poverty, over 4.4 million children do not get to attend primary school. In Malawi, schools are so overcrowded that each primary school teacher is responsible for around sixty-seven students.[13] Almost 3 million children a year die from hunger-related factors.[14] An estimated 300–600 million people a year suffer from malaria, largely in developing countries.[15] This is despite one of the most effective preventative measures against malaria being the provision of a $10 bed net that prevents contact with mosquitos while the user sleeps. Finally, the gap between rich and poor countries is perhaps most striking when one compares life expectancy rates. In Japan, one of the world's wealthiest and most developed societies, individuals live an average of 83.7 years. In my home country of Canada, the average is about 82.2 years. Contrast that with the Central African Republic, again the world's poorest country as determined by looking at GDP per capita, in which individuals live an average of 52.5 years, or more than 30 years less than individuals living in Japan. Individuals in Sierra Leone bottom out the list as inhabitants of the country with the lowest life expectancy in the world. An individual in Sierra Leone is expected to live approximately 50.1 years, or almost 34 years less than a citizen of Japan and 32 years less than a Canadian.[16] Put starkly, this means that individuals in the world's wealthiest countries get to enjoy a lifespan that is roughly two-fifths longer than that enjoyed by individuals in the world's poorest countries. Given the extraordinary arbitrariness in the distribution of wealth and resources, and the aforementioned history of colonialism and oppression that is in part to blame for many of these countries' current levels of poverty and civil strife, this seems absolutely unjustifiable. Moreover, it seems especially egregious given that many of the social and economic rights of individuals can be successfully realized at relatively minimal cost to states and without necessarily sacrificing economic growth overall. Recent empirical research on the steps taken by states to fulfil their obligations under the ICESCR by Fukuda-Parr, Lawson-Remer and Randolph seems to bear this out. This is strikingly good news for all proponents of human rights.

> Do countries face a trade-off between fulfilling social and economic rights today and promoting per capita income growth to enable higher social and economic rights attainment tomorrow? Our analysis reveals that there is no necessary trade-off. Quite the contrary, fulfilling social and economic rights and economic growth can be synergistic; countries with policies and institutions promoting social and economic rights tend to enjoy a virtuous cycle in which social and economic rights promote growth and growth promotes the further extension of social and economic rights.[17]

All these tendencies demonstrate the tremendous need to treat inequality more seriously, both in itself and due to its considerable material consequences on those who are negatively impacted by policies that favour the wealthy and hurt the poor or insecure. But how to go about rectifying these inequities is a complex question without readily available answers. This is true even among progressives. For most left liberals since Rawls,[18] the proper response to inequality is to provide a robust welfare state that will enable individuals to enjoy true equality of opportunity by ensuring relatively equal starting points for all participants in the global economy. Often, the Nordic models of Sweden, Denmark and Norway are held up as exemplars of such a welfarist model.[19] For more radical egalitarians, even these proposals do not go far enough. Though they are preferable to more 'meritocratic' societies in which those with morally arbitrary advantages are able to get ahead, they fall short of the ideal of true equality of outcome for all, which is the only justifiable distribution of resources and capabilities.[20] My own argument for an equality of capabilities except where inequities are justified by morally significant choices straddles the middle ground between these two positions. It draws on the liberal tradition, with its appreciation for moral arbitrariness, while retaining concern for the significance of individual life choices. But it also regards equality as the default moral position for we should be arguing if we are to take dignity seriously. Equality may not be the natural condition of any living species, as some have pointed out.[21] But our status as natural beings is related in complex ways to our status as moral beings who have obligations to bring about a just state of affairs. Given that, taking the dignity of each individual seriously means ascribing them equal worth and a consonant set of capabilities in life to make something of themselves. The only reason that this should be qualified is the choices that individuals themselves make, ideally under conditions of sufficient knowledge to recognize the potential capability-inhibiting consequences that might ensue. In ideal conditions, this is the model of distributive justice that I feel states would adopt in order adequately to amplify human dignity.

This brings us to the heart of the matter: how international human rights law might play an important role in ensuring such an equality of human capabilities. Discussing how international law can amplify dignity through realizing the economic and social rights of citizens is challenging, since little jurisprudence on the issue has stuck. Much of international human rights law that relates to economic and social rights is aspirational and is not enforced even to the minimal degree that human rights law that relates to civil and political rights is. Therefore, I will be relying more on treaty law and principled argument to develop a normative case on why we *should* take these rights far more seriously, including making them enforceable against states. However, I will invoke the reasoning of the Committee on Economic, Social and Cultural Rights to argue that some major legal decisions suggest how and why courts should take a more active approach to economic, social and cultural rights. Again, many of these cases take place within the Eurozone. Major cases involving economic, social and cultural rights include *Moldovan II*, which concerned living conditions, and *DH v Czech Republic*, which concerned the right to an education. I will discuss the latter in order to formulate how the right to an education can be more concretely realized.

Some domestic decisions also provide useful guidance. South African jurisprudence is a good example. In *Government of South Africa and Others v Grootboom*, the Constitutional Court ruled that the state is obliged to look after the well-being of its citizens. While the earlier *Soobramoney* decision revealed some of the limitations of this approach, I still think that it is a salient example.[22] It shows law being used to push the state more actively to establish the rightful condition for the amplification of human dignity. My argument will be that international human rights law can play a more active role in framing contemporary liberal constitutions in a more egalitarian way, both by emphasizing this robust account of dignity and by penalizing those who do not work to realize it. These cases provide valuable precedents that should be adhered to, and their underpinning principles should be deepened.

DH v Czech Republic and Securing the Right to an Education

The right to a good education is integral to the amplification of an individual's entire set of expressive capabilities. This is because education is fundamentally linked to the amplification of many capabilities within an individual's total set. Here I will invoke Nussbaum's pioneering list of the central capabilities. A good education is integrally linked to a capability to deploy 'senses, imagination, (and) thought' and to have these 'cultivated by education and a participatory culture'. It is linked to being capable of 'exercising practical reason' by forming a conception of the good life and reflecting on it. And, of course, an education is also essential for an individual capably to participate in democratic politics and, in many situations, materially advance through life. Indeed, in many countries across the globe, a good education is almost a prerequisite for the attainment of economic success.[23] Moreover, education is essential as a prerequisite to the establishment of a well-functioning democratic polity, since (ideally) it enables individuals better to evaluate the substantive issues at play in political debates and to make less partial assessments. Indeed, as Nussbaum has indicated, one of the great worries facing liberal democratic polities today is the declining importance that is ascribed to a liberal education and the development of critical thinking abilities.[24] Instead, a growing number of individuals are being pushed into neo-liberal education systems that encourage them exclusively to foster economically marketable skill sets without asking more fundamental questions about the justice of the contemporary order. This limits their capacity critically to evaluate politics and to attempt to reconstruct their political practices and institutions in line with their interests. This is a serious problem that demonstrates the need to foster rights to a robust education, in no small part because of its integral connection to amplifying the consonant rights of individuals to become democratic authors of their communities.

This highlights the issues at play in the case of *DH and Others v Czech Republic*. Between 1996 and 1999, the applicants, who were members of the Roma community from the Ostrava region in the Czech Republic, were assigned to special schools for children with learning difficulties. They formed the majority of the students in these schools, in which the children received an inferior education based on a diluted curriculum allegedly designed to compensate for their intellectual disabilities. In 2000, eighteen former Romani students, represented by the European Roma Rights Centre, submitted an application to the ECtHR, seeking compensation for their discriminatory treatment at the hands of the Czech education system.[25] At the time when the case was brought forward, Roma children were twenty-seven times more likely than non-Roma children to be placed in schools for children with learning difficulties. Moreover, even when Roma students were not placed into schools for children with learning disabilities, many of them were placed in schools that were substandard compared with those who went to schools in predominantly non-Roma regions of the country. The applicants were between the ages of nine and fifteen years old at the time they submitted their application to the ECtHR.[26]

On 15 June 1999 the applicants launched an appeal to the Czech Constitutional Court. They argued that the 'special' treatment that they had received was not based on any 'objective and reasonable' justification and amounted to degrading treatment that had resulted in their being denied their rights to education. They also argued that nothing in their individual files indicated that oversight was being maintained with an orientation towards determining whether the children should be transferred to a regular primary school. The conclusion was that the decision to keep the children in 'special schools' had been based not on their intellectual ability but on judgements that the children showed 'insufficient' command of the Czech language, that their parents were not sufficiently concerned about their education, and that social and cultural differences would make them ill adapted to education in one of the better primary schools.[27]

Both the special schools and the Czech Ministry of Education denied that any discrimination had taken place. They argued that the placement of Roma children in the inferior special schools was predicated on the recommendation of a psychological centre that had assessed each child's intellectual capacity. They also noted that the transfer of the children had initially been consented to by representatives and parents. Finally, the Ministry of Education also defended the placement of the children by arguing that Roma parents tended to take a 'negative attitude' towards the school work of their children.[28]

The Czech Constitutional Court found that it had no grounds to hear the complaint, because many of the individual applicants had not filed complaints against the decisions concerned. However, it did decide to assess the merits of the claim. In making its assessment, the court noted that it had no reason to believe that any unconstitutional measures had been taken. All the teachers and educational administrators were vested with the authority to make decisions about the capacity of the children, and had done so in this case with the consent of the relevant representatives and the parents of the children. More disconcertingly, the court also determined that it was not in its purview to assess whether insufficient monitoring and racial discrimination had taken place, when deciding either whether the Roma children should go to the special school or whether they should remain there rather than being transferred to an ordinary primary school. It also concluded that the applicants had submitted insufficient concrete evidence to support their claims of insufficient monitoring and racial discrimination. The court also determined that the applicants and their representatives had not been sufficiently active in acquiring information about the potential consequences of being placed in a special school, nor had they had shown any particular interest in being transferred to an ordinary private school. The Constitutional Court therefore rejected the applicants' appeal.[29]

The applicants appealed the Constitutional Court's decision to the ECtHR, where their claim was initially rejected by the First Chamber. The First Chamber accepted the Government's claims that the special schools had not been established exclusively to cater to Roma children, and that such schools were designed to assist those who required additional help in obtaining a decent primary education. Moreover, they found that the applicants had not sufficiently refuted the expert's claims that their learning difficulties would prevent them from succeeding in an ordinary primary school setting. Finally, the First Chamber accepted the Czech Government's claim that it was not easy to develop an educational system that 'reconciled' a considerable number of different and competing interests, and that it was impossible to reach an 'ideal' solution. It accepted that the Roma applicants had presented 'worrying figures' about the quality of education provided in the special schools. However, it did not believe that this statistical evidence warranted finding that the placement of the Roma children in special schools was the result of racial prejudice. The applicants appealed to have their complaint heard by the Grand Chamber of the ECtHR.[30]

The Grand Chamber delivered its ruling in November 2007. It extensively reviewed a broad array of international legal sources and jurisprudence on the right to an education and the nature of racial discrimination generally. It also reviewed whether the applicants had any further domestic remedies available to them. The Czech Government reiterated its claim that none of the applicants had initially complained or appealed the decision to be placed in a special school. Moreover, it echoed the Constitutional Court's finding that only five of the twelve applicants who lodged the constitutional appeal had initially contested the decision to place them in special schools. It also presented highly personalized information about the history of the individual applicants,[31] noting the following:

> Two applicants were currently in their final year at primary school. Seven had begun vocational training in a secondary school in September 2006. Four had started but later abandoned their secondary school studies, the majority through a lack of interest, and

> had instead signed on at the job centre. Lastly, five of the applicants had not sought to pursue their studies at secondary-school level but had registered at the job centre. Those applicants who had registered at a job centre had not cooperated with it or shown any interest in the offers of training or employment that had been made, with the result that some of them had already been struck off the job-applicants register (in some instances repeatedly).[32]

This information was presented to demonstrate that the psychological experts who had made the initial assessments as to the applicants' educational and intellectual capacities had made the correct judgements. The applicants disputed these claims and reiterated their arguments that the Czech Government's policy had been predicated on racial discrimination that had negatively impacted them as Roma people and children in a vulnerable situation.

In making its judgment, the Grand Chamber reiterated the importance of eliminating discrimination on the basis of ethnic origin, stating that this constituted a form of racial discrimination that could not be tolerated in modern European societies. Indeed, it went so far as to stress that the elimination of racial discrimination in education must be so prioritized by member states that 'all available means' needed to be committed to combat it.

> Discrimination on account of, inter alia, a person's ethnic origin is a form of racial discrimination. Racial discrimination is a particularly invidious kind of discrimination and, in view of its perilous consequences, requires from the authorities special vigilance and a vigorous reaction. It is for this reason that the authorities must use all available means to combat racism, thereby reinforcing democracy's vision of a society in which diversity is not perceived as a threat but as a source of enrichment.[33]

However, it also reiterated that this position did not indicate that governments were not permitted to treat groups differently as a means to combat inequality between them. Indeed, it noted that in some circumstances a failure to do so would constitute a breach of a state's human rights obligations towards minorities:

> The Court has established in its case-law that discrimination means treating differently, without an objective and reasonable justification, persons in relevantly similar situations (see Willis v. the United Kingdom, no. 36042/97, § 48, ECHR 2002-IV, and Okpisz v. Germany, no. 59140/00, § 33, 25 October 2005). However, Article 14 does not prohibit a member State from treating groups differently in order to correct "factual inequalities" between them; indeed in certain circumstances a failure to attempt to correct inequality through different treatment may in itself give rise to a breach of the Article.[34]

The Grand Chamber then went on to observe that statistical evidence was increasingly accepted as a way of determining whether a given practice was discriminatory. Discrimination could be established empirically, whether or not the stated intent of a given policy was to engage in discriminatory practices if the effect of a policy was to do so. It also observed that there was an emerging consensus among EU member states that they had obligations to take steps to protect minority populations. Interestingly, it observed that this was not just beneficial to the minority populations. The cultural diversity that they contributed was beneficial to the entire community.

> In Chapman (cited above, §§ 93–94), the Court also observed that there could be said to be an emerging international consensus among the Contracting States of the Council of Europe recognizing the special needs of minorities and an obligation to protect their security, identity and lifestyle, not only for the purpose of safeguarding the interests of the minorities themselves but to preserve a cultural diversity of value to the whole community.[35]

After analysing the statistical evidence in this case, the Court determined that discrimination had indeed taken place. While, on the face of it, the policy of sending intellectually needy children to special schools did not seem discriminatory, the number of such students who were Roma was 'disproportionately high'. The Court also found that the Czech Government had not sufficiently established that the measure was reasonably justifiable or proportionate. It also noted that the Government had not taken reasonable measures to ensure that the parents of the Roma children received information about the potential consequences of attending the special school, which might have helped them to make a more informed decision. This was especially important given the established link between attending such a school and subsequently losing job opportunities.

> The facts of the instant case indicate that the schooling arrangements for Roma children were not attended by safeguards (see paragraph 28 above) that would ensure that, in the exercise of its margin of appreciation in the education sphere, the State took into account their special needs as members of a disadvantaged class (see, mutatis mutandis, Buckley, cited above, § 76, and Connors, cited above, § 84). Furthermore, as a result of the arrangements the applicants were placed in schools for children with mental disabilities where a more basic curriculum was followed than in ordinary schools and where they were isolated from pupils from the wider population. As a result, they received an education which compounded their difficulties and compromised their subsequent personal development instead of tackling their real problems or helping them to integrate into the ordinary schools and develop the skills that would facilitate life among the majority population. Indeed, the Government has implicitly admitted that job opportunities are more limited for pupils from special schools.[36]

As a result of these various discriminatory consequences, the Grand Chamber ruled that the distinction in treatment between Roma and non-Roma children was sufficiently justified and proportionate to the issues at hand. It therefore ruled in favour of the children and ordered the Czech Government to pay damages to them.

Unfortunately, the ruling was not unanimous. Judge Jungwiert offered a stinging dissent to the majority in this case. He began by observing that the Czech Republic had accepted tens of thousands of Roma immigrants in recent years. Many of them were 'illiterate and completely uprooted, they did not speak the Czech language'. To Judge Jungwiert, this presented a problem for the Czech Government in the education field. This was compounded by the fact that absenteeism and truancy were significantly higher among Roma children generally, in contrast to the general Czech population, in which almost 100 per cent of students attend school. Judge Jungwiert stated:

> The population of the Roma community is estimated (by the same source) at 400,000 in Slovakia, 600,000 in Hungary, 750,000 in Bulgaria and 2,100,000 in Romania. In total, there are more than 4,000,000 Roma children in Europe, approximately 2,000,000 of whom will, in all probability, never attend school in their lifetimes.[37]

He then asked what standards and minimum requirements needed to be met in order to respect the right of the Roma children to an education, especially given these cultural and demographic difficulties. To Judge Jungwiert, it was clear that the Government had done all that could be expected in these circumstances. Indeed, he observed that the policies that had the effect of discriminating were in fact established with an emancipatory intention. The Czech Government wanted to ensure that more Roma and intellectually needy children were able to attend school and succeed there. Invoking Schopenhauer, Judge Jungwiert criticized the majority for being excessively demanding:

> In a way, the Czech Republic has thereby established an education system that is inegalitarian. However, this inegalitarianism has a positive aim: to get children to attend school in order to have a chance to succeed through positive discrimination in favour of a disadvantaged population. Despite this, the majority feel compelled to say that it is not satisfied that the difference

> in treatment between Roma children and non-Roma children pursued the legitimate aim of adapting the education system to the needs of the former and that there existed a reasonable relationship of proportionality between the means used and the aim pursued (see paragraph 208 of the judgment). No one has conveyed the following opinion better than Arthur Schopenhauer, who was the first to express it: 'This peculiar satisfaction in words contributes more than anything else to the perpetuation of errors. For, relying on the words and phrases received from his predecessors, each one confidently passes over obscurities and problems.'[38]

Judge Jungwiert then observed that, while it was possible that more could have been done to help the Roma children, this was expecting too much. He observed that few countries in Europe had done more to assist the Roma. He therefore found that the majority was 'wholly' unreasonable in its expectation that more could have been done. The policy adopted by the Czech Government was reasonable and proportionate. Judge Jungwiert's argument was largely accepted by Judge Sikuta, who echoed this reasoning in his own dissenting judgment in this case.

A different form of dissenting argument was given by Judge Borrego. He felt that the Grand Chamber had overstepped its boundaries as a court of law, by making an assessment about the effectiveness of a given social policy. This usurped the state's control over the making of policy assessments and was therefore unjustifiable. This included making judgements on the disadvantaged status of various minority groups.

> In contradiction with the role which all judicial bodies assume, the entire judgment is devoted to assessing the overall social context – from the first page ('historical background') to the last paragraph, including a review of the 'Council of Europe sources' (fourteen pages), 'Community law and practice' (five pages), United Nations materials (seven pages) and 'other sources' (three

> pages, which, curiously, with the exception of the reference to the European Monitoring Centre, are taken exclusively from the Anglo-American system, that is, the House of Lords and the United States Supreme Court). Thus, to cite but one example, the Court states at the start of paragraph 182: 'The Court notes that as a result of their turbulent history and constant uprooting the Roma have become a specific type of disadvantaged and vulnerable minority.' Is it the Court's role to be doing this?[39]

Judge Borrego then went on to make a more interesting statement about the majority's patrimonial approach to the children's parents. It found that the parents lacked sufficient knowledge and 'capacity' to decide whether to place their children in special schools. Judge Borrego regarded this as very patronizing and reflective of the growing 'ivory tower' mentality characteristic of the Court. He noted the irony of fighting discriminatory policies by invoking such patronizing rhetoric.

> I find this particularly disquieting. The Grand Chamber asserts that all parents of Roma children, 'even assuming' them to be capable of giving informed consent, are unable to choose their children's school. Such a view can lead to the awful experiences with which we are only too familiar of children being 'abducted' from their parents when the latter belong to a particular social group because certain 'well intentioned' people feel constrained to impose their conception of life on all. An example of the sad human tradition of fighting racism through racism.[40]

I believe the majority made the right decision in this case, and that, for a variety of reasons, the rationale of Judges Jungwiert and Sikuta is flawed. However, I do believe that there is a valid point to the reasoning of Judge Borrego, which is whether that state can justifiably appropriate the decision-making responsibility of individuals in order to optimize the realization of their social and economic rights or, in this case, the rights of a parent's children. I do not find it justifiable, and will explain why in some detail. This will help us to understand the relationship between the twinned rights and why the first right must take priority over the second.

Judges Jungwiert and Sikuta effectively made two interrelated decisions as to why we should reject the claims of the students. The first operates at the level of principle and the second is an empirical claim. The principled first argument is that the sovereign right of states to decide how they will resolve social issues, and the resources that they will devote to them, should be respected. They see the majority as essentially usurping this sovereign right in this case. The second empirical claim is that the Czech Government had devoted adequate resources and care to resolving a pressing social problem – the lower educational status of many Roma children and families. Given this, the Government could be said to have met its obligations to respect their right to an education by providing resources in a manner that balanced this obligation with the need to address other social problems.

I do not believe that this argument is adequate. This is because the dissenting judges focus too much on the quantitative dimensions of the social problem, and not enough on its qualitative dimensions. All the judges in this case accept that there are substantial economic, social and cultural barriers to ensuring that Roma children will receive an adequate education that meets the threshold required by the ECHR. The need to ensure that this right is realized must be balanced against other, competing claims on resources. But Judges Jungwiert and Sikuta approach this issue only from the standpoint of material resources without ever addressing the root of the case: did the Czech Government seek to realize the right of Roma children to an education in a manner that was sufficiently sensitive to their specific cultural needs? Whatever the expense and resources devoted to them, the special schools that were assembled were inadequately designed to ensure that children from this background would receive an adequate education that took their unique background and its challenges into account. This is integral to the realization of the economic, social, and cultural rights of individuals; especially those belonging to cultural minorities and marginalized groups. It is especially key when, as Judge Jungwiert and Borrego acknowledge, the people in question – the Roma – have long been the victims of marginalization, and even genocide, and have a very distinct set of cultural practices. Policies to realize a right to an education must be very finely tailored in such instances to ensure a high success rate.[41] This is not just a quantitative and formal matter of providing a solution, but a complex qualitative issue of determining, through genuine dialogue, how best to suit the needs of the children. The fact that the parents appear to have been largely misinformed – or at least not given a comprehensive overview of what would happen to their children – heavily suggests that this qualitatively oriented dialogue did not take place in any sufficient manner.

This brings me to the more powerful objections of Judge Borrego. He makes the plausible claim that the majority patronizes the Roma parents by assuming that they simply lacked the capacity to understand what was going on, and that the Court therefore had an obligation to rectify their mistaken assessment. It does so without providing a robust account of what such a capacity would be, opening the door to setting a highly paternalistic precedent wherein the Roma parents would be regarded as unable to make their own legitimate decisions about what to do with their children.

In my model, this would deeply infringe the dignity of both the individuals and the children, by inhibiting their capacity to be authors of their own lives and the political contexts that govern them. This demonstrates why it is key for the first right – to democratic self-authorship – to trump the second right to an equality of expressive capabilities. Where Roma parents make a decision concerning how their children will have the economic, social and cultural rights respected, that decision should be accepted by the state in all but extreme cases where doing so might potentially violate other rights enjoyed by the child. In this case the Czech Government erred by not adequately respecting these rights – indeed, the very compact made with the parents to ensure a proper education was provided to their children – by ensuring that it was realized in a culturally sensitive way. This could have been achieved through a more dialogical approach that would have brought out more explicitly what the needs of the Roma children were. In such a circumstance, dialogue on the nature of realizing the educational rights of children would have been a bridge to ensuring adequate respect of the democratic rights of the parents. Dialogue serves more deeply to link the twinned rights to democratic authorship and equality of capabilities without ever forcing them to collapse together in an unacceptable manner.

The case of *DH v Czech Republic* is highly instructive on the pitfalls and challenges of adequately realizing a right to an equality of expressive capabilities. Where individuals are members of a historically marginalized group, their positive economic, social and cultural rights must be respected in a manner consonant with their culture and expectations. Moreover, this must be achieved through continuous dialogue to ensure that the provision of opportunities is carried out in a non-patronizing manner, with the full participation of the individuals exercising their primary right to democratic self-authorship.

The Right to Housing: *Government of South Africa and Others v Grootboom*

The ECtHR has pioneered the justiciability of economic, social and cultural rights at the level of international law. This makes its jurisprudence ideal when examining how international legal institutions can serve as a steering mechanism for states guiding them to the realization of the rightful condition. But, needless to say, international jurisprudence does not operate in a vacuum, and cannot be influential unless states acquiesce to being guided by it. This is quite possible in highly developed countries that are members of a well-functioning and respected international organization such as the EU.[42] In such contexts, pressure to ensure the realization of economic, social and cultural rights can be formidable, since the resources are available and the expectations consequently high. It is quite another to ask that less-developed states fulfil their obligations to respect the economic, social and cultural rights of their citizens to even a minimal degree, let alone ask them to ensure that all enjoy an equality of expressive capabilities. In this section, I wish to demonstrate that it is still possible to make economic, social and cultural rights justiciable in a manner that would meet the international legal obligations of developing states. There is formidable jurisprudence in

South Africa that deals with these matters, some of which has gone a reasonably way towards respecting the rights of citizens to an equality of expressive capabilities. Perhaps the most noteworthy case in this respect is the *Grootboom* decision. It is a crucial case for being among the first instances in domestic jurisprudence in which a court determined that the state had not met its obligations to respect the economic, social and cultural rights of citizens and ordered them to change their policy. Unfortunately, it also demonstrates the limitations of courts, and how far we need to go in giving 'teeth' to the justiciability of economic, social and cultural rights.

Mrs Irene Grootboom and her fellow respondents had initially lived in a slum in Wallacedene while awaiting access to better low-income housing. The waiting list for such housing meant that individuals could wait as long as seven years. A quarter of the individuals in Wallacedene had no income whatsoever, and two-thirds made less than R500 a month. Roughly half the population were children, and all lived in shacks. There was no running water or sewage removal, and only 5 per cent of the houses had electricity.[43] In addition, the homes were dangerously close to the main thoroughfare of the town, and the streets were often waterlogged. Unwilling to tolerate such a situation for herself and her children, Mrs Grootboom and others uprooted and moved on to unused land that had been allocated for later building low-income housing. There, they built a very modest but still improved set of homes on the then unused land. Sadly, as the Constitutional Court itself highlighted at the opening of its judgment, Mrs Grootboom's situation was hardly exceptional in South Africa. It also noted, with bitter irony and surprising empathy, that the understandable actions of individual poor people to assist themselves and their children often had a negative impact on the capacity of the Government to ameliorate broader problems affecting marginalized groups in society as a whole.

> The people of South Africa are committed to the attainment of social justice and the improvement of the quality of life for everyone. The Preamble to our Constitution records this commitment. The Constitution declares the founding values of our society to be

> '[h]uman dignity, the achievement of equality and the advancement of human rights and freedoms'. [...] This case grapples with the realisation of these aspirations for it concerns the state's constitutional obligations in relation to housing: a constitutional issue of fundamental importance to the development of South Africa's new constitutional order. The issues here remind us of the intolerable conditions under which many of our people are still living. The respondents are but a fraction of them. It is also a reminder that unless the plight of these communities is alleviated, people may be tempted to take the law into their own hands in order to escape these conditions. The case brings home the harsh reality that the Constitution's promise of dignity and equality for all remains for many a distant dream. People should not be impelled by intolerable living conditions to resort to land invasions. Self-help of this kind cannot be tolerated, for the unavailability of land suitable for housing development is a key factor in the fight against the country's housing shortage.[44]

As a result of their eviction from the illegally seized land, Mrs Grootboom, her children and the other respondents were rendered homeless. They went and sheltered in the Wallacedene sports field, under temporary structures such as tents with plastic sheeting. Shortly afterwards, the winter rains began. Unwilling to accept this situation, they applied to the Cape of Good Hope High Court to provide them with shelter and subsistence while they waited for the Government to grant them a more permanent residence. The Court agreed, and ordered the Government to provide them with tents for shelter, as well as basic supplies such as water and portable latrines, as a bare minimum to enable them to get by. The Government challenged this ruling, but ultimately agreed to provide assistance. However, four months later, Mrs Grootboom and the other respondents made an urgent application to the Constitutional Court, alleging that the Government had not complied with its side of the bargain.

The Constitutional Court began its analysis by recognizing that the root cause of many of the housing problems in the country, like so much else, were the discriminatory policies aimed against black people by the previous apartheid regime. While, officially, apartheid had been ended, South Africa's long history of racial oppression very much continued.

> The cause of the acute housing shortage lies in apartheid. A central feature of that policy was a system of influx control that sought to limit African occupation of urban area. Influx control was rigorously enforced in the Western Cape, where government policy favoured the exclusion of African people in order to accord preference to the coloured community: a policy adopted in 1954 and referred to as the 'coloured labour preference policy.' In consequence, the provision of family housing for African people in the Cape Peninsula was frozen in 1962. This freeze was extended to other urban areas in the Western Cape in 1968. Despite the harsh application of influx control in the Western Cape, African people continued to move to the area in search of jobs. Colonial dispossession and a rigidly enforced racial distribution of land in the rural areas had dislocated the rural economy and rendered sustainable and independent African farming increasingly precarious. Given the absence of formal housing, large numbers of people moved into informal settlements throughout the Cape peninsula. The cycle of the apartheid era, therefore, was one of untenable restrictions on the movement of African people into urban areas, the inexorable tide of the rural poor to the cities, inadequate housing, resultant overcrowding, mushrooming squatter settlements, constant harassment by officials and intermittent forced removals.[45]

The Court also recognized that, according to section 26 of the South African Constitution, the Government had an obligation 'progressively' to realize the rights of its citizens to adequate housing. It also noted that, according to section 28(1)(c), the Government had an obligation to provide all children with 'shelter', among other basic goods. Given this, the Court maintained that the question was not whether these rights existed, since they clearly did, according to the language of the Constitution. The question was how to enforce these rights in any given context, especially given the limited resources available to the Government.[46]

The Court began by expressly linking the realization of these socio-economic rights to respect for human dignity. Interestingly, it was well ahead of its time in noting that social and economic rights and civil and political rights should not be regarded in isolation from each other. Instead, they must be understood as 'mutually supporting'.

> Our Constitution entrenches both civil and political rights and social and economic rights. All the rights in our Bill of Rights are inter-related and mutually supporting. There can be no doubt that human dignity, freedom and equality, the foundational values of our society, are denied those who have no food, clothing or shelter. Affording socio-economic rights to all people therefore enables them to enjoy the other rights enshrined in Chapter 2. The realisation of these rights is also key to the advancement of race and gender equality and the evolution of a society in which men and women are equally able to achieve their full potential.[47]

The Court then noted that the right to adequate housing had a special relationship to other social and economic rights, and stressed that the Constitution needed to be read as a whole when deciding how to interpret them. Invoking the *Soobramoney* decision, the judges determined that, in a poor society such as South Africa, the immense disparities in wealth and the persistence of gross poverty made claims that the state adequately respected human dignity ring 'hollow'.[48] They then noted that public international human rights law also had a bearing in this case, since its logic meshed well with the aspirations of the South African constitutional order. They noted that Article 11.1 of the ICESCR specified that states must take all appropriate steps to provide an adequate standard of living for all their citizens.

> The States Parties to the present Covenant recognize the right of everyone to an adequate standard of living for himself and his family, including adequate food, clothing and housing, and to the

> continuous improvement of living conditions. The States Parties will take appropriate steps to ensure the realization of this right, recognizing to this effect the essential importance of international co-operation based on free consent.[49]

The judges noted that this Article had considerable bearing when interpreting the South African Constitution's right to 'access to adequate housing'. Specifically, South Africa could not be said to meet its domestic or international legal duties if it ignored what the UN Committee on Economic, Social and Cultural Rights called the minimum 'core obligations' to provide a floor below which no citizen was permitted to drop.[50] This was especially pertinent when considering 'vulnerable' groups who are especially in need of the protections guaranteed by the right. Given all this, the Court homed in on the fundamental issue of the case:[51] whether South Africa had taken all the steps necessary progressively to respect the rights of citizens to be cared for to the standard set out as 'core obligations' given available resources and paying due mind to what I have elsewhere in this work termed 'socio-historical contexts'.

> The determination of a minimum core in the context of 'the right to have access to adequate housing' presents difficult questions. This is so because the needs in the context of access to adequate housing are diverse: there are those who need land; others need both land and houses; yet others need financial assistance. There are difficult questions relating to the definition of minimum core in the context of a right to have access to adequate housing, in particular whether the minimum core obligation should be defined generally or with regard to specific groups of people. As will appear from the discussion below, the real question in terms of our Constitution is whether the measures taken by the state to realise the right afforded by Section 26 are reasonable. There may be cases where it may be possible and appropriate to have regard to the content of a minimum core obligation to determine whether the measures taken by the state are reasonable. However, even if it were appropriate to do so, it could not be done unless sufficient

> information is placed before a court to enable it to determine the minimum core in any given context. In this case, we do not have sufficient information to determine what would comprise the minimum core obligation in the context of our Constitution. It is not in any event necessary to decide whether it is appropriate for a court to determine in the first instance the minimum core content of a right.[52]

The judges then carried on with their substantive analysis. They started by recognizing that a right of access to adequate housing meant more than just providing basic shelter. It required access to land, and the provision of water and sewage systems, as well as the construction of a house. Innovatively, they also observed that obligations to provide such adequate housing went beyond the state. Individuals and social actors were also responsible for the realization of the right, and needed to be 'enabled by legislative and other measures' to provide for it.[53] The state 'must create the conditions for access to adequate housing for people at all economic levels in [South African] society'.[54] The judges then went on to find that this could be realized in different ways. For those able to afford adequate housing, it meant unlocking the system and enabling them to access the land and resources needed to build their home. For those who could not independently afford adequate housing, the requirements were different.

The judges then went on to analyse what constituted reasonable measures to ensure the progressive realization of the right of access to housing. They began by noting that the South African Constitution establishes different levels of government with different responsibilities. They therefore stipulated that attempts to realize such a holistic right must be co-ordinated and comprehensive, entailing dialogue between the different levels of government. The judges also went out of their way to stipulate that such co-ordination must pay constant attention to the 'social, economic, and historical context' of those requiring aid, to ensure that the right will be successfully realized in the short, medium and long terms.[55] Finally, the judges went on to acknowledge that progressive realization of the right to housing needed to be carried out with an awareness that the resources available to the state were, sadly, very far from bountiful. They accepted the need to remain prudent with such limited resources, but also maintained that the state must attempt to realize the right 'expeditiously and effectively'.[56]

Given this rich theoretical overview, the judges then went on to analyse whether the state had met its obligations to provide housing to all citizens. They began by noting two important factors. The first is that the Government had indeed made significant, and in many cases effective, efforts to resolve the housing crisis. However, the second is that, despite these efforts, many South Africans either remained in very poor-quality housing or were homeless. This, of course, included Mrs Grootboom and the other respondents. The judges therefore concluded that, despite its admirable efforts, the Government had not met its obligations to the respondents and others in Cape Metro, as stipulated under section 26(2) of the Constitution. They also noted that the state was not meeting its section 28 obligations and was failing to abide by international law.

> The extent of the state obligation must also be interpreted in the light of the international obligations binding upon South Africa. The United Nations Convention on the Rights of the Child, ratified by South Africa in 1995, seeks to impose obligations upon state parties to ensure that the rights of children in their countries are properly protected. Section 28 is one of the mechanisms to meet these obligations. It requires the state to take steps to ensure that children's rights are observed. In the first instance, the state does so by ensuring that there are legal obligations to compel parents to fulfil their responsibilities in relation to their children. Hence, legislation and the common law impose obligations upon parents to care for their children. The state reinforces the observance of these obligations by the use of civil and criminal law as well as social welfare programmes.[57]

The judges went on to dismiss the claim that, just because Mrs Grootboom and other parents were with their children on the squatted land, this meant that the state had no special duty to provide the children with a higher standard of living than inhabiting squalor:

> This does not mean, however, that the state incurs no obligation in relation to children who are being cared for by their parents or families. In the first place, the state must provide the legal and administrative infrastructure necessary to ensure that children are accorded the protection contemplated by section 28. This obligation would normally be fulfilled by passing laws and creating enforcement mechanisms for the maintenance of children, their protection from maltreatment, abuse, neglect or degradation, [...] and the prevention of other forms of abuse of children mentioned in section 28. In addition, the state is required to fulfil its obligations to provide families with access to land in terms of section 25, access to adequate housing in terms of section 26 as well as access to health care, food, water and social security in terms of section 27. It follows from this judgment that sections 25 and 27 require the state to provide access on a programmatic and coordinated basis, subject to available resources. One of the ways in which the state would meet its section 27 obligations would be through a social welfare programme providing maintenance grants and other material assistance to families in need in defined circumstances.[58]

This brings us to the final part of the judgment. The Court observed, morosely, that the situation in Wallacedene was undeniably tragic. It also observed that much the same could be said about thousands of other South Africans who did not enjoy access to an adequate standard of living. The Court acknowledged that, given these problems, it was acceptable for the Government to engage in the challenging business of determining trade-offs concerning which rights to prioritize. But the Court also observed that the Constitution would be nothing but a scrap of paper, and justiciable social and economic rights rendered useless, if 'teeth' were not given to the claims of the respondents. It then went on directly to connect this imperative to the broader need to respect and amplify human dignity; indeed, in a manner extremely close to what is required by my mode of dignity and rights. Given that living in such conditions was a serious affront to the dignity of Mrs Grootboom and the other respondents, something needed to be done.

> But section 26 is not the only provision relevant to a decision as to whether state action at any particular level of government is reasonable and consistent with the Constitution. The proposition that rights are interrelated and are all equally important is not merely a theoretical postulate. The concept has immense human and practical significance in a society founded on human dignity, equality and freedom. It is fundamental to an evaluation of the reasonableness of state action that account be taken of the inherent dignity of human beings. The Constitution will be worth infinitely less than its paper if the reasonableness of state action concerned with housing is determined without regard to the fundamental constitutional value of human dignity. Section 26, read in the context of the Bill of Rights as a whole, must mean that the respondents have a right to reasonable action by the state in all circumstances and with particular regard to human dignity. In short, I emphasise that human beings are required to be treated as human beings. This is the backdrop against which the conduct of the respondents towards the appellants must be seen.[59]

Given this, the Court ruled that the state had violated the rights of Mrs Grootboom and the other respondents. It recognized that limited resources were available to enable these rights to be realized fully, and that compromises needed to be made. However, it stressed, for a final time, that these socio-economic rights were *rights*, and that the Constitution 'obliges the state to give effect to them'. The judges also observed that, since these rights were constitutional, the law obligated the Court to enforce them:

> I am conscious that it is an extremely difficult task for the state to meet these obligations in the conditions that prevail in our country. This is recognised by the Constitution which expressly provides

> that the state is not obliged to go beyond available resources or to realise these rights immediately. I stress however, that despite all these qualifications, these are rights, and the Constitution obliges the state to give effect to them. This is an obligation that courts can, and in appropriate circumstances, must enforce.[60]

It therefore required the state to develop a comprehensive and reasonable plan to ensure that Mrs Grootboom, her children and the other respondents had their right of access to housing respected. This included providing relief to those who had no land, and no roof over their heads, and who lived in inadequate conditions.

The *Grootboom* decision is a model for how to make socio-economic rights justiciable. While the ECtHR was admirably willing to take a non-formalistic approach to the realization of education rights in *DH v Czech Republic*, the case was seriously hampered by the paternalism shown to the parents involved, and an unwillingness to enter into a dialogue with them in a serious manner. This seriously infringed the dignity of the Roma parents and children, by not adequately respecting their democratic rights to participate in the formulation of policies that impacted them, posing serious challenges to the parents' and children's capacity to participate in Czech society as dignified self-authors. In *Grootboom*, the South African Court takes very seriously the far more severe socio-historical contexts impacting Mrs Grootboom and the other respondents. It discusses in considerable detail how the history of apartheid, and the consequent racist policies, continue to impact her many years after the formal legal restrictions had vanished. After a thorough analysis, the judges indicate that these socio-historical contexts need to be overcome to afford all South Africans an equal opportunity to participate in the polity as individuals possessing equal dignity. The Court also recognizes the important role that international human rights law plays in framing what is required for the full realization of human dignity. In addition to citing the ICESCR at multiple points, they also look to other UN committees and precedents for guidance on how best to realize socio-economic rights in a manner that respects the dignity of their citizens and conforms to their international legal obligations. In this respect, the *Grootboom* decision demonstrates very nicely how international human rights law can steer a state towards the fuller realization of the rightful condition. It is especially inspiring given South Africa's long and difficult history as an international pariah, propagating an unambiguously wicked legal regime.[61]

The *Grootboom* decision is also a good test case on the more substantial difficulties of how to realize the economic, social and cultural rights of citizens progressively. While it does not go as far as my model in calling for a full equality of human capabilities except where inequities are otherwise justified, there is no doubt that its references to the stark inequality facing South Africans and the urgent need to remedy this situate it quite closely to this ideal. But the Court also acknowledged that the way to go about this is a complex task, given the limited resources, the scope of the problems and the need to make policy choices.

I think that the Court largely made the correct decision in this case, by ordering the Government to provide a solution while largely refraining from specifying how to go about doing so. This is because this course of action pays greater respect to the first right of citizens, to democratic self-authorship. Involving courts in making public policy choices would ultimately prove an impediment to the full realization of the first of the twinned rights. The way in which to balance the need to respect democratic self-authorship with the need to realize the right to an equality of capabilities will offer to provide an overall guide for policymakers on how best to amplify human dignity. This is also important for a second and often articulated reason: that judges are not policymakers, and may well lack the necessary information or skills to develop sound policy.

Unfortunately, these limitations can only go so far and, here as well, the *Grootboom* decision is more tragically instructive.[62] Despite winning her case, Mrs Grootboom died in a shack, still poor and without adequate lodging.[63] This was in part due to the unwillingness of the Court to order more specific remedies for her situation, which might have forced the Government to take more concrete and long-term action. It is also indicatory of the well-known discrepancy between how law operates in books, and its concrete implications. This has been well studied by a host of socio-legal scholars, many of whom note that even the most noble legal decisions are often underwhelming when put into practice.

The *Grootboom* decision is almost an ideal case in point on this issue. As a piece of legal reasoning concerned to amplify human dignity and rectify gross injustices that emerged from racist socio-historical contexts, it is an ideal decision. In terms of its practical consequences for those in need, it fell considerably short of the mark. *Grootboom* was an inspiring legal precedent protecting the rights of the poor, but it shows that even justiciable rights are not a complete remedy for gross inequalities in a society so deeply riven by corruption, racism and the worst forms of neo-liberal hegemony. Here, some critical legal scholars may point to the relative uselessness of law in achieving true social justice. And, in part, we should take this critique seriously. Simply pushing for legal remedies and change will not be enough to rectify gross injustices. What one needs is critical advocacy and activism along a broad number of different fronts in order to undertake a more substantial transformation of society. In many contexts, especially those such as South Africa, this is the only way to truly establish the rightful condition for the full flourishing of human dignity. However, I do not think that this means that law should simply be avoided or dismissed. Indeed, the point of this entire book is that we should deploy such critical advocacy and activism to push for more robust international and domestic protections for a broad and egalitarian conception of rights and dignity. In this respect the *Grootboom* decision remains inspiring, since it was movement in the right direction. That it was insufficient only shows us the greater efforts to which critical scholars must commit themselves in order to bridge the gap between what is and what ought to be.

Can the Economic, Social and Cultural Rights of Non-Citizens be Made Justiciable?

Throughout the previous sections of this chapter I have shown why and how the economic, social and cultural rights of citizens should be justiciable. It is clear that, while we still have a long way to go in ensuring that states take adequate care to amplify the economic, social and cultural rights of their citizens to the degree that is required to respect human dignity, some progress has been made. Moreover, we have seen how international human rights law and its affiliated institutions can play an important role in realizing these rights, both independently and via their influence on domestic courts. This brings me to my final discussion of the chapter, which is whether one might make the economic, social and cultural rights of non-citizens similarly justiciable.

I have already provided an extensive philosophical argument on why there are good principled reasons for non-citizens being given such rights, and why it is morally correct to require more developed states to provide them with the resources that they need to enjoy a minimally dignified life. In this section, I will discuss the more practical challenges and possibilities that are required to make this a reality. More centrist liberals, and even some progressives who reject the argument that states have such substantial obligations to non-citizens, may well think that such a discussion is beside the point, because we have no business establishing such broad rights to begin with. If that is the case, I would encourage them to go through the more abstract discussion in Chapter 4 in order to deal with the issue at a more principled level.

The most obvious practical argument against my position is prudential and has two dimensions to it. The first would be to acknowledge that many developed states do not even feel sufficiently compelled adequately to respect the minimal level of economic, social and cultural rights for their own citizens. Trying to broaden the obligation to include non-citizens and other states is likely to be a waste of resources and time. Instead, one should focus on comprehensively making economic, social and cultural rights justiciable for the citizens of individual states, as this is a more realistic goal. I do not find this to be an especially compelling line of reasoning, since it is predicated on a false dualism of objectives. To invoke the reasoning of the South African court, rights are rights and should belong to all human beings regardless of the arbitrary factors of their birth. This suggests that we should be pushing to respect the socio-economic rights of all individuals regardless of where they happen to be born as part of a comprehensive project aimed at adequately respecting the human dignity of all. Indeed, drawing such a stark moral distinction between citizens and non-citizens waters down the universalistic dimension of human rights and international human rights law. While the distinction is significant from practical and moral points of view – and I have already indicated why we should reject the argument that states do not have any special obligations to their own citizens – we should not go so far as simply ignoring the pressing obligations that we have to others.

The second dimension of a practical argument against my position is considerably more powerful and politically savvy. Its most powerful iteration comes via the objections of Slavoj Žižek, who limited it to commenting on the refugee crisis, but the same logic applies here.[64] It is that trying to extend economic, social and cultural rights to non-citizens might well prove disastrous for progressive causes. This is because the backlash that might result from even attempting such an audacious move would ultimately be tremendously damaging. This is especially true in today's political climate, in which various iterations of postmodern conservative quasi-authoritarianism have seized control in states such as Italy, Hungary, Poland and, of course, the United States, largely on the back of anti-refugee and anti-immigrant rhetoric and platforms. The argument would be that in such a tempestuous political climate it is not just impractical but outright dangerous to attempt to force an even broader recognition of rights. The consequence could well be that we would do greater harm than good.

I think that this is an important, though ultimately conditional, objection. It depends for its force on the current ghoulish political climate persisting into the near future. We should all work towards preventing that. But, in any event, I think that the argument loses some of its force when one actually examines its inner logic. Žižek seems to be saying that attempts to provide mass assistance to non-citizens will result in a backlash.

Žižek is right, but I am not convinced that that is a compelling reason to desist, in and of itself. We must recognize that, in today's political climate, postmodern populists will never be satisfied with even the most minimal efforts to assist people beyond their national borders and who belong to a given ethnic identity. This has little to do with the volume or impact of assistance, since the incremental efforts already made have already provided tremendous fodder for the populist grinder. Confronting postmodern conservative populism cannot entail moderating or acquiescing to their demands, since this will simply empower them to take more. Instead, we must stridently assert virtues of a more cosmopolitan and egalitarian world, in which the dignity of all should be respected.

Moreover, Žižek's reasoning occasionally falters when he implies that policies that benefit non-citizens must invariably produce a populist backlash. This takes such policies in isolation and does not recognize that there are more complex reasons for populist outrage being directed against non-citizens and the vulnerable in the first place. Žižek is, of course, well aware of this, and has spoken at great length of the socio-political and psychic roots[65] of xenophobia in liberal societies.[66] However, at times he seems to give in to an excessively pessimistic programme, aligned to his dark outlook. Many xenophobic and racist attitudes towards non-citizens may be predicated simply on prejudice and fear of the 'Other'. There is little chance of shifting such perspectives. But my argument is that, with the realization of the twinned rights for a broader cross-section of domestic societies, we may well be able to ameliorate the socio-political and psychic propensity towards nativism. By enabling individuals to enjoy far greater authorship of their societies, and rectifying gross inequalities in expressive capabilities, individuals can feel far more capable of dignified self-authorship and have less to fear from the mysterious Other seizing their resources and time. This could foster a willingness to extend the rights to non-citizens in other states so as to provide them with the minimal capacity that is required to lead a dignified life.

With these more politically oriented arguments out of the way, we can move to discussing how such rights could be made justiciable. Here there are very few instances on which we can draw. There are certainly long-standing precedents involving individuals using international law to push for their rights in a foreign state. Here, Canada is perhaps ahead of the curve. There has recently been some momentum towards expanding such rights via decisions such as 2013's *Choc v*

Hudbay Minerals Inc,[67] in which an Ontario court agreed to hear a suit against a Canadian mining company that was responsible for infringing the rights of its workers and other affiliated individuals in Guatemala. However, even these limited gains have been almost exclusively related to pushing for violations of civil and political rights in domestic courts. Canadian courts have been considerably more reticent when enforcing the economic, social and cultural rights of non-citizens: for instance, in the disappointing *Ontario (Attorney General) v Fraser* decision of 2011 it denied seasonal agricultural workers from Latin America the right to form labour unions.[68] So even countries who were willing to entertain the idea that non-citizens who do not permanently reside in the state have justiciable rights are not yet willing to go so far.

Perhaps the most worthwhile precedent to look to would be international refugee law, which does impose obligations on states to accept refugees and provide them with resources in the event of gross forms of oppression. Ever since Hannah Arendt's pioneering examination in *The Origins of Totalitarianism*,[69] refugees have been a paradigmatic example of how the international community needs to grant non-citizens substantial entitlements to realize their 'right to have rights'. In many respects the United Nations Convention Relating to the Status of Refugees is intended to address this need. Signatory states are obligated to take in refugees when they are fleeing from situations of extreme danger and prejudice. Article 16 also obligates states to provide refugees with access to courts; Articles 17, 18 and 19 obligate states not to discriminate against refugees with regard to employment; Articles 20–24 require states not to discriminate in providing refugees with the same social and economic benefits as citizens; and finally Article 25 obligates states to provide refugees with administrative assistance when relocating. Many states have set up institutions designed to assess the truth and legality of refugee claims, and a formidable apparatus to ensure that their rights are respected in an effective manner.[70]

The international and legal provisions and institutions set up around refugees may well be a worthwhile precedent when examining how to establish justiciable economic, social and cultural rights for non-citizens successfully. Those who can demonstrate that they are in positions of tremendous precarity should be enabled to file suits arguing for the redistribution of resources from developed countries to ensure they do not fall below a minimum floor. How to accomplish such an ambitious scheme in practice goes well beyond the purview of this work.

Obviously, since tremendous challenges are involved in accessing domestic legal systems in many developing countries, international legal institutions would have to provide significant assistance to ensure that vulnerable individuals and communities enjoyed meaningful access to economic and social justice. Here, well-established international courts such as the ECtHR may well play a crucial role. This would mean bucking its worrying recent trend of ignoring the concerns of refugees fleeing from hardship, as in cases such as *AS v Switzerland*[71] and *AME v The Netherlands*.[72] The ECtHR would do well to remember that human dignity is a matter that crosses borders, much as international law does, and that one of its primary functions is to engender respect for both rather than simply deferring to nationalist concerns. Domestic courts in developed countries will also have to be more willing to hear cases brought forward by non-citizens, and work to entrench a degree of respect for their economic, social and cultural rights in national jurisprudence. Here, Canadian precedents such as *Choc v Hudbay Minerals Inc* may be worth looking at.[73]

The practical challenges involved in making the economic, social and cultural rights of non-citizens justiciable are the most formidable explored in this work. This is especially true given the current rightward shift across the developed world. Many countries increasingly see it as their duty to take care of their own citizens' needs at the expense of all concern for the world at large (for example, the United States' policy to put 'America first' (as if the modern world has ever seen anything but the that country putting itself first). This should be deeply worrying for all critical scholars and anyone concerned to promote a world in which the dignity of all human beings is respected. It is not at all clear what the path should be going forward at a time in which paranoid 'strong' men are attempting to take control. But we should not cease in our efforts to move past such narrow concerns and towards the goal of a more just world in which the dignity and rights of all are respected.

7

Concluding Remarks on What it Means to Overcome False Necessity

Earlier in this work I promised to sketch out a novel theory of human dignity, and an affiliated set of rights, that would broadly mesh with the critical legal tradition. I then linked this account to a reorientation of international human rights law, to demonstrate how it could be used to establish a world in which human dignity was more broadly respected. My motivations for engaging in such a project were twofold.

First, I wanted to demonstrate that it was possible to operate within that tradition without succumbing exclusively to the temptation to engage in 'trashing' non-progressive viewpoints and institutions – although the book has done plenty of that! At its core, the theory of human dignity, and the affiliated set of rights, is most deeply inspired by the philosophical outlook of Roberto Unger. The title of this chapter, expressly invoking Unger, is meant to signal that human dignity is fundamentally about enabling individuals to be the authors of their own lives and the socio-political institutions that govern them. Far too often, individuals are compelled or determined to act in a manner that they would choose to reject if given the opportunity, and that runs highly counter to their general interests. This constitutes a deep injustice if we have decided to take dignity seriously. We therefore have compelling reasons radically to transform societies in a manner that would be more amenable to the dignified self-authorship of all individuals. I believe that the best way to do this would be to adopt dignity as a mother right, which most immediately gives birth to the twinned rights to democratic self-authorship and an equality of expressive capabilities. States that respected and amplified these rights would be more just than those that failed to do so. Unfortunately, most states are not especially close to such a standard.

This brings me to my second motivation, which is more concrete. I wanted to show how international human rights law could be reoriented so as to move states towards the 'rightful condition' for the flourishing of human dignity. It can do this by steering states in the direction of policies and more specific positive laws that would sufficiently entrench the twinned rights. Moreover, I also argued that states have obligations beyond their borders. Rich states must ensure that the world's poorest people enjoy the minimal standard of living required for the enjoyment of some dignified self-authorship. This minimum falls below what they owe to their citizens, but would entail undertaking significantly greater efforts than they do today. Finally, I concretized this argument by looking at several major cases in international human rights law that concern both democratic rights and economic, social and cultural rights. This analysis drew primarily on European international law, since it is one of the few global legal systems that actually has the power to enforce its decisions. I also looked at South Africa's *Grootboom* decision as a formal model for how domestic courts may be steered in the direction of the rightful condition through appealing to international human rights law. This case also demonstrates the limits of my account, since it showcases that even the most well-meaning legal system cannot rectify all socio-political injustices. Finally, I briefly discussed some cases in refugee law and the domestic jurisprudence of various legal systems to demonstrate how we might theoretically proceed to make the economic, social and cultural rights of non-citizens justiciable.

I will conclude this work by briefly looking to the future, attempting to preview what I take to be my approach's limitations and how they might be rectified at some later time. To begin, this work does not deal with many important theoretical issues on the nature of law. This includes many substantial and important debates about the nature of legal interpretation, neutrality and the relationship between law and a given political and/or moral theory. For the purposes of this volume, I ignored such questions and focused instead on presenting a very specific political and moral account of dignity and discussed how international human rights law could be used as a tool to achieve this. For some domestic legal theorists and jurists, such an account of law might seem far too instrumental and normatively weighted down, though such complaints are less common in the more overtly political and philosophical literature on international human rights law.

This brings me to a second, and related, limitation. One of the most obvious assumptions of this work has been its focus on law as a tool of emancipation and social transformation. This runs counter to the grain of most critical and socio-legal scholarship, which has rightly demonstrated the many ways in which law serves as a tool of oppression. As highlighted, in doing so my intention was to provide a more optimistic and constructive account. But the power of law as a potential tool of oppression should by no means be dismissed. Even many reasonably just legal systems are still marked by oppressive practices. The issue becomes even darker, and more conceptually complicated, when one considers truly wicked 'legal' systems, such as those that operated in Nazi Germany and apartheid South Africa. In these cases, some have argued that it is wrong even to characterize such systems as 'law', as they go so far beyond the logic typically associated with legality.[1]

One could even go beyond this objection and claim, as some have, that legal concerns are in some sense peripheral to more general political and historical movements. On this reading, 'legalizing' politics may well be dangerous, since it grants a great deal of power to enact social change to a small group of unelected judges from elite institutions.[2] But this argument has never struck me as being especially powerful, since it was based primarily on the empirical claim that judges would simply be hostile to any major attempts at reform. As we have seen in many of the cases discussed here, that has not been exclusively true at the international level. This should be cause for some optimism. Moreover, such an argument can have only limited weight when directed against an expressly principled project that is aimed at reorienting law.

We must see the project that is developed here as part of a far wider effort to try to take back the political agenda that has been increasingly seized by dangerous authoritarians and various forms of postmodern conservatism. To do so, we must both propose alternatives to the status quo that would establish a more egalitarian world, and engage in a substantial critique of those institutions, ideologies and personalities who prevent such a project from coming to fruition. This work clearly falls more into the former category and, ideally, will be read as such. How to go about the second task is a question for another book at another time.

Notes

Chapter 1

1. This echoes the sentiments of those, like Macklin and Pinker, who feel that dignity is too deeply affiliated with religious thought to be of any significant use to scientifically minded liberals.
2. See Eve Darian-Smith, *Laws and Societies in Global Contexts: Contemporary Approaches* (Cambridge: Cambridge University Press, 2013).
3. See Peter Gabel, 'Critical Legal Studies as Spiritual Practice', *Pepperdine Law Review*, 36 (2012), 523–4.
4. Even by then Marxism, at least in its orthodox formulations, was somewhat passé.
5. Jean-François Lyotard, *The Postmodern Condition: A Report on Knowledge*, trans. Geoff Bennington and Brian Massumi (Minneapolis: University of Minnesota Press, 1984), p. 37.
6. See Lyotard, *The Postmodern Condition.*
7. This echoes the claims of some positivist international lawyers who see references to dignity as little more than window dressing. It is worth noting that positivist jurists tend to be more sceptical of moral ideas playing a role than positivist legal theorists. See Joseph Raz, *The Authority of Law*, 2nd edn (Oxford: Oxford University Press, 2009).
8. See, for example, Ruth Macklin, 'Dignity is a Useless Concept', *British Medical Journal*, 327 (2003).
9. See Steven Pinker, 'The Stupidity of Dignity', *The New Republic*, 28 May 2008.
10. This association is not without merit. Indeed, the emphasis placed on dignity by Roman Catholic authors persists down to the modern era. See John Coughlin, 'Pope John Paul II and the Dignity of the Human Being', *Harvard Journal of Law and Social Policy*, 27 (2003).
11. See Immanuel Kant. Groundwork to the Metaphysics of Morals, trans. H. J. Paton (New York: Harper Torchbooks, 1964).
12. Sen refers to it as 'freedom'. Because of the classical liberal connotations of the word, I refer to 'agency' throughout.
13. I will define this below.

14. My approach is significantly different than other recent attempts to do the same. The most prominent is likely to be Capps's work. See Patrick Capps, *Human Dignity and the Foundations of International Law* (London: Bloomsbury Publishing, 2009).
15. I do, of course, draw on Kant's own writings on the subject. However, my conception of dignity is more voluntarist than the anti-humanist interpretation of Kant given by some authors. See Michael Rosen, *Dignity: Its Meaning and History* (Cambridge: Harvard University Press, 2012), p. 151.
16. See Jeremy Waldron. *Dignity, Rank, and Rights* (Oxford: Oxford University Press, 2015).
17. The capacity for context transcendence is emphasized throughout Unger's work, though he connotes it in different ways. For the most updated iteration, see Roberto Unger. *The Self Awakened: Pragmatism Unbound* (Cambridge: Harvard University Press, 2007), p. 127. It is also a major theme in Roberto Unger. *Passion: An Essay on Personality* (London: The Free Press, 1986).
18. See Roberto Unger, *Politics Volume Three: Plasticity Into Power (Comparative-Historical Studies on the Institutional Conditions of Economic and Military Success)* (London: Verso Press, 2004), 206.
19. Part of the reason I am willing to give more weight to individualism and liberal rights is I do not think Unger was sufficiently charitable in his interpretation of them. See William Ewald, 'Unger's Philosophy: A Critical Legal Study', *Yale Law Journal*, 97 (1988) for a comprehensive defence of liberal values and a criticism of Unger's position.
20. This also makes my work more individualistic than Unger's, which tends to have a more left-communitarian bent. Saying that, I would argue his work has shifted in that direction since his earliest writings, which tended to be sharply critical of liberal atomism and its affiliated psychology. See Roberto Unger, *Knowledge and Politics* (New York: The Free Press, 1973).
21. I believe law and human rights can play a crucial role in respecting and amplifying an individual's expressive capabilities. This is where I deviate from some critical legal scholars, who tend to exclusively associate rights with hegemonic forces. For an account of this debate see Adamantia Pollis and Peter Schwab, 'Human Rights: A Western Construct with Limited Applicability' in Pollis and Schwab (eds), *Human Rights: Cultural and Ideological Perspectives* (New York: Praeger, 1979), 1 with regard to international law. My own country also has its critical legal sceptics of human rights law. See Allan Hutchinson, *Waiting for C.O.R.A.F.* (Toronto: University of Toronto Press, 1995).
22. The term 'functionings' is Sen's. See Amartya Sen, *Inequality Re-Examined* (Cambridge: Harvard University Press, 1992), p. 39. See also Amartya Sen, *Commodities and Capabilities* (Oxford: Oxford University Press, 1999), 17–21.

23. One of the ways in which I develop the account given by Sen and Nussbaum is by looking more extensively at how law and constitutionalism can be organized to amplify human dignity. The reasoning that I apply here echoes some of the points made by Daniel Weinstock on the distribution of goods, for instance when he claims that a refined theory of distributive justice with regard to health 'will have more to do with the manner in which societies organize the delivery and distribution of goods that have not usually been thought of as having to do with health'. See Daniel Weinstock, 'Integrating Intermediate Goods to Theories of Distributive Justice: The Importance of Platforms', *Res Publica*, 21 (2015), 172.
24. See Roberto Unger, *Politics Volume One: False Necessity* (London: Verso Press, 2004), p. 4.
25. See Kant, *Groundwork to the Metaphysics of Morals*.
26. Sen and Nussbaum tirelessly stress this point. See Amartya Sen, *Development as Freedom* (New York: Anchor Books, 1999) and Martha Nussbaum, *Creating Capabilities: The Human Development Approach*. (Cambridge: Harvard University Press 2011).
27. For the most part I will eschew discussing questions related to natural talents, except briefly in Chapter 3.
28. The latter qualification is a key point with an immense literature surrounding it. In a later work, I hope to explore the idea of moral significance more thoroughly.
29. Nagel refers to this discord between liberty and equality as the 'problem of convergence'. Thomas Nagel, *Equality and Partiality* (Oxford: Oxford University Press, 1991), pp. 75–85. My focus is on democratic authorship of social institutions and coercive rule on the one hand, and capabilities on the other.
30. See Benhabib, *The Rights of Others*.
31. I regard this right as agency enhancing because the aggregate consequence of a more equal distribution of capabilities would be so. This is not to suggest that for some individuals with far greater wealth and power, a more equal distribution might decrease their overall level of agency because redistributive policies would be required to transfer resources from the wealthy to the more impoverished. However, I feel for a variety of different reasons that the egalitarian impulse on this point trumps marginal decreases in the agency of those who already enjoy a great deal of it. Part of this is due to the utilitarian dimension of the capabilities approach highlighted earlier, which stresses that there are some empirical choices that need to be made concerning how to make things generally go best. I think the decreases in marginal utility experienced by individuals with a great deal of agency would be more than compensated for by increases in marginal utility enjoyed by those who now

enjoyed a far more robust set of expressive capabilities due to redistributive efforts. However, this solution would be rejected by many libertarians. The most powerful objection I can think of is Nozick's. See Robert Nozick, *Anarchy, State, and Utopia* (New York: Basic Books, 1974). While I have some thoughts on how to push against his deeply compelling criticisms, I cannot address them here.

32. This is not to imply that the second right is at a lower tier of importance in some scheme, lexical or other. The metaphor of twinned rights is meant to show that the two are paired so intimately that modern democracies may be unable to function meaningfully without substantive change, for instance by rectifying a grossly unequal distribution of human capabilities. Marx, here, is a useful historical lesson, especially the Marxist tradition of deterministic historical materialism. Individuals must recognize that the precondition for the amplification of their individual expressive capabilities is the realization of the expressive capabilities of all. But they cannot be forced to reach this conclusion, and none should attempt to do so either theoretically or in reality.
33. Some domestic legal systems come quite close to this already. Germany for instance places tremendous constitutional weight on dignity, and judges have often been called upon to engage in robust theoretical interpretation to demonstrate its centrality. See David Robertson, *The Judge as Political Theorist: Contemporary Constitutional Review* (Princeton: Princeton Press, 2010), pp. 40–82.
34. See Aharon Barak, *Human Dignity: The Constitutional Value and the Constitutional Right* (Cambridge: Cambridge University Press, 2015). Also important is the work of Benhabib and Waldron on this subject. See Seyla Benhabib, *Dignity in Adversity: Human Rights in Troubled Times* (Cambridge: Polity, 2011) and Waldron, *Dignity, Rank, and Rights* though both accounts differ from mine. Again, it would be good to indicate briefly how these authors differ, i.e. the major elements of divergence.
35. Some modern critical legal scholars have become so sceptical of this that they encourage the rejection of the entire human rights project, both internationally and domestically. Ironically, they tend to move towards communitarian solutions that I consider to be far less egalitarian, and far more conservative, than my own account. For an indicative example see Costas Douzinas, *The End of Human Rights: Critical Thought at the Turn of the Century* (Oxford: Hart Publishing, 2000).
36. Here I am drawing on the less classically liberal and engaging the more contextually minded dimensions of Kant's thought on law and politics. Several authors have emphasized this. For instance, see Arthur Ripstein, *Force and Agency: Kant's Legal and Political Philosophy* (Cambridge: Harvard University

Press, 2009), pp. 325–52 and Allen W. Wood *Kant's Ethical Thought* (Cambridge: Cambridge University Press, 1999).

37. This is one of the areas where I feel that my approach overlaps with the communitarian claims of many other critical legal scholars. I believe international human rights law, in amplifying the dignity of all individuals, must protect their right to forms of cultural expression and practical reasoning that may reasonably intrude on the wishes of state authorities. Where those same authorities push back in an attempt to re-establish hegemony, international human rights law should ally with the marginalized individuals.
38. This echoes a point made by Daniel Weinstock: that the nation state is not a natural entity with the right to do whatever it wishes. See Daniel Weinstock, 'Motivating the Global Demos', *Metaphilosophy*, 40 (2009).
39. My position here echoes Beitz's. See Charles R. Beitz, 'Human Rights and the Law of Peoples', in D. K. Chatterjee, *The Ethics of Assistance: Morality and the Distant Needy* (Cambridge: Cambridge University Press, 2004), p. 193.
40. See Unger, *Politics Volume One* supra n. 24.
41. This bears some resemblance to the dialogically oriented horizontal and vertical forms of legitimation discussed by Habermas in his work on international law. See Jürgen Habermas, *The Crisis of the European Union: A Response*, trans. Ciaran Croni (Cambridge: Polity, 2012).
42. In some senses I am extending the jurisgenerative logic of Benhabib's account of rights to a global context. See Seyla Benhabib, *The Rights of Other: Aliens, Residents, and Citizens* (Cambridge: Cambridge University Press, 2004).
43. One source of moral weight I will draw upon to justify this position is the isolation paradox formulated by Sen, which demonstrates that there is no rational reason why actors would not be willing to share resources if they were aware that others would contribute as well. See Amartya Sen, 'Isolation, Assurance, and the Social Rate of Discount', *Quarterly Journal of Economics*, 81(1), 1967.
44. I draw some inspiration here from Macklem. See Patrick Macklem, 'What is International Human Rights Law: Three Applications of a Distributive Account', *McGill Law Journal*, 52 (2007). My account is considerably more individualistic than his, though this is tempered by my focus on the set of expressive capabilities and the social-historical contexts that inhibit their development.
45. I believe that looking to Article 13 of the ICESCR would be a good place to start engaging the project in more practical terms. While it lacks the striking economy of references found in the Preambles to the ICCPR and the ICESCR, Article 13 programmatically delineates the connection between dignity, human rights, and economic and social well-being in a fairly comprehensive manner. And, most importantly, it is already legally enforceable.

46. For an informative modern look into this topic, see Christopher D. Wraight, *The Ethics of Trade and Aid: development, charity or waste?* (London: Continuum Press, 2011) and Lesley Jacobs, *Pursuing Equal Opportunities: The Theory and Practice of Equality* (Cambridge: Cambridge University Press, 2004).
47. See Oisin Suttle, 'Equality in Global Commerce: Towards a Political Theory of International Economic Law', *European Journal of International Law*, 25 (2015) for an informative look. My own project will not touch on this extensively, except to note the importance of overlapping orientations.

Chapter 2

1. Jack Donnelly, *Universal Human Rights in Theory and Practice*, 3rd edn (Ithaca: Cornell University Press, 2013), p. 131.
2. See Steven Pinker, 'The Stupidity of Dignity', *The New Republic*, 28 May 2008.
3. For instance, references to dignity appear in the catechism of the Catholic Church, which insists that the 'dignity of the human person is rooted in his or her creation in the image and likeness of God'. Similarly the *Cairo Declaration on Human Rights in Islam* states that 'true faith is the guarantee for enhancing such basic human dignity along the path to human perfection'.
4. See Michael Rosen, *Dignity: Its Meaning and History* (Cambridge: Harvard University Press, 2012).
5. Pico Della Mirandola, 'Oration on the Dignity of Man', *The Website of Professor Paul Brians*, Washington State University, accessed November 2017: *https://brians.wsu.edu/2016/11/14/pico-della-mirandola-oration-on-the-dignity-of-man-15th-c-ce/*
6. Mirandola, 'Oration on the Dignity of Man'.
7. See Michael Rosen, *Dignity: Its Meaning and History* (Cambridge: Harvard University Press, 2012), Chapter 1 Part II.
8. David Hume, 'Of the Dignity or Meanness Of Human Nature', *Commonlit*, accessed 20 June 2018: *https://commonlit.s3.us-west-2.amazonaws.com/texts/student_pdfs/000/000/324/original/*.
9. My account of Kant's conception of dignity is intended to be as uncontroversial as possible since an extended exegesis on his profound work is not my intention here. For this reason I have avoided addressing any of the major interconnections which do a better job of systematizing the apparently disparate strands of his thinking together.
10. These challenges are hardly unique to Kant's conception of dignity. Many commentators have discussed how, despite his insistence on systematicity, Kant's moral philosophy is hardly free of inconsistencies, ambiguities, and theoretical tensions. One need only peruse the vast literature that exists

comparing and examining the different formulations of the categorical imperative given in the *Groundwork*. Despite Kant's insistence that all three of the different formulations operate together, as the form, substance, and end of the categorical imperative, very few commentators have accepted this. Many commentators feel that there is a substantial tension between how one might apply the first formulation, to will universal law; and the second, to treat all individuals as ends in themselves and never as means. Perhaps it is as Parfit claims: truly original thinking in moral theory may well come at the price of consistency and full coherence. See Derek Parfit, *On What Matters: Volume One* (Oxford: Oxford University Press, 2011), p. XLII.

11. See Kant, *Groundwork to the Metaphysics of Morals*.
12. It is sometimes unclear whether Kant intends these to be different moral imperatives, or different formulations of the same imperative. His own belief seems to have been the latter, but this makes it unclear why he saw fit to give such different formulations.
13. There is some difficulty here in determining what Kant meant. It is unclear whether he meant dignity stems from an individual's capacity simply to will any ends, including those which might be amoral or immoral, or whether it stems purely from an individual's capacity to will moral ends. This is a difficult and nuanced complication, which I will not discuss at length here.
14. Jack Donnelly, *Universal Human Rights in Theory and Practice*, 3rd edn (Ithaca: Cornell University Press, 2013), p. 127.
15. See J. B. Schneewind, *The Invention of Autonomy: A History of Modern Moral Philosophy* (Cambridge: Cambridge University Press, 1998), p. 518.
16. The centrality of autonomy to Kant's overall theory has been attacked by those who feel it is overly simplistic. At times Kant is treated as a moralistic theorist, who held that we always possess the full autonomy needed to act morally and there is therefore little we can do and, indeed, little we need to do in order to make it easier. And indeed, at times Kant does seem to write that way. However, there are many works in which Kant seems to be more empirically minded, and sensitive to the influence of history, state institutions, religion, and individual psychology. Many academic works explore this subject. See Rachel Bayefsky, 'Dignity, Honor, and Human Rights: Kant's Perspective', *Political Theory*, 41 (2013) for an indicatory example. Longer works include Arthur Ripstein, *Force and Agency: Kant's Legal and Political Philosophy* (Cambridge: Harvard University Press, 2009) and Allen. W. Wood, *Kant's Ethical Thought* (Cambridge: Cambridge University Press, 1999). Personally, I do not believe that Kant ever successfully managed to reconcile all these competing aspects of his moral thought on the subject into a fully coherent framework. This is not intended as a criticism of course. The mark of a great and original

thinker is often a certain eclecticism. What makes his work valuable is the continued engine it has proven for thought.

17. See David Robertson, *The Judge as Political Theorist: Contemporary Constitutional Review* (Princeton: Princeton Press, 2010), pp. 40–82.
18. There is another dimension to this that cannot be discussed at length in this work but should be noted. In addition to Kant's works in political and legal philosophy, one can point to his religious beliefs, as in some respects reflecting the limitations of this absolute commitment to *a priori* freedom and human dignity without guarantees. There are some respects in which Kant's God seems compelled to guarantee this status even in circumstances where socio-historical contexts seem to diminish freedom. This is because even the apparent inequality in life circumstances is rectified after death, since the immortality of the soul guarantees that we will all be held morally accountable for what we have willed in the prior life. This means that the slave who struggled to will the moral law will enjoy a dignity in death that the slave owner might not.
19. See Ripstein, *Force and Agency.*
20. See Karl Marx, *Capital Volume One: A Critique of Political Economy*, trans. Ernest Mandel (London: Penguin Books, 1990).
21. See Samuel Moyn, 'The Secret History of Constitutional Dignity', *Yale Human Rights and Development Journal*, 17 (2014), 44.
22. Moyn, 'The Secret History of Constitutional Dignity', p. 47.
23. See Samuel Moyn, *The Last Utopia: Human Rights in History* (Cambridge: Harvard University Press, 2012). Because this text deals primarily with human rights rather than with dignity per se, I will address its arguments more comprehensively in later chapters dealing with that topic.
24. Carl Schmitt, *The Concept of the Political* (Chicago: University of Chicago Press, 1996), p. 54.
25. See Ronald Dworkin, 'Objectivity and Truth: You Better Believe It', *Philosophy and Public Affairs*, 25, 1996.
26. See Hannah Arendt, *The Origins of Totalitarianism* (San Diego: Harcourt Inc, 1976), p. 275.
27. See Moyn, *The Last Utopia.*
28. My (brief) reading of Dworkin's conception draws on Kenneth Simon's review. See Kenneth Simon, 'Dworkin's Two Principles of Dignity: An Unsatisfactory Nonconsequentialist Account of Interpersonal Moral Duties', *Boston University Law Review*, 90 (2010).
29. See Ronald Dworkin, *Justice for Hedgehogs* (Cambridge: Harvard University Press, 2010), p. 132.
30. Dworkin, *Justice for Hedgehogs*, p. 132.

31. See Simon, 'Dworkin's Two Principles of Dignity', p. 715.
32. See George Kateb, *Human Dignity* (Cambridge: Belknap Press, 2011), p. 10.
33. See Kateb, *Human Dignity*, p. 12.
34. See Kateb, *Human Dignity*, pp. 79–92.
35. My reading of these authors is in part inspired by my interpretation of their work in deliberative democracy. For an accessible guide on this point, see Seyla Benhabib, *Democracy and Difference: Contesting the Boundaries of the Political* (Princeton: Princeton University Press, 1996).
36. In this respect, rights normatively operate as a kind of empirical *a priori* to political discourse.
37. The term 'realistic utopia' was, as far as I know, coined by Rawls. Strangely, Habermas does not cite him on this point.
38. See Jürgen Habermas, 'Human Dignity and the Realistic Utopia of Human Rights', *Metaphilosophy*, 41 (2010), 469.
39. Habermas, 'Human Dignity and the Realistic Utopia of Human Rights', 472.
40. See Jeremy Waldron, *Dignity, Rank, and Rights: The Tanner Lectures on Human Value*. Delivered at UC Berkeley, 21–23 April 2009.
41. See Waldron, *Dignity, Rank, and Rights*, p. 229.
42. This point is also made in her book on rights. See Seyla Benhabib, *The Rights of Others: Aliens, Residents, and Citizens* (Cambridge: Cambridge University Press, 2004).
43. See Seyla Benhabib, *Dignity in Adversity: Human Rights in Troubled Times* (Cambridge: Polity Press, 2011).
44. This relates back to her fascinating account of deliberative democracy and political legitimacy. See the paper 'Toward a Deliberative Model of Democratic Legitimacy' in Benhabib, *Democracy and Difference*, pp. 67–94.
45. For objections to this view, see Derek Parfit, *On What Matters: Volume Two* (Oxford: Oxford University Press, 2011) and Derek Parfit, *Reasons and Persons* (Oxford: Oxford University Press, 1986). I will unpack my own comments on his work more thoroughly elsewhere.
46. Duncan Kennedy, 'Form and Substance in Private Law Adjudication', *Harvard Law Review*, 89 (1976).
47. See John Finnis, 'On The Critical Legal Studies Movement', *The American Journal of Jurisprudence*, 21 (1985).
48. See Roberto Unger, *Knowledge and Politics* (New York: The Free Press, 1973).
49. See Costas Douzinas, *The End of Human Rights: Critical Thought at the Turn of the Century* (Oxford: Hart Publishing, 2000).
50. See Allan Hutchinson, *Waiting for C.O.R.A.F.* (Toronto: University of Toronto Press, 1995) and Michael Mandel, *The Charter of Rights and the Legalization of Politics in Canada* (Toronto: Thompson Educational Publishing, 1994).

51. Duncan Kennedy, 'The Critique of Rights in Critical Legal Studies' in Brown and Halley (eds), *Left Legalism/Left Critique* (Durham: Duke University Press, 2002).
52. See John Rawls, 'The Idea of Public Reason Revisited', *University of Chicago Law Review*, 64 (1997), at 805.

Chapter 3

1. There might be some confusion about whether dignity, self-authorship, or agency is the central conception being argued for here. I will clarify this shortly by setting out how all three occupy a unique place in the theoretical architecture I am assembling, but come together in a way that animates all. At times, however, I will refer to 'dignified self-authorship', which seems to conflate them but is just an expression combining dignity, self-authorship, and agency together in an economical fashion.
2. See Roberto Unger, *Politics Volume Three: Plasticity Into Power (Comparative-Historical Studies on the Institutional Conditions of Economic and Military Success)* (London: Verso Press, 2004), 206.
3. See Unger, *Knowledge and Politics* (New York: The Free Press, 1973).
4. See Ewald, 'Unger's Philosophy: A Critical Legal Study' for probably the sharpest criticisms.
5. This point has been made by many other critical legal scholars. One of the more convincing accounts is Schlag's. See Pierre Schlag, 'The Empty Circles of Liberal Justification', *Michigan Law Review*, 96 (1997).
6. Indeed, he has sometimes characterized his approach as a kind of 'super-liberalism' with its strong emphasis on context-transcendence and critical mindedness. Whether this is an accurate label depends, I suspect, on how one understands liberalism. See Roberto Unger, *The Critical Legal Studies Movement: Another Time, Another Task* (Cambridge: Harvard University Press, 2015), p. 125 for the reference to super-liberalism.
7. Later, I will draw upon Kant to argue this can be characterized as realizing the 'rightful condition'.
8. My account of socio-historical contexts is derived from many of Unger's different works. He has reworked and relabelled the idea in several different manners throughout his career. Mainly I draw on his work in *Passion* where he discusses 'context breaking' at length. See Roberto Unger, *Passion: An Essay on Personality* (London: The Free Press, 1986), p. 9.
9. He does not accede to either Hayekian or Marxist forms of social determinism in this respect. Since there is always some respect in which socio-historical contexts are open, the particular form they assume and their perpetuation is in some respects dependent on deliberate human choice.

10. Whether and how transhumanism and genetic engineering might correspond to my conception of dignity I do not take up here. Overall, I am inclined to be more sympathetic than certain traditional views, such as those found in Roman Catholicism and Kantianism.
11. This, I take it, is the weakness of Waldron's approach.
12. See Giorgio Agamben, *Homo Sacer: Sovereign Power and Bare Life*, trans. Daniel Heller-Roazen (Stanford: Stanford University Press, 1998), p. 1.
13. See Jeremy Waldron, *Dignity, Rank, and Rights* (Oxford: Oxford University Press, 2015).
14. I am by no means restricting my argument to just states and their citizens here. Indeed, I feel there is a great deal we could say about the obligations of states and international legal and political institutions towards non-citizens and internationals, or the obligations of non-state institutions, such as international corporations, towards people. But since this is a far more robust question, I will leave it aside for now.
15. Sen is more inclined to understand the capabilities approach as being concerned with amplifying human freedom.
16. See Amartya Sen, *Inequality Re-Examined* (Cambridge: Harvard University Press, 1992), p. 59. See also Amartya Sen, *Commodities and Capabilities* (Oxford: Oxford University Press, 1999), pp. 17–21.
17. His most systematic account of these philosophical questions is found in Amartya Sen, *The Idea of Justice* (Cambridge: Belknap, 2009).
18. Amartya Sen, *Inequality*, p. 150.
19. Sen, *Inequality*, p. 61.
20. My account is informed by Thomas Wells. See Thomas Wells, 'Sen's Capability Approach', *Internet Encyclopedia of Philosophy: A Peer Reviewed Academic Source.*
21. This links to the emphasis that Sen places on 'freedom' in his work. My own preference is to focus on dignity. See Ananta Giri, 'Rethinking Human Well-being: A Dialogue with Amartya Sen', *Journal of International Development*, 12 (2000) and also Sen, *The Idea of Justice*.
22. See Sen, *Development as Freedom*, for a systematic account.
23. See Unger, *Politics Volume One: False Necessity* (London: Verso Press, 2004), p. 4.
24. See Kant, *Groundwork to the Metaphysics of Morals*.
25. See Noam Chomsky, *On Language: Chomsky's Classic Works Language and Responsibility and Reflections on Language* (New York: The New Press, 2007).
26. See Roberto Unger, *The Self Awakened: Pragmatism Unbound* (Cambridge: Harvard University Press, 2007), p. 127.
27. This is especially important given the ideological connotations that can be associated with established semantic formations.

28. See his account of context transcending powers in Unger, *Politics: Volume One*, pp. 319–24.
29. See Unger, *Politics Volume Three*, p. 206.
30. See Matthew McManus, 'Making Human Dignity Central to International Human Rights Law', *The New Jurist*, 24 March (2017).
31. See Derek Parfit, *On What Matters: Volume One* (Oxford: Oxford University Press, 2011), at 404–411 for the most eloquent account of the triple theory and its Kantian Consequentialism.
32. See Derek Parfit, *On What Matters: Volume Two* (Oxford: Oxford University Press, 2011), pp. 378–401 for his most sophisticated treatment; and Derek Parfit, *Reasons and Persons* (Oxford: Oxford University Press, 1986).
33. See Derek Parfit, *Reasons and Persons* (Oxford: Oxford University Press, 1986) and Derek Parfit, 'Personal Identity', *Philosophical Review*, 80(1), 1971 for his most elaborate account of selfhood and personal identity. See Derek Parfit, *On What Matters: Volume One* (Oxford: Oxford University Press, 2011) for the triple theory's account of why we should try to make everything 'go best'.
34. See Roberto Unger and Lee Smolin, *The Singular Universe and the Reality of Time: A Proposal in Natural Philosophy* (Cambridge: Cambridge University Press, 2014) for his account of time.
35. See Unger, *Passion* and Unger, *The Self Awakened* for his elaboration on these points.
36. The idea of stringency was drawn from Samuel Scheffler. See Samuel Scheffler, *Human Morality* (Oxford: Oxford University Press, 1992), pp. 26–8.
37. See Henry Sidgwick, *The Methods of Ethics* (Indianapolis: Hackett Press, 1981).
38. See Søren Kierkegaard, *Concluding Unscientific Postscript to Philosophical Fragments*, trans. Howard Hong (Princeton: Princeton University Press, 1992), p. 190.
39. See Martin Heidegger, *Being and Time*, trans. John Macquarrie and Edward Robinson (San Francisco: Harper Collins, 1962).
40. See Jeff Nicholas, *Reason, Tradition, and the Good: MacIntyre's Tradition Constituted Reason and Frankfurt School Critical Theory* (Notre-Dame: University of Notre-Dame Press, 2012).
41. The typical opponent here is the Kantian tradition. Kant famously declared that individuals were ends in themselves, or elsewhere, that human individuals were unique in being able to decide which ends they wished to pursue. Later Kantians, such as Rawls, pursued this further, arguing that human beings should be free to choose which interests and life plans they wish to pursue. Communitarians regard this as a dangerous and damaging position.

42. See Michael Walzer, *Spheres of Justice: A Defence of Pluralism and Equality* (New York: Basic Books, 1983).
43. Richard Rorty, *Philosophy and Social Hope* (London: Penguin Books, 1999), Richard Rorty, 'Solidarity and Objectivity' in Michael Krausz (ed.), *Relativism: Interpretation and Confrontation* (Notre-Dame: University of Notre-Dame Press, 1989) and Robert Brandom, 'Intentionality and Language: A Normative, Pragmatist, Inferentialist Approach', in N. J. Enfield, Paul Kockelman and Jack Sidnell (eds), *The Cambridge Handbook of Linguistic Anthropology* (Cambridge: Cambridge University Press, 2014).
44. See A. N. Whitehead, *Adventures of Ideas* (New York: The Free Press, 1967), p. 103.
45. This account of rights bears an unrelated affiliation to John Finnis's seminal account of natural rights in *Natural Law and Natural Rights*. In particular, the focus on universal expressive capabilities bears some resemblance to the list of 'basic forms of the good' given in Chapter IV of the 2nd edition of the book. These basic goods include: practical reflection, life, knowledge, play, aesthetic experience, sociability (friendship), practical reasonableness, and friendship. To my mind this list is accurate insofar as it goes, since any conception of human flourishing and dignity which did not take into account these 'basic forms of the good' would be inadequate. However, I also think the list is far too short and lacks sufficient political bite. For instance, Finnis's list contains few overt connections to any more robust conception of political legitimacy, and how legal subjects should be involved in processes of governance. Where Finnis does provide a more robust account of what constitutes political legitimacy, I have largely found it too conservative. Indeed, there is a strange respect in which the work of his positive opponents, most notably Joseph Raz, is more radical in granting subjects greater moral license to defy the law if they disagree with its substantive content. To some extent, I find Finnis's neo-Thomistic invocation of natural law to have a strangely reactionary dimension, in that at points it seems to eschew heightened concern with consent and political participation in favour of discussing whether legal systems adequately conform to his list of what law should do. This can occasionally lead him to suggest that, whether the subjects of law agree with his list of basic goods or not, so long as the legal system conforms to them, they have little basis for complaint. This is too strong a claim for me. Moreover, it also inverts the problem of modern liberalism by placing too much weight on the 'good' over the 'right', resulting in a host of meta-ethical and meta-political problems about what in turn justifies Finnis's openly axiomatic claims about what knowledge of the good, and the good itself is. This strikes me as unconvincing for a host of reasons adequately criticized by John Rawls and other egalitarian liberals

who (I think wisely) prioritize the 'right' over the 'good' to the extent one can conceptually and practically distinguish the two. While it may be impossible to truly make a clean cut, in this day and age I think there is little place for a thinker to simply impose his or her preferred comprehensive doctrine by fiat-like appeal to axioms about what is good for all. These are simply a few of the major problems I have with Finnis's work. Needless to say, as a result, this work should in no way be construed as connected to the natural law position he pioneered. However, this does not preclude it from perhaps aligning with other, more radical variants of natural law doctrine in the future. For my references, see John Finnis, 'The Critical Legal Studies Movement', *American Journal of Jurisprudence* (30), 1985 for his own account of the critical legal studies movements, and John Finnis, *Natural Law and Natural Rights*, 2nd edn (Oxford: Oxford University Press, 2011), pp. 85–90 for the argument about 'basic forms of the good'. For the reference to Rawlsian type liberalism, see John Rawls, *Political Liberalism* (New York: Columbia University Press, 1993). For Raz's positivist account of legal legitimacy, see Joseph Raz, *The Authority of Law: Second Edition* (Oxford: Oxford University Press, 2009). As to why I do not ultimately think the distinction between the 'right' and the 'good' entirely holds water, see Pierre Schlag, 'The Empty Circles of Liberal Justification', *Michigan Law Review* 96 (1997).

46. See Karl Marx, 'On the Jewish Question' in *Early Writings*, trans. Rodney Livingstone (London: Penguin Classics, 1992), pp. 211–42.
47. See Adamantia Pollis and Peter Schwab, 'Human Rights: A Western Construct with Limited Applicability' in Pollis and Schwab (eds), *Human Rights: Cultural and Ideological Perspectives* (New York: Praeger, 1979).
48. At points this has extended to an outright critique of individualism in favour of a more communitarian outlook. Not surprisingly, I feel this often leads radicals to gradually embrace more conservative outlooks, since their concern shifts from an individual's capacity to reinvent society towards maintaining the identity of both individuals and society as they are. MacIntyre is perhaps the most famous example, starting as a Marxist and gradually moving towards a sophisticated and compelling, but in my opinion ultimately reactionary, advocacy of Aristotelian virtue ethics. See Alasdair MacIntyre, *After Virtue: A Study in Moral Theory* (Notre-Dame: University of Notre-Dame Press, 1981). Unger's own romanticism and distrust of liberal atomism has occasionally pushed him in this direction. However he never abandoned his commitments to overcoming false necessity, trying to argue that more authentic and deep communitarian ties could only emerge in a society that was a reflection of the sincere interests and commitments of all individuals rather than as a product of hegemony.

49. Edmund Burke, *Reflections on the Revolution in France* (Oxford: Oxford University Press, 2009).
50. See Douzinas, *The End of Human Rights*, pp. 147–82.
51. See Saul Kripke, 'Speaker's Reference and Semantic Reference' in Saul Kripke, *Philosophical Troubles* (Oxford: Oxford University Press, 2011), pp. 105–6.
52. See Aharon Barak, *Human Dignity: The Constitutional Value and the Constitutional Right* (Cambridge: Cambridge University Press, 2015). Justice Barak's own work is more descriptive than my own project.
53. The term 'jurisgenerative' is drawn from Benhabib, who has engaged in a similar project of linking human rights to a more radical critical project. See Seyla Benhabib, *The Rights of Other: Aliens, Residents, and Citizens* (Cambridge: Cambridge University Press, 2004), p. 25.
54. I characterize the model as critical for two reasons. The first is that it would strongly entail more involvement of individuals in the formation and maintenance of social institutions. Secondly, realizing the model would require a very substantial redistribution of wealth and power to ensure a greater equality of expressive capabilities.
55. I believe this constitutes a dimension of self-authorship rather than simply political participation. The two have occasionally been separated, for instance by the existential tradition, and I believe falsely. The right to have a meaningful say in determining the form of governing structures and the laws which flow from these is key to engaging in robust self-authorship. Hierarchical political systems which deny individuals such rights limit the capacity of individuals to engage in self-authorship because they calcify the socio-historical boundaries. At best this is justified in the name of benevolent patrimony. At worst a hierarchical political system is designed in the naked self-interest of one group over another – for instance, in apartheid South Africa. Since self-authorship is predicated on an individual's capacity to define himself by redefining the socio-historical boundaries within which he exists, such a hierarchical political system would not be the ideal setting for the type of individualism I espouse to flourish. That said, there may be other virtues to hierarchical political systems that are not captured in a democracy. Plato certainly thought so.
56. On these points I draw substantial inspiration from Benhabib and others in a useful collection. See Seyla Benhabib, *Democracy and Difference: Contesting the Boundaries of the Political* (Princeton: Princeton University Press, 1996).
57. The latter qualification is a key point with an immense literature surrounding it. In a later work, I hope to explore the idea of moral significance more thoroughly.
58. See Nussbaum, *Frontiers*, pp. 107–8.

59. Nagel refers to this discord between liberty and equality as the 'problem of convergence'. Thomas Nagel, *Equality and Partiality* (Oxford: Oxford University Press, 1991), pp. 75–85. My focus is on democratic authorship of social institutions and coercive rule on the one hand, and capabilities on the other.
60. See Seyla Benhabib, *The Rights of Other: Aliens, Residents, and Citizens* (Cambridge: Cambridge University Press, 2004).
61. I regard this right as agency enhancing because the aggregate consequence of a more equal distribution of capabilities would be so. This is not to suggest that for some individuals with far greater wealth and power, a more equal distribution of wealth might decrease their overall level of agency because redistributive policies would be required to transfer resources from the wealthy to the more impoverished. However, I feel for a variety of different reasons that the egalitarian impulse on this point trumps marginal decreases in the agency of those who already enjoy a great deal of it. Part of this is due to the utilitarian dimension of the capabilities approach highlighted earlier, which stresses that there are some empirical choices that need to be made concerning how to make things generally go best. I think the decreases in marginal utility experienced by individuals with a great deal of agency would be more than compensated for by increases in marginal utility enjoyed by those who would enjoy a far more robust set of expressive capabilities due to redistributive efforts. However, this solution would be rejected by many libertarians. The most powerful objection I can think of is Nozick's. See Robert Nozick, *Anarchy, State, and Utopia* (New York: Basic Books, 1974). While I have some thoughts on how to push against his deeply compelling criticisms, I cannot address them here.
62. This is not to imply that the second right is at a lower tier of importance in some scheme, lexical or other. The metaphor of twinned rights is meant to show that the two are paired so intimately that modern democracies may be unable to function meaningfully without substantive change, for instance by rectifying a grossly unequal distribution of human capabilities. Marx, here, is a useful historical lesson, especially the Marxist tradition of deterministic historical materialism. Individuals must recognize that the precondition for the amplification of their individual expressive capabilities is the realization of the expressive capabilities of all. But they cannot be forced to reach this conclusion, and none should attempt to do so either theoretically or in reality.
63. Of course, Nozick's entire point in that work was to encourage us to reject such patterned distributions. Interestingly, I do not think that left wing critics who would accept Nozick's criticism of the state have ever done enough to answer his comment about patterned distributions. Many just seem to suppose that with the destruction of state power, a more egalitarian distribution

of goods would or could emerge. This might be the case, but it needn't be. As Nozick shows, it might instead just lead us to support a minimalist libertarian state where some acquire a great deal based on their providing goods and services that others desire. Nor do I see why, if I am to be left free and not treated as a means to an end in any circumstance, there could be any strong moral reasons why I should feel compelled to redistribute wealth in a non-state context if that is not the end I choose to pursue. See Robert Nozick, *Anarchy, State, and Utopia* (New York: Basic Books, 1974).

64. I say 'historically' because it is important to realize the first right before pursuing the second one in actual history. This is to ensure that individuals remain capable of robust democratic self-authorship even while using the power of the state and international institutions to redistribute capabilities. This, again, runs counter to some egalitarian theorists, notably Singer, who believe we have stringent duties to redistribute resources. While Singer himself does not argue for this as far as I know, such a position does lend support to the idea that the state and international institutions can legitimately force individuals to redistribute resources where doing so would increase aggregate utility. While I am deeply sympathetic to aspects of this egalitarian urge, I do not think such an attempt can end with anything but violent appropriation of goods. So we need to undertake the first step of creating a more democratic forum for marginalized voices to be heard. After this acquires greater degrees of legitimation across the entire body politic, egalitarians can push for the redistribution of capabilities. For a representative account of Singer's theory see Peter Singer, *The Most Good You Can Do: How Effective Altruism is Changing Ideas About Living Ethically* (New Haven: Yale University Press, reprinted 2016) and also his earlier seminal essay Peter Singer, 'Famine, Affluence, and Morality', *Philosophy and Public Affairs*, 1 (1972).

65. This seemingly relativistic claim might appear at odds with the universalistic pretensions that have pervaded the rest of this piece, but should not be understood that way. It is not a concession to pragmatic reality, but rather testifies to the dignified nature of individualistic self-authorship. If people are empowered to live authentically by becoming authors of their lives, then they will invariably decide to make decisions that a theorist might eschew. Increasing the capacity of individuals to make such choices, far from posing a problem for my theory, would only testify to the expansion of human dignity in the world. The crucial issue is not whether people should make decisions a theory will preclude, but what (if any) limitations should be imposed on the employment of human expressive capabilities. This is where one gets into all the classic dilemmas about how to balance the rights of different citizens who might have competing interests and commitments.

Obviously this is an exceptionally important problem which I hope to take up at a different time.

66. Shockingly, courts have historically been willing to defend these laws. See *Richardson v Ramirez*, 418 U.S. 24 (1974). For a classic and still relevant articulation of these problems, see Lani Guinier, *The Tyranny of the Majority: Fundamental Fairness in Representative Democracy* (New York: The Free Press, 1995).
67. See Thomas Piketty, *Capital in the Twenty-First Century*, trans. Arthur Goldhammer (Cambridge: Belknap Press, 2014).
68. This is one of the reasons why the twinned rights should, in ideal circumstances, be concurrently realized. The decision to characterize them as 'twinned' was motivated by concerns that focusing excessively on one or the other might paradoxically be self-defeating. A democracy defined by immense levels of inequality can easily slide back into more hierarchical forms of governance. This is true even in developed societies like the United States, which increasingly looks more like a liberal polyarchy; a state with some democratic features, but one largely oriented around protecting the rights of the most advantaged. This is where permanent efforts to realize a right to democratic authorship can be abetted by concurrent efforts to secure a greater equality of expressive capabilities for all. The term polyarchy is Dahl's. See Robert Dahl, *Democracy and Its Critics* (New Haven: Yale University Press, 1991).

Chapter 4

1. Jean H. Quataert, *Advocating Dignity: Human Rights Mobilizations in Global Politics* (Philadelphia: University of Philadelphia Press, 2009), p. 304.
2. Martti Koskenniemi is perhaps the most prominent critical legal scholar who has done so.
3. John Finnis is the most contemporary representative of this field. See John Finnis, *Natural Law and Natural Rights*, 2nd edn (Oxford: Oxford University Press, 2011).
4. My account here is somewhat inspired by Schmitt. See Carl Schmitt, *The Nomos of the Earth in the International Law of Jus Publicum Europeaum* (Candor: Telos Press, 2006).
5. See Edward Said, *Orientalism: 25th Anniversary Edition* (New York: Vintage Books, 2004).
6. Robert Jackson, 'Opening Statement Before the International Military Tribunal' *Robert H. Jackson Center*. Retrieved 5 April 2018: *https://www.roberthjackson.org/speech-and-writing/opening-statement-before-the-international-military-tribunal/*
7. See Thucydides, *The History of The Peloponnesian War*, trans. Richard Crawley (e-book: Project Gutenberg, 1 May 2009). Last Updated 7 February 2013,

accessed 3 March 2018: *https://www.gutenberg.org/files/7142/7142-h/7142-h.htm#link2HCH0026* (Chapter XVII).

8. The references to Schmitt abound in his work, but the most important engagement for my purposes appears in Habermas's work on international law. See Jürgen Habermas, *The Divided West*, trans. (London: Polity Press, 2006).
9. Carl Schmitt, *Constitutional Theory*, trans. Jeffrey Seitzer (Durham: Duke University Press, 2008), pp. 260 and 272.
10. See Jean-Jacques Rousseau, *The Social Contract* (London: Penguin Books, 1968).
11. See John Rawls, *Justice as Fairness: A Restatement* (Cambridge: Belknap Press, 2001).
12. See Martha Nussbaum, *Frontiers of Justice: Disability, Nationality, Species Membership* (Cambridge: Belknap Press, 2006), Ch. One.
13. Carl Schmitt, *Political Theology* (Chicago: The University of Chicago Press, 2005), p. 1; and Carl Schmitt, *The Concept of the Political: Expanded Edition* (Chicago: The University of Chicago Press, 2007).
14. Carl Schmitt, *Political Theology* (Chicago: The University of Chicago Press, 2005), p. 13.
15. See John Rawls, *Political Liberalism* (New York: Columbia University Press, 1993).
16. This is not to suggest that I am exclusively critical. I believe there is much that is extremely valuable in Schmitt's work. His observation that liberal democracies are never capable of demonstrating the full degree of tolerance they purport to believe in is very well taken, especially in a modern context. We can see the pushback against tolerance and liberal cosmopolitanism with the nationalist movements which have taken hold in the United States, Hungary, Britain, and Poland. Under the pressure of postmodern fragmentation, powered by the deconstructive capacity of capitalism, these states have cracked down on difference under the auspices of preserving a liberal way of life against hordes of odd looking refugees and migrants who often hold to theologies which are not our own. This demonstrates that Schmitt and his ideas will remain eerily relevant for a long period of time.
17. Carl Schmitt, *The Leviathan in the State Theory of Thomas Hobbes* (Chicago: University of Chicago Press, 2008), p. 62.
18. See Ernesto Laclau and Chantal Mouffe, *Hegemony and Socialist Strategy*, 2nd edn (London: Verso Press, 2014).
19. Martti Koskenniemi has brilliantly unpacked this hagiographic vision of international law as 'the gentle civilizer of nations' throughout his work.
20. See Georg Wilhelm Friedrich Hegel, *The Philosophy of Right*, trans. S. W. Dyde (New York: Dover Press, 2005); and Immanuel Kant, *On History*, trans.

Lewis White Beck, Robert E. Anchor and Emil L. Fackenheim (United States: The Library of Liberal Arts, 1957).

21. See Hans Kelsen, *The Pure Theory of Law*, trans. Max Knight (United States: Lawbook Exchange Limited, 2008); and H. L. A. Hart, *The Concept of Law* 2nd edn (Oxford: Oxford University Press, 1997).
22. See Thomas Hobbes, *Leviathan* (London: Penguin Books, 1982); and Michael Oakeshott, *Rationalism in Politics and Other Essays* (Indianapolis: Liberty Fund, 1991).
23. Interestingly, Costas Douzinas has recently been developing a left wing equivalent to this same argument. Having not read his chief works on this point, I am unable to comment on them extensively. But, like all else he does, it is sure to be an interesting and enlightening contribution.
24. See John Austin, *The Province of Jurisprudence Determined (and The Uses of the Study of Jurisprudence)* (Indianapolis: Hackett Publishing, 1998).
25. Hart at least entertained the idea that if the empirical situation changed then so could the status of international law.
26. See Scott Shapiro, *Legality* (Cambridge: Belknap Press, 2011).
27. See J. G. Herder, *Another Philosophy of History and Selected Political Writings*, trans. Ioannis D. Evrigenis and Daniel Pellerin (Indianapolis: Hackett Publishing Inc, 2004) and Hobbes, *Leviathan*.
28. Herder, *Another Philosophy of History*.
29. See Robert Bork, *Coercing Virtue: The Worldwide Rule of Judges* (Toronto: Vintage Canada, 2002) and Antonin Scalia, *A Matter of Interpretation: Federal Courts and the Law* (Princeton: Princeton University Press, 1997).
30. See Antony Anghie, 'Francisco de Vitoria and the Colonial Origins of International Law', *Social Legal Studies*, 5 (1996).
31. See Costas Douzinas, *The End of Human Rights: Critical Thought at the Turn of the Century* (Oxford: Hart Publishing, 2000).
32. My sensitivity to this question has grown over the years – especially since, despite the claims of realist critics, there is one branch of international law which wields substantial real power: international economic law. Sadly, in many instances this power is wielded against the interests of oppressed peoples, thereby giving weight to the arguments of post-colonial critics. Europeans have recently had this brought home to them. As I write this, the European Union is currently engaging in a systematic process to undermine the Greek state through the application of austerity measures which even neoliberal economists have maintained will not help the economy in any notable fashion. These measures will, however, have the devastating effect of punishing the Greek people for the incompetence of their leaders, the corruption of the rich, and most importantly, the systematic failings of global capital.

33. See Ronald Dworkin, *Law's Empire* (Cambridge: Harvard University Press, 1986), p. 214.
34. This is implied in his most systematic work of moral theory. See Ronald Dworkin, *Justice for Hedgehogs* (Cambridge: Belknap Press, 2012).
35. See Immanuel Kant, *The Metaphysics of Morals*, trans. Mary Gregor (Cambridge: Cambridge University Press, 1996).
36. See Seyla Benhabib, *The Rights of Other: Aliens, Residents, and Citizens* (Cambridge: Cambridge University Press, 2004) between pp. 176 and 183.
37. This issue was at the heart of Rawls's book on international justice. See John Rawls, *The Law of Peoples: With the 'Idea of Public Reason Revisited'* (Cambridge: Harvard University Press, 2001).
38. As with my critique of contractarianism, I believe that a state can be legitimated only by real democratic consent, and not by an appeal to metaphysical or transcendental arguments. This is doubly so when such ideological appeals to culture are meant to mask the very real, and deeply hierarchical, power structures which often favour the ruling elites.
39. The reality is much more complex. As is increasingly recognized, the classical liberal state was probably never a truly 'minimal' state as its proponents desired. The classical liberal states of the United Kingdom and the United States, even in their nineteenth-century heyday, may have been domestically smaller. But they were highly dependent on immense imperialist and colonial projects to establish new markets and develop new labour pools. Within the imperial peripheries, one saw comparatively little respect or interest for the hallowed liberal rights.
40. See Barak, *Human Dignity*.
41. Barak, *Human Dignity*, p. 157.
42. I have drawn the term 'archetype' from Jeremy Waldron, though I have employed it in a more basic sense. Waldron leaves open to question whether there can be a plurality of constitutional archetypes. While possible, if this is true, it becomes difficult to see how an archetype fulfills a different and more foundational role in Waldron's theory of jurisprudence than any other 'principle' does in Dworkin's approach. According to Waldron, archetypes 'differ from Dworkinian principles and policies in that they also operate as foreground provisions. They do foreground work – as rules or precedents – but in doing that work they sum up the spirit of a whole body of law that goes beyond what they require on their own terms. The idea of an archetype, then, is the idea of a rule or positive law provision that operates not just on its own account, and does not just stand simply in a cumulative relation to other provisions, but operates also in a way that expresses or epitomizes the spirit of a whole structured area of doctrine, and does so vividly, effectively,

publicly, establishing the significance of that area for the entire legal enterprise'. Unfortunately this does not clarify things for me, since Dworkin makes quite the same claim about those principles which flow from a commitment to integrity in the law. For this reason I have adapted the term archetype to mean a singular, unifying commitment; in this case to human dignity. See Jeremy Waldron, 'Torture and Positive Law: Jurisprudence for the Whitehouse', *Colombia Law Review*, 105 (2005), 47.

43. See Barak, *Human Dignity*.
44. See Amartya Sen, *Development as Freedom* (New York: Anchor Books, 1999); Martha Nussbaum, *Creating Capabilities: The Human Development Approach* (Cambridge: Harvard University Press, 2011).
45. See John Rawls, *A Theory of Justice* (Cambridge: Harvard University Press, 1971).
46. The most notable has been the United States, which has been uniquely hostile towards both international law and any non-liberty-oriented approach to agency.
47. See Immanuel Kant, *The Metaphysics of Morals*, trans. Mary Gregor (Cambridge: Cambridge University Press, 1996).
48. Perhaps the most novel and important development in this area is the formulations of 'extra-territorial obligations' based upon existing international law. While the argument for ETOs was once largely moral and principled, recent years have seen considerable movements in the direction of providing legal teeth to what was once a highly abstract claim. The most obvious development was the adoption of the Maastricht Principles in 2011. While the Maastricht Principles are not themselves legal, they constitute a formidable step forward in clarifying and systematizing the existing international law on ETOs. Moreover, as the opinions of learned scholars are considered a source of international law (albeit a controversial and softer one than sources like treaties), and the Maastricht Principles have garnered widespread acclaim and acceptance by prestigious human rights bodies such as Amnesty International and Human Rights watch, they are due for a legal promotion in the near future. The largely theoretical arguments formulated here, while distinct from the Maastricht Principles, none the less draw from the same outlook. They should be understood as providing philosophical clarity and guidance on why and how ETOs should be understood and implemented. In particular, I stress the need to not let the demands of market actors undermine the realization of economic, social, and cultural rights for all. These rights have for too long been ignored or marginalized by neo-liberal actors, many of whom are now paying a political price for their indifference to inequality and the marginalization of peoples across

the globe. Where I differ from these right-wing critiques of neo-liberalism is in arguing that we should absolutely maintain an internationalist outlook in trying to realize economic, social, and cultural rights for all. This is why generating support for the legalization of ETOs is such a crucial project for international lawyers in the future.

49. Traditional jurists argue that the formation of the modern state system began with the Treaty of Westphalia in 1648. This is increasingly regarded as a Eurocentric vision of history; not one that is without ideological purpose. The characterization of the pre-1945 international order as consisting of sovereign states largely minding their own business effaces the immense history of colonialism, and the complex processes through which colonial peoples were excluded from the European and later white international order. For an interesting account of this process at the level of legal discourse, see Antony Anghie, 'Francisco de Vitoria and the Colonial Origins of International Law', *Social Legal Studies*, 5 (1996). For a more comprehensive, but often opaque, look at how these same processes operated throughout society, see Gayatri Spivak, *A Critique of Post-Colonial Reason: Toward A History of the Vanishing Present* (Cambridge: Harvard University Press, 1996).
50. For an informative look at these processes, see Rogers Brubaker, *Citizenship and Nationhood in France and Germany* (Cambridge: Harvard University Press, 1992).
51. Michel Foucault, *The Birth of Biopolitics: Lectures at the College de France 1978–1979*, trans. Graham Burchell (New York: Picador, 2008).
52. This is why many conservative accounts of an 'organic community' centred on national identity have an especially strange quality to them. Ignoring the metaphysical problems with the language of organic totality, national identity is no more natural than other forms of social organization, if by natural one means emerging without state intervention and manipulation. This is also why many arguments against the formation of a more international polity, and establishing affective and democratic attachments that might secure its longevity, seem to fall flat. Over a long enough period of time I do not see why it would be impossible to establish such affective and democratic attachments, though of course this should be achieved without the violence and crass manipulation which was often necessary to establish a sense of national identity. Perhaps the most articulate modern defender of this view is Roger Scruton. See Roger Scruton, *Conservatism: An Invitation to the Great Tradition* (New York: All Points Books, 2017), between pp. 79 and 102, for his most recent contribution discussing this form of 'cultural conservatism'.
53. See Edmund Burke, *Reflections on the Revolution in France* (Oxford: Oxford University Press, 2009).

54. Michael Walzer, *Spheres of Justice: A Defence of Pluralism and Equality* (New York: Basic Books, 1983).
55. My intuition is that in some cases affective attachment might generate normative obligations of a special kind. For instance, the helplessness of children at birth and their total dependence on their parents would seem to create special obligations on the part of the latter party. There is no space to discuss this here at any length, though I will touch on it in my response to Singer below. Needless to say I do not believe the idea of special obligations can be generalized so broadly to claim that the state has a special obligation to exclusively look after its citizens and pay no concern to anyone else.
56. See H. L. A. Hart, *The Concept of Law*, 2nd edn (Oxford: Oxford University Press, 1997).
57. For an interesting and non-utilitarian argument for rectifying inequality which is rather different from my own, see Scanlon's book on the topic: T. M. Scanlon, *Why Does Inequality Matter?* (Oxford: Oxford University Press, 2018).
58. One feature of the conflict that Singer does not discuss is whether Western states had obligations to the people of Bangladesh given their own colonial pasts, which contributed a great deal to the post-colonial ethnic conflicts as peoples behind lazily drawn borders fought for independence and rights against autocratic successor states. This tendency to de-historicize moral analysis, and to develop theories of moral obligation in isolation from the relevant context, is a consistent weakness in Singer's work. For instance, he observes with moderate approval that Britain has given 'rather more' than other countries, having donated £14,750,000. Nowhere does he observe that this amount might be grossly inadequate given Britain's failure to ensure the relative stability of the region in a post-colonial context. This observation will be developed shortly when I offer criticisms of Singer's position and attempt to develop a more robust account of the rights of non-citizens.
59. Singer, 'Famine, Affluence and Morality', p. 235.
60. Singer, 'Famine, Affluence and Morality', p. 232.
61. See Immanuel Kant, *On History*, trans. Lewis White Beck, Robert E. Anchor and Emil L. Fackenheim (United States: The Library of Liberal Arts, 1957), p. 111.
62. See Immanuel Kant, *The Metaphysics of Morals*, trans. Mary Gregor (Cambridge: Cambridge University Press, 1996).
63. See John Rawls, *The Law of Peoples: With the 'Idea of Public Reason Revisited'* (Cambridge: Harvard University Press, 2001).
64. See Franz Fanon, *The Wretched of the Earth* (New York: Grove Press, 2004).
65. See Robert Nozick, *Anarchy, State, and Utopia* (New York: Basic Books, 1974).

66. This is an adaption of two of Singer's points. First, it combines a deontological argument about fairness with a consequentialist dimension. My argument is that after a threshold, the fair thing to do would be to redistribute resources to those who would get more marginal utility out of them. The second point, of course, is that the arbitrariness of distance (and belonging to a given state) should not determine our sense of moral obligation.
67. In some respect, the distribution of goods is not arbitrary, but in historical fact has deliberately or consequently discriminated against many. This is the point of my first argument.
68. He has numerous papers on this subject. See, for example, Amartya Sen, 'Isolation, Assurance, and the Social Rate of Discount', *Quarterly Journal of Economics*, 81(1), 1967, 113.
69. There are also good historical reasons to adopt such a principle. Many rich states became so through the gross exploitation of former colonies which are now independent, though poor, states. The current position, that we give back as a matter of generosity, is therefore unfounded since the superior position of rich states was predicated on their morally reprehensible behavior towards those who are now to be their beneficiaries.
70. I thank Marion Trejo for her informative discussions on this topic, and for reviewing early iterations of the presented arguments.
71. See Michael Hardt and Antonio Negri, *Empire* (Cambridge: Harvard University Press, 2000).
72. Some might claim there is a tension here between my demand that citizens be the authors of the political and legal institutions which govern them, and thence the laws that flow from these, and my claim that international human rights law should steer states in the direction of the rightful condition. But this argument is too coarsely grained. International human rights law steers states in the direction of the rightful condition to the extent necessary for the realization of the twinned rights, including the democratic right. Where a state is not sufficiently accountable to its citizens, indeed international human rights law should infringe on its sovereignty to steer it in the right direction. But as states become increasingly democratic (and egalitarian), the necessity of such steering will abate until a point where the state will be operating in a manner entirely consistent with their normative and legal obligations. At this point there should no longer be any need for international human rights law to play any role at all.

Chapter 5

1. See John Bolton, 'Is There Really "Law" in International Affairs?', *Transnational and Contemporary Problems*, 1 (2000), 3.

2. In its most extreme iterations, this conspiratorial sentiment can manifest as hostility towards the very idea the international law is law at all. See Bolton, 'Is There Really Law in International Affairs?'.
3. See John Bolton, 'John Bolton on Law, International Law, and American Sovereignty' *American Enterprise Institute*. 11 January 2011: *http://www.aei.org/publication/john-bolton-on-law-international-law-and-american-sovereignty/*
4. See Antonin Scalia, *A Matter of Interpretation: Federal Courts and the Law* (Princeton: Princeton University Press, 1997)
5. See ACLU, 'Voting with a Criminal Record' American Civil Liberties Union, accessed March 2018: *https://www.aclu.org/other/voting-criminal-record-executive-summary*
6. Bolton, 'Is There Really Law in International Affairs?', p. 37.
7. One supposes Bolton takes 'international law' to be an insufferable usurpation of the right of the strong to do as they will and the weak to suffer what they must. His position on this issue is never argued for, but only rhetorically defended by invoking the claim that a state's ultimate responsibility is the preservation of national security. Indeed, that is so. But the argument of international criminal law experts and proponents has never been that states should not be permitted to act to preserve their national security. Indeed, for cosmopolitans as far back as Kant, who argued that war should increasingly become illegal, states always retained the right to self-defence. The entire purpose of the international criminal legal system and the laws of war especially is to constrain states to only conduct actions that are necessary for their self-defence. *Jus ad bellum* principles were developed to determine whether a state is truly acting in self-defence or merely pursuing what Bolton characterizes as a state's 'interests'. One would have thought at this point that permitting war for the pursuit of 'interests', rather than the absolute necessity of self-defence or in rare cases to prevent imminent mass atrocities, is the source of great evil to humankind. I cannot see any reason why it should be permitted. The *jus in bello* principles on international law which Bolton also scorns are more controversial and obviously up for debate. But I also can see no moral reasons why states should not at least aspire to a global order where indiscriminate weapons which primarily harm civilians and other non-combatants should be banned. No doubt Bolton and his advocates would argue that such *jus in bello* restrictions would be morally damaging since they tie the hands of righteous states like the United States during conflicts with wicked ones. But this is self-defeating since righteousness is not an inherent virtue. It is cultivated by action, and in a wartime setting can only be maintained by actions such as avoiding the use of weapons, tactics, and strategies that would have an immensely negative impact on civilians and other non-combatants. Given this, if a state truly is righteous

in its decision to wage war, it should not try to bar efforts to orient a conflict situation as closely as possible towards justice and respect for human life.

8. Patricia Ewick and Susan Silbey, *The Common Place of Law: Stories From Everyday Life* (Chicago: University of Chicago Press, 1998).
9. The classic expression of the legal realist position is Holmes'. See Oliver Wendell Holmes, 'The Path of the Law', *Harvard Law Review*, p. 457.
10. See Allan Hutchinson, 'Judges and Politics: An Essay From Canada', *Supreme Court Law Review*, 25 (2004), 275.
11. Marie-Bénédicte Dembour, 'Gaygusuz Revisited: The Limits of the European Court of Human Rights' Equality Agenda', *Human Rights Law Review*, 12 (2012).
12. Thierry Cruvellier, 'The ICC, Out of Africa', *The New York Times*, 6 November 2016: *https://www.nytimes.com/2016/11/07/opinion/the-icc-out-of-africa.html*
13. Alexandra R. Harrington, 'Don't Mind the Gap: The Rise of Individual Complaint Mechanisms Within International Human Rights Treaties', *Duke Journal of Comparative and International Law*, 22 (2012).
14. See *Lovelace v Canada, Communication No. 24/1977*: Canada 30/07/81, UN Doc. CCPR/C/13/D/24/1977.
15. See *Aziz v Cyprus (No. 2) (application no. 69949/01)* [2004] ECHR.
16. See *Aziz v Cyprus (No. 2)*.
17. *Aziz v Cyprus (No. 2)* at para. 13.
18. *Aziz v Cyprus (No. 2)* at para. 15.
19. *Aziz v Cyprus (No. 2)*.
20. *Aziz v Cyprus (No. 2)* at para. 18.
21. *Aziz v Cyprus (No. 2)* at para. 22.
22. *Aziz v Cyprus (No. 2)* at para. 23.
23. *Aziz v Cyprus (No. 2)* at para. 24.
24. *Aziz v Cyprus (No 2)*.
25. *Aziz v Cyprus (No 2)* at para. 28.
26. See *Aziz v Cyprus (No 2)* at para. 22.
27. *Aziz v Cyprus (No 2)* at para. 15.
28. See John Stuart Mill, 'Some Considerations on Representative Government' in John Gray (ed.), *On Liberty and Other Essays* (Oxford: Oxford University Press, 2008).
29. See Kant, *The Metaphysics of Morals.*
30. See Immanuel Kant, *'Perpetual Peace'* in *On History*, trans. Lewis White Beck, Robert E. Anchor and Emil L. Fackenheim (United States: The Library of Liberal Arts, 1963), pp. 85–136.
31. My approach here is guided by Habermas. See Jürgen Habermas, *The Crisis of the European Union: A Response*, trans. Ciaran Cronin (Cambridge: Polity, 2012).

32. *Hirst v United Kingdom (No. 2) (application no.74025/01)* [2005] ECHR 681 (6 October 2005).
33. *Hirst v United Kingdom (No. 2)* at para. 42.
34. *Hirst v United Kingdom (No. 2)* at para. 43.
35. *Hirst v United Kingdom (No. 2)*.
36. *Hirst v United Kingdom (No. 2)* at para. 44.
37. *Hirst v United Kingdom (No. 2)* at para. 45.
38. *Hirst v United Kingdom (No. 2)* at para. 47.
39. *Hirst v United Kingdom (No. 2)*.
40. *Hirst v United Kingdom (No. 2)* at para. 47.
41. *Hirst v United Kingdom (No. 2)* at para. 48.
42. *Hirst v United Kingdom (No. 2)* at para. 50.
43. *Hirst v United Kingdom (No. 2)*.
44. *Hirst v United Kingdom (No. 2)* at para. 51.
45. *Hirst v United Kingdom (No. 2)* at para. 52.
46. They also made stranger arguments I feel barely warrant serious consideration. The Government maintained that the impact of the ban on Mr Hirst would not change since he was imprisoned for life and was therefore unlikely to benefit from a more targeted ban. Beyond making this argument, unusually particular for a legal case being decided at the ECtHR, the logic of this position is very unusual. It amounts to saying that, since any policy shift beyond outright enfranchisement for all prisoners would not benefit Mr Hirst, the European Court should refrain from ruling in his favour. Perhaps this salient point is why the European Court simply decided to push the UK towards enfranchising all prisoners regardless of the duration of their sentence.
47. See *Hirst v United Kingdom (No. 2)* at para. 56.
48. *Hirst v United Kigdom (No. 2)*.
49. *Hirst v United Kingdom (No. 2)* at para. 59.
50. *Hirst v United Kingdom (No. 2)*.
51. *Hirst v United Kingdom (No. 2)* at para. 62.
52. *Hirst v United Kingdom (No. 2)* at para. 62.
53. *Hirst v United Kingdom (No. 2)* at para. 62.
54. *Hirst v United Kingdom (No. 2)* at para. 69.
55. *Hirst v United Kingdom (No. 2)* at para. 70
56. *Hirst v United Kingdom (No. 2)* at para. 45.
57. *Hirst v United Kingdom (No. 2)* at para. 2.
58. *Hirst v United Kingdom (No. 2)* at para. 4.
59. See *Hirst v United Kingdom (No. 2)* and the dissenting opinion at para. 3.
60. *Hirst v United Kingdom (No. 2)* at para. 9.

61. See the dissenting opinion of Judge Costa in *Hirst v United Kingdom (No. 2)* at paras 8–9.
62. See Plato, '*Crito*' in *The Republic and Other Works*, trans. Benjamin Jowett (United States: Anchor Books, 1960).
63. See *Riza and Others v Bulgaria (applications nos. 48555/10 and 48377/10).*
64. *Riza and Others v Bulgaria.*
65. *Riza and Others v Bulgaria.*
66. *Riza and Others v Bulgaria.*
67. See *Riza and Others v Bulgaria* at para. 137.
68. *Riza and Others v Bulgaria.*
69. *Riza and Others v Bulgaria* at para. 142.
70. *Riza and Others v Bulgaria* at para. 148.
71. *Riza and Others v Bulgaria* at para. 141.
72. *Riza and Others v Bulgaria* at para. 178.
73. *Riza and Others v Bulgaria* at para. 179.
74. Mahita Gajanan, 'Here Are The Only Times The US Government Can Revoke Your Citizenship', *Times Magazine*, 29 November 2016: *http://time.com/4584784/donald-trump-flag-burn-citizenship/*
75. 'Bulgaria Muslim Mayor to Alarm Europe About Ethnic Terror', *Novinite.com*, 29 September 2009: *http://www.novinite.com/articles/108301/Bulgaria+Muslim+Mayor+to+Alarm+Europe+about+Ethnic+Terror*
76. For an interesting account of these problems in a domestic legal system, see Hazel Genn, *Paths to Justice: What People Do and Think about Going to Law* (Oxford: Hart Publishing, 1999).
77. See *Citizens United v Federal Election Commission*, No. 08-205, 558 U.S. 310 (2010).

Chapter 6

1. Sakiko Fukuda-Parr, Terra Lawson-Remer and Susan Randolph, *Fulfilling Social and Economic Rights* (Oxford: Oxford University Press, 2015), p. 7.
2. For a summary, see, among other pieces, Matthew McManus, 'What is Post-modern Conservatism?' *Philosophical Salon*, 18 December 2017*: https://thephilosophicalsalon.com/post-modern-conservatism/*
3. Jack Donnelly. *Universal Human Rights in Theory and Practice: Third Edition* (Ithaca: Cornell University Press, 2013), pp. 43–44.
4. Thomas Piketty, *Capital in the Twenty-First Century*, trans. Arthur Goldhammer (Cambridge: Belknap Press, 2014).
5. See Jordan Peterson, 'The Inequality of Wealth and Productivity': *https://www.youtube.com/watch?v=6QOPCDEJWek*

6. Patrick Deneen, 'After Liberalism: Can We Imagine a Humane, Post-Liberal Future?', *Religion and Ethics*, December 2014: *http://www.abc.net.au/religion/articles/2014/12/11/4146762.htm*
7. Josh Hoxie,'Trump's Tax Cuts are the Biggest Wealth Grab in Modern History', *Fortune*, 3 November 2017: *http://fortune.com/2017/11/03/trump-gop-tax-plan-cuts-2017/*
8. Juliette Legendre, 'Emmanuel Macron was Supposed to be the Anti-Trump. He's not', *Inequality*, 22 February 2018: *https://inequality.org/research/macron-economic-policy-labor-taxes/*
9. Noah Kirsch, 'The 3 Richest Americans Hold More Wealth Than the Bottom 50% of the Country', *Forbes*, 9 November 2017: *https://www.forbes.com/sites/noahkirsch/2017/11/09/the-3-richest-americans-hold-more-wealth-than-bottom-50-of-country-study-finds/#18fa42b23cf8*
10. Joe Myers, 'Millennials will be the First Generation to Earn Less than their Parents', *World Economic Forum*, 19 July 2016: *https://www.weforum.org/agenda/2016/07/millennials-will-be-the-first-generation-to-earn-less-than-their-parents/*
11. World Bank, 'Poverty Overview' World Bank IBRD+IDA: *http://www.worldbank.org/en/topic/poverty/overview*, last updated 11 April 2018.
12. Jonathan Gregson, 'The World's Richest and Poorest Countries', *Global Finance*, 3 February 2017: *https://www.gfmag.com/global-data/economic-data/worlds-richest-and-poorest-countries*
13. Oxfam, 'Global Campaign for Education', *Oxfam*, 2010: *https://www.oxfamblogs.org/eastafrica/wp-content/uploads/2010/09/Global-Campaign-for-Education-report1.pdf*, at p. 5
14. Oxfam, 'Food, Farming, and Hunger', *Oxfam*: *https://www.oxfamamerica.org/explore/stories/food-farming-and-hunger/*
15. UNICEF, 'The Reality of Malaria', *UNICEF*: *https://www.unicef.org/health/files/health_africamalaria.pdf*
16. WHO, 'Annex B: Tables of Health Statistics by Country, WHO Region and Globally', *World Health Organization 2015: World Health Statistics. http://www.who.int/gho/publications/world_health_statistics/2016/EN_WHS2016_AnnexB.pdf?ua=1*
17. Fukuda-Parr, Lawson-Remer and Randolph, *Fulfilling Social and Economic Rights*, p. 158.
18. See John Rawls, *A Theory of Justice* (Cambridge: Harvard University Press, 1971).
19. Special Report, 'The Secret of Their Success: The Nordic Countries Are Probably the Best Governed in the World', *The Economist*, 2 February 2013: *https://www.economist.com/special-report/2013/02/02/the-secret-of-their-success*

20. See the work of G. A. Cohen as a model for arguing for such a conception of justice: G. A. Cohen, *Karl Marx's Theory of History: A Defence* (Princeton: Princeton University Press, 1980).
21. See Jordan Peterson, *12 Rules for Life: An Antidote to Chaos* (Toronto: Random House Canada, 2018) Chapter One.
22. *Soobramoney v Minister of Health (Kwazulu-Natal) (CCT32/97)* [1997] ZACC 17; 1998 (1) SA 765 (CC); 1997 (12) BCLR 1696 (27 November 1997).
23. See Martha Nussbaum, *Creating Capabilities: The Human Development Approach* (Cambridge: Harvard University Press, 2011), pp. 33–5.
24. See Martha Nussbaum, *Not for Profit: Why Democracy Needs the Humanities* (Princeton: Princeton University Press, 2012).
25. *DH and Others v Czech Republic (No. 57325/00).*
26. *DH and Others v Czech Republic).*
27. *DH and Others v Czech Republic)* at para. 7.
28. *DH and Others v Czech Republic* at para. 26.
29. *DH and Others v Czech Republic.*
30. *DH and Others v Czech Republic* at para. 147.
31. *DH and Others v Czech Republic.*
32. *DH and Others v Czech Republic* at para. 158.
33. *DH and Others v Czech Republic* at para. 176.
34. *DH and Others v Czech Republic* at para. 175.
35. *DH and Others v Czech Republic* at para. 181.
36. *DH and Others v Czech Republic* at para. 207.
37. *DH and Others v Czech Republic* (dissenting opinion of Judge Jungweirt at para. 7).
38. *DH and Others v Czech Republic* (dissenting opinion of Judge Jungweirt at para. 11).
39. *DH and Others v Czech Republic* (dissenting opinion of Judge Borrego at para. 5).
40. *DH and Others v Czech Republic* (dissenting opinion of Judge Borrego at para. 14).
41. I am deploying this as a case study rather than ultimately trying to solve the issue at hand. Not being an expert on either educational policy or the Roma people, I am unsure of what steps might be taken to respect the right of the children to an education. However, given the dramatically low success rate of the special schools, and their tendency to substantively discriminate against Roma children, I am confident in saying with the majority that more efforts should have been made to develop a viable solution.
42. Though of course, given the fallout from the financial crises, Brexit, and the rise of new forms of right-wing populism along the eastern edges of the

continent, even the States within the European Union have occasionally struggled to maintain their legitimacy in the face of mounting criticism.

43. *Government of the Republic of South Africa and Others v Grootboom and Others (CCT11/00)* [2000] ZACC 19; 2001 (1) SA 46; 2000 (11) BCLR 1169.
44. *Government of the Republic of South Africa and Others v Grootboom and Others* at paras 1 and 2.
45. *Government of the Republic of South Africa and Others v Grootboom and Others* at para. 6.
46. *Government of the Republic of South Africa and Others v Grootboom and Others* at para. 27.
47. *Government of the Republic of South Africa and Others v Grootboom and Others* at para. 23.
48. *Government of the Republic of South Africa and Others v Grootboom and Others* at para. 25.
49. *Government of the Republic of South Africa and Others v Grootboom and Others* at para. 27.
50. *Government of the Republic of South Africa and Others v Grootboom and Others* at para. 29.
51. *Government of the Republic of South Africa and Others v Grootboom and Others* at para. 31.
52. *Government of the Republic of South Africa and Others v Grootboom and Others (CCT11/00)* [2000] ZACC 19; 2001 (1) SA 46; 2000 (11) BCLR 1169 at para. 33.
53. *Government of the Republic of South Africa and Others v Grootboom and Others* at para. 35.
54. *Government of the Republic of South Africa and Others v Grootboom and Others* at para. 35.
55. *Government of the Republic of South Africa and Others v Grootboom and Others*at para. 43.
56. *Government of the Republic of South Africa and Others v Grootboom and Others* at para. 45.
57. *Government of the Republic of South Africa and Others v Grootboom and Others* at para. 75.
58. *Government of the Republic of South Africa and Others v Grootboom and Others* at para. 78.
59. *Government of the Republic of South Africa and Others v Grootboom and Others* at para. 83.
60. *Government of the Republic of South Africa and Others v Grootboom and Others* at para. 94.

61. As well noted by Hart throughout *The Concept of Law* and other works. For Hart, the South African apartheid regime, alongside Nazi Germany, was a paradigm case of a bad legal system. It was also instructive when clarifying his distinction between those who are 'obliged' by coercion to obey the law, and those who feel 'obligated' to obey it for social and other normative reasons. Hart's observation is that there is no need to have a substantial majority of the citizens onside in order for a legal system to operate functionally. In the South African context, the black majority may very well have felt 'obliged' to obey the laws passed by the apartheid regime, while feeling few moral 'obligations' to do so. Interestingly enough, Mrs Grootboom's act of civil disobedience in seizing land to provide shelter for herself and her family after suffering from decades of racial oppression can be linked to more general and philosophical questions about legal obligation. Interestingly enough, the South African court in the *Grootboom* case seems to toe a careful line between positioning itself as the positivistic arbiter of the law, since "rights" are now justiciable and they are obligated to enforce them, and adopting a borderline natural law position invoking human dignity as a normative orientation for the entire legal system. Naturally I am quite inclined towards the second position, though as I indicated before, this work should not unambiguously seem to adhere to most features normally affiliated with the natural law tradition. For the reference to Hart's work, see H. L. A. Hart, *The Concept of Law*, 2nd edn (Oxford: Oxford University Press, 1997).
62. A worthwhile scholarly look at these topics is Darian-Smith's. See Eve Darian-Smith, *Laws and Societies in Global Contexts: Contemporary Approaches* (Cambridge: Cambridge University Press, 2013).
63. See Pearlie Joubert, 'Grootboom Dies Homeless and Penniless', *Mail and Guardian*, 8 August 2008: *https://www.mg.co.za/article/2008-08-08-grootboom-dies-homeless-and-penniless*
64. Slavoj Žižek, 'In the Wake of the Paris Attacks the West Must Embrace Its Radical Western Roots', *In These Times*, 16 November 2015: *http://inthesetimes.com/article/18605/breaking-the-taboos-in-the-wake-of-paris-attacks-the-left-must-embrace-its*
65. For an elaboration of the philosophical dimensions of this view, see Slavoj Žižek, *Less than Nothing: Hegel and the Shadow of Dialectical Materialism* (London and New York: Verso Press, 2012); and Slavoj Žižek. *The Parallax View* (Boston: MIT Press, 2006).
66. Slavoj Žižek, 'Liberal Multiculturalism Masks an Old Barbarism With A Human Face', *The Guardian*, 3 October 2010: *https://www.theguardian.com/commentisfree/2010/oct/03/immigration-policy-roma-rightwing-europe*

67. *Choc v Hudbay Minerals Inc.*, 2013 ONSC 1414.
68. *Ontario (Attorney General) v Fraser*, 2011 SCC 20.
69. Hannah Arendt, *The Origins of Totalitarianism* (New York: Harcourt, 1955), p. 177.
70. These institutional apparatuses are variably effective, and have come under considerable strain in recent years; especially in the European Union, which has been rocked by formidable controversies about whether and how to resettle primarily Islamic refugees fleeing from conflicts in Syria and elsewhere. And there has been the recent travel ban imposed by the American Trump administration preventing individuals, primarily from Muslim majority countries, from entering the United States.
71. *A.S. v Switzerland (application no. 39350/13).*
72. *A.M.E. v The Netherlands (application no. 51428/10)*, 13.
73. *Choc v Hudbay Minerals Inc.*, 2013 ONSC 1414.

Chapter 7

1. See Lon Fuller, *The Morality of Law*, revised edn (New Haven and London: Yale University Press, 1969) and Ronald Dworkin, *Law's Empire* (Cambridge: Harvard University Press, 1986) for representative examples. Fuller and Dworkin both believe that law is fundamentally a moral idea which places restraints on what can viably be done by states in the name of legality. To the extent that the state goes beyond these constraints, even if it claims to be acting in a legal manner, its policies and rules are not law. The reasons given for this position are complex and powerful, and to my mind far more convincing than the classical natural law type reasoning given by individuals such as Finnis, who I already discussed in an earlier footnote. Fuller and Dworkin appeal to the nature of legal reasoning and the logic of morality, arguing that there is no integral or logical way to push the law to do certain things while having it remain law. An example would be not treating like cases alike. Though this does certainly essentialize he concept of legal beyond what I would be willing to accept, it is a compelling claim. Unfortunately, there was no space to deal with it in this work.
2. This was a common complaint of more dogmatic Marxists. See Michael Mandel, *The Charter of Rights and the Legalization of Politics in Canada* (Toronto: Thompson Educational Publishing, 1994).

Bibliography

Books, Reports and Articles

ACLU, 'Voting with a Criminal Record' American Civil Liberties Union, accessed March 2018: *https://www.aclu.org/other/voting-criminal-record-executive-summary*

Agamben, Giorgio, *Homo Sacer: Sovereign Power and Bare Life*, trans. Daniel Heller-Roazen. (Stanford: Stanford University Press, 1998)

Anghie, Antony, 'Francisco de Vitoria and the Colonial Origins of International Law' *Social Legal Studies*, 5 (1996)

Arendt, Hannah, *The Origins of Totalitarianism* (New York: Harcourt, 1955)

Austin, John, *The Province of Jurisprudence Determined (and The Uses of the Study of Jurisprudence)* (Indianapolis: Hackett Publishing, 1998)

Barak, Aharon, *Human Dignity: The Constitutional Value and the Constitutional Right* (Cambridge: Cambridge University Press, 2015)

Bayefsky, Rachel, 'Dignity, Honor, and Human Rights: Kant's Perspective', *Political Theory*, 41 (2013)

Beitz, Charles R, 'Human Rights and the Law of Peoples', in D. K. Chatterjee, *The Ethics of Assistance: Morality and the Distant Needy* (Cambridge: Cambridge University Press, 2004)

Benhabib, Seyla, *Democracy and Difference: Contesting the Boundaries of the Political* (Princeton. Princeton University Press, 1996)

Benhabib, Seyla, *Dignity in Adversity: Human Rights in Troubled Times* (Cambridge: Polity, 2011)

Benhabib, Seyla, *The Rights of Other: Aliens, Residents, and Citizens* (Cambridge: Cambridge University Press, 2004)

Bolton, John, 'Is There Really "Law" in International Affairs?', *Transnational and Contemporary Problems*, 1 (2000)

Bolton, John, 'John Bolton on Law, International Law, and American Sovereignty', *American Enterprise Institute*, 11 January 2011: *http://www.aei.org/publication/john-bolton-on-law-international-law-and-american-sovereignty/*

Bork, Robert, *Coercing Virtue: The Worldwide Rule of Judges* (Toronto: Vintage Canada, 2002)

Brandom, Robert, 'Intentionality and Language: A Normative, Pragmatist, Inferentialist Approach', in N. J. Enfield, Paul Kockelman and Jack Sidnell (eds), *The Cambridge Handbook of Linguistic Anthropology* (Cambridge: Cambridge University Press, 2014)

Brubaker, Rogers, *Citizenship and Nationhood in France and Germany* (Cambridge: Harvard University Press, 1992)

Burke, Edmund, *Reflections on the Revolution in France* (Oxford: Oxford University Press, 2009)

Capps, Patrick, *Human Dignity and the Foundations of International Law* (London: Bloomsbury Publishing, 2009)

Chomsky, Noam, *On Language: Chomsky's Classic Works Language and Responsibility and Reflections on Language* (New York: The New Press, 2007)

Cohen, G. A., *Karl Marx's Theory of History: A Defence* (Princeton: Princeton University Press, 1980)

Coughlin, John, 'Pope John Paul II and the Dignity of the Human Being' *Harvard Journal of Law and Social Policy*, 27 (2003)

Cruvellier, Thierry, 'The ICC, Out of Africa' *The New York Times*, 6 November 2016: *https://www.nytimes.com/2016/11/07/opinion/the-icc-out-of-africa.html*

Darian-Smith, Eve, *Laws and Societies in Global Contexts: Contemporary Approaches* (Cambridge: Cambridge University Press, 2013)

Dembour, Marie-Bénédicte, 'Gaygusuz Revisited: The Limits of the European Court of Human Rights' Equality Agenda', *Human Rights Law Review* 12 (2012)

Deneen, Patrick, 'After Liberalism: Can We Imagine a Humane, Post-Liberal Future?' *Religion and Ethics*, December 2014: *http://www.abc.net.au/religion/articles/2014/12/11/4146762.htm*

Donnelly, Jack, *Universal Human Rights in Theory and Practice*, 3rd edn (Ithaca: Cornell University Press, 2013)

Douzinas, Costas, *The End of Human Rights: Critical Thought at the Turn of the Century* (Oxford: Hart Publishing, 2000)

Dworkin, Ronald, *Justice for Hedgehogs* (Cambridge: Harvard University Press, 2010)

Dworkin, Ronald, *Law's Empire* (Cambridge: Harvard University Press, 1986)

Dworkin, Ronald, 'Objectivity and Truth: You Better Believe It' *Philosophy and Public Affairs*, 25, 1996

Economist-Lessons, 'The Secret of Their Success: The Nordic Countries Are Probably the Best Governed in the World' *The Economist*, 2 February 2013: *https://www.economist.com/special-report/2013/02/02/the-secret-of-their-success*

Ewald, William, 'Unger's Philosophy: A Critical Legal Study', *Yale Law Journal*, 97 (1988)

Ewick, Patricia and Silbey, Susan, *The Common Place of Law: Stories From Everyday Life* (Chicago: University of Chicago Press, 1998)

Fanon, Frantz, *The Wretched of the Earth* (New York: Grove Press, 2004)

Finnis, John, 'The Critical Legal Studies Movement', *American Journal of Jurisprudence* (30), 1985

Finnis, John, *Natural Law and Natural Rights*, 2nd edn (Oxford: Oxford University Press, 2011)

Foucault, Michel, *The Birth of Biopolitics: Lectures at the College de France 1978–1979*, trans. Graham Burchell (New York: Picador. 2008)

Fukuda-Parr, Sakiko, Terra Lawson-Remer and Susan Randolph, *Fulfilling Social and Economic Rights* (Oxford: Oxford University Press, 2015)

Fuller, Lon, *The Morality of Law*, revised edn (New Haven and London: Yale University Press, 1969)

Gabel, Peter, 'Critical Legal Studies as Spiritual Practice', *Pepperdine Law Review*, 36 (2012)

Gajanan, Mahita, 'Here Are The Only Times The US Government Can Revoke Your Citizenship' *Times Magazine*, 29 November 2016: *http://time.com/4584784/donald-trump-flag-burn-citizenship/*

Genn, Hazel, *Paths to Justice: What People Do and Think about Going to Law* (Oxford: Hart Publishing, 1999).

Giri, Ananta, 'Rethinking Human Well-being: A Dialogue with Amartya Sen', *Journal of International Development*, 12 (2000)

Gregson, Jonathan, 'The World's Richest and Poorest Countries', *Global Finance*, 3 February 2017: *https://www.gfmag.com/global-data/economic-data/worlds-richest-and-poorest-countries*

Habermas, Jürgen, *The Crisis of the European Union: A Response*, trans. Ciaran Cronin (Cambridge: Polity, 2012)

Habermas, Jürgen, *The Divided West*, trans. (London: Polity Press, 2006)

Habermas, Jürgen, 'Human Dignity and the Realistic Utopia of Human Rights', *Metaphilosophy*, 41, 2010

Hardt, Michael and Antonio Negri, *Empire* (Cambridge: Harvard University Press, 2000)

Harrington, Alexandra R., 'Don't Mind the Gap: The Rise of Individual Complaint Mechanisms Within International Human Rights Treaties', *Duke Journal of Comparative and International Law*, 22 (2012)

Hart, H. L. A., *The Concept of Law*, 2nd edn (Oxford: Oxford University Press, 1997)

Hart, H. L. A., 'Positivism and the Separation of Law and Morals', *Harvard Law Review*, 71, 1958

Hegel, Georg Wilhelm Friedrich, *The Philosophy of Right*, trans. S. W. Dyde (New York: Dover Press, 2005)

Heidegger, Martin, *Being and Time*, trans. John Macquarrie and Edward Robinson (San Francisco: Harper Collins, 1962)

Herder, J. G., *Another Philosophy of History and Selected Political Writings*, trans. Ioannis D. Evrigenis and Daniel Pellerin (Indianapolis: Hackett Publishing Inc, 2004)

Hobbes, Thomas, *Leviathan* (London: Penguin Books, 1982)

Holmes, Oliver Wendell, 'The Path of the Law', *Harvard Law Review*, 457

Hume, David, 'Of the Dignity or Meanness Of Human Nature' *Commonlit*, accessed 20 June 2018: *https://commonlit.s3.us-west-2.amazonaws.com/texts/student_pdfs/000/000/324/original/*

Hutchinson, Allan, 'Judges and Politics: An Essay From Canada', *Supreme Court Law Review*, 25 (2004)

Hutchinson, Allan, *Waiting for C.O.R.A.F.* (Toronto: University of Toronto Press, 1995)

Jackson, Robert, 'Opening Statement Before the International Military Tribunal' *Robert H. Jackson Center*, retrieved 5 April 2018: *https://www.roberthjackson.org/speech-and-writing/opening-statement-before-the-international-military-tribunal/*

Joubert, Pearlie, 'Grootboom Dies Homeless and Penniless' *Mail and Guardian*, 8 August 2008: *https://www.mg.co.za/article/2008-08-08-grootboom-dies-homeless-and-penniless*

Kant, Immanuel, *Groundwork to the Metaphysics of Morals*, trans. Herbert James Paton (New York: Harper Torchbooks, 1964)

Kant, Immanuel, *The Metaphysics of Morals*, trans. Mary Gregor (Cambridge: Cambridge University Press, 1996)

Kant, Immanuel, *On History*, trans. Lewis White Beck, Robert E. Anchor and Emil. L. Fackenheim (United States: The Library of Liberal Arts, 1957)

Kateb, George, *Human Dignity* (Cambridge: Belknap Press, 2011)

Kelsen, Hans, *The Pure Theory of Law*, trans. Max Knight (United States: Lawbook Exchange Limited, 2008)

Kennedy, Duncan, *A Critique of Adjudication (Fin De Siècle)* (Cambridge: Harvard University Press, 1997)

Kierkegaard, Søren, *Concluding Unscientific Postscript to Philosophical Fragments* trans. Howard Hong. (Princeton: Princeton University Press, 1992)

Kirsch, Noah, 'The 3 Richest Americans Hold More Wealth Than the Bottom 50% of the Country' *Forbes*, 9 November 2017: *https://www.forbes.com/sites/noahkirsch/2017/11/09/the-3-richest-americans-hold-more-wealth-than-bottom-50-of-country-study-finds/#18fa42b23cf8*

Kripke, Saul, 'Speaker's Reference and Semantic Reference', in Saul Kripke, *Philosophical Troubles* (Oxford: Oxford University Press, 2011)

Laclau, Ernesto and Chantal Mouffe, *Hegemony and Socialist Strategy*, 2nd edn (London: Verso Press, 2014)

Legendre, Juliette, 'Emmanuel Macron was Supposed to be the Anti-Trump. He's not', *Inequality*, 22 February 2018: https://inequality.org/research/macron-economic-policy-labor-taxes/

Lyotard, Jean-François, *The Postmodern Condition: A Report on Knowledge*, trans. Geoff Bennington and Brian Massumi (Minneapolis: University of Minnesota Press, 1984)

Macklem, Patrick, 'What is International Human Rights Law?: Three Applications of a Distributive Account', *McGill Law Journal*, 52 (2007)

Macklin, Ruth, 'Dignity is a Useless Concept', *British Medical Journal*, 327 (2003)

Mandel, Michael, *The Charter of Rights and the Legalization of Politics in Canada* (Toronto: Thompson Educational Publishing, 1994)

Marx, Karl, *Capital Volume One: A Critique of Political Economy*, trans. Ernest Mandel (London: Penguin Books, 1990)

McManus, Matthew, 'Making Human Dignity Central to International Law', *The New Jurist*, 24 March 2017

McManus, Matthew, 'What is Post-modern Conservatism?', *Philosophical Salon*, 18 December 2017: *https://thephilosophicalsalon.com/post-modern-conservatism/*

Mill, John Stuart, 'Some Considerations on Representative Government', in John Gray (ed.), *On Liberty and Other Essays* (Oxford: Oxford University Press, 2008)

Mirandola, Pico Della, 'Oration on the Dignity of Man', *The Website of Professor Paul Brians*, Washington State University, accessed November 2017: *https://*

brians.wsu.edu/2016/11/14/pico-della-mirandola-oration-on-the-dignity-of-man-15th-c-ce/

Moyn, Samuel, *The Last Utopia: Human Rights in History* (Cambridge: Harvard University Press, 2012)

Moyn, Samuel, 'The Secret History of Constitutional Dignity', *Yale Human Rights and Development Journal*, 17 (2014)

Myers, Joe, 'Millennials will be the First Generation to Earn Less than their Parents', *World Economic Forum*, 19 July 2016: *https://www.weforum.org/agenda/2016/07/millennials-will-be-the-first-generation-to-earn-less-than-their-parents/*

Nagel, Thomas, *Equality and Partiality* (Oxford: Oxford University Press, 1991)

Nicholas, Jeff, *Reason, Tradition, and the Good: MacIntyre's Tradition Constituted Reason and Frankfurt School Critical Theory* (Notre-Dame: University of Notre Dame Press, 2012)

Nozick, Robert, *Anarchy, State, and Utopia* (New York: Basic Books, 1974)

Nussbaum, Martha, *Creating Capabilities: The Human Development Approach* (Cambridge: Harvard University Press, 2011)

Nussbaum, Martha, *Frontiers of Justice: Disability, Nationality, Species Membership* (Cambridge: Belknap Press, 2006)

Nussbaum, Martha, 'Political Liberalism and Respect: A Response to Linda Barclay', *SATS: The Northern European Journal of Philosophy*, 4 (2003)

Nussbaum, Martha, *Not for Profit: Why Democracy Needs the Humanities* (Princeton: Princeton University Press, 2012)

Oakeshott, Michael, *Rationalism in Politics and Other Essays* (Indianapolis: Liberty Fund, 1991)

Oxfam, 'Food, Farming, and Hunger', *Oxfam*: *https://www.oxfamamerica.org/explore/stories/food-farming-and-hunger/*

Oxfam, 'Global Campaign for Education', *Oxfam*, 2010: *https://www.oxfamblogs.org/eastafrica/wp-content/uploads/2010/09/Global-Campaign-for-Education-report1.pdf*

Parfit, Derek, *On What Matters: Volume One* (Oxford: Oxford University Press, 2011)

Parfit, Derek, *On What Matters: Volume Two* (Oxford.: Oxford University Press, 2011)

Parfit, Derek, *Reasons and Persons* (Oxford: Oxford University Press, 1986)

Peterson, Jordan, *12 Rules for Life: An Antidote to Chaos* (Toronto: Random House Canada, 2018)

Piketty, Thomas, *Capital in the Twenty-First Century*, trans. Arthur Goldhammer (Cambridge: Belknap Press, 2014)

Pinker, Steven, 'The Stupidity of Dignity', *The New Republic*, 28 May 2008

Pollis, Adamantia and Peter Schwab, 'Human Rights: A Western Construct with Limited Applicability' in Pollis and Schwab (eds), *Human Rights. Cultural and Ideological Perspectives* (New York: Praeger, 1979)

Quataert, Jean H., *Advocating Dignity: Human Rights Mobilizations in Global Politics* (Philadelphia: University of Philadelphia Press, 2009)

Rawls, John, 'The Idea of Public Reason Revisited', *University of Chicago Law Review*, 64, 1997

Rawls, John, *Justice as Fairness: A Restatement* (Cambridge: Belknap Press, 2001)

Rawls, John, *The Law of Peoples: With the 'Idea of Public Reason Revisited'* (Cambridge: Harvard University Press, 2001)

Rawls, John, *Political Liberalism* (New York: Columbia University Press, 1993)

Rawls, John, *A Theory of Justice* (Cambridge: Harvard University Press, 1971)

Raz, Joseph, *The Authority of Law*, 2nd edn (Oxford: Oxford University Press, 2009)

Raz, Joseph, *Between Authority and Interpretation: On the Theory of Law and Practical Reason* (Oxford: Oxford University Press, 2010)

Ripstein, Arthur, *Force and Agency: Kant's Legal and Political Philosophy* (Cambridge: Harvard University Press, 2009)

Robertson, David, *The Judge as Political Theorist: Contemporary Constitutional Review* (Princeton: Princeton Press, 2010)

Rorty, Richard, *Philosophy and Social Hope* (London: Penguin Books, 1999)

Rorty, Richard, 'Solidarity and Objectivity', in Michael Krausz (ed.), *Relativism: Interpretation and Confrontation* (Notre Dame: University of Notre-Dame Press, 1989)

Rosen, Michael, *Dignity: Its Meaning and History* (Cambridge: Harvard University Press, 2012)

Rousseau, Jean-Jacques, *The Social Contract* (London: Penguin Books, 1968)

Said, Edward, *Orientalism: 25th Anniversary Edition* (New York: Vintage Books, 2004)

Scalia, Antonin, *A Matter of Interpretation: Federal Courts and the Law* (Princeton: Princeton University Press, 1997)

Scanlon, T. M., *Why Does Inequality Matter?* (Oxford: Oxford University Press, 2018)

Scheffler, Samuel, *Human Morality* (Oxford: Oxford University Press, 1992)

Schlag, Pierre, 'The Empty Circles of Liberal Justification', *Michigan Law Review*, 96 (1997)

Schmitt, Carl, *The Concept of the Political* (Chicago: University of Chicago Press, 1996)

Schmitt, Carl, *The Concept of the Political: Expanded Edition* (Chicago: University of Chicago Press, 2007)

Schmitt, Carl, *Constitutional Theory*, trans. Jeffrey Seitzer (Durham: Duke University Press, 2008)

Schmitt, Carl, *The Leviathan in the State Theory of Thomas Hobbes* (Chicago: University of Chicago Press, 2008)

Schmitt, Carl, *The Nomos of the Earth in the International Law of Jus Publicum Europeaum* (Candor: Telos Press, 2006)

Schmitt, Carl, *Political Theology* (Chicago: University of Chicago Press, 2005)

Schneewind, J. B., *The Invention of Autonomy: A History of Modern Moral Philosophy* (Cambridge: Cambridge University Press, 1998)

Scruton, Roger, *Conservatism: An Invitation to the Great Tradition* (New York: All Points Books, 2017)

Sen, Amartya, *Commodities and Capabilities* (Oxford: Oxford University Press, 1999)

Sen, Amartya, *Development as Freedom* (New York: Anchor Books, 1999)

Sen, Amartya, *Inequality Re-Examined* (Cambridge: Harvard University Press, 1992)

Sen, Amartya, 'Isolation, Assurance, and the Social Rate of Discount', *Quarterly Journal of Economics*, 81(1)

Sidgwick, Henry, *The Methods of Ethics* (Indianapolis: Hackett Press, 1981)

Simon, Kenneth, 'Dworkin's Two Principles of Dignity: An Unsatisfactory Nonconsequentialist Account of Interpersonal Moral Duties', *Boston University Law Review*, 90 (2010)

Singer, Peter, 'Famine, Affluence, and Morality', *Philosophy and Public Affairs*, 1 (1972)

Singer, Peter, *The Most Good You Can Do: How Effective Altruism is Changing Ideas About Living Ethically* (New Haven: Yale University Press, reprinted 2016)

Shapiro, Scott, *Legality* (Cambridge: Belknap Press, 2011)

Spivak, Gayatri, *A Critique of Post-Colonial Reason: Toward A History of the Vanishing Present* (Cambridge: Harvard University Press, 1996)

Suttle, Oisin, 'Equality in Global Commerce: Towards a Political Theory of International Economic Law', *European Journal of International Law*, 25 (2015)

Thucydides, *The History of The Peloponnesian War*, trans. Richard Crawley (E-Book: Project Gutenberg, 1 May 2009), last updated 7 February 2013; accessed 3 March 2018: *https://www.gutenberg.org/files/7142/7142-h/7142-h.htm#link2HCH0026*

Unger, Roberto, *The Critical Legal Studies Movement: Another Time, Another Task* (Cambridge: Harvard University Press, 2015)

Unger, Roberto, *Knowledge and Politics* (New York: The Free Press, 1973)

Unger, Roberto, *Politics Volume One: False Necessity* (London: Verso Press, 2004)

Unger, Roberto, *Politics Volume Three: Plasticity Into Power (Comparative-Historical Studies on the Institutional Conditions of Economic and Military Success)* (London: Verso Press, 2004)

Unger, Roberto, *Passion: An Essay on Personality* (London: The Free Press, 1986)

Unger, Roberto, *The Self Awakened: Pragmatism Unbound* (Cambridge: Harvard University Press, 2007)

Unger, Roberto and Lee Smolin, *The Singular Universe and the Reality of Time: A Proposal in Natural Philosophy* (Cambridge: Cambridge University Press, 2014)

UNICEF, 'The Reality of Malaria', *UNICEF*: https://www.unicef.org/health/files/health_africamalaria.pdf

Waldron, Jeremy. *Dignity, Rank, and Rights* (Oxford: Oxford University Press, 2015)

Waldron, Jeremy, 'Dignity, Rank, and Rights: The Tanner Lectures on Human Value', lecture delivered at UC Berkeley, 21–23 April 2009

Waldron, Jeremy, 'Torture and Positive Law: Jurisprudence for the Whitehouse', *Columbia Law Review*, 105 (2005)

Walzer, Michael, *Spheres of Justice: A Defence of Pluralism and Equality* (New York: Basic Books, 1983)

Weinstock, Daniel, 'Integrating Intermediate Goods to Theories of Distributive Justice: The Importance of Platforms', *Res Publica*, 21 (2015)

Weinstock, Daniel, 'Motivating the Global Demos', *Metaphilosophy*, 40 (2009)

Wells, Thomas, 'Sen's Capability Approach', *Internet Encyclopedia of Philosophy: A Peer Reviewed Academic Source*

Whitehead, Alfred North, *Adventures of Ideas* (New York: The Free Press, 1967)

WHO, 'Annex B: Tables of Health Statistics by Country, WHO Region and Globally' *World Health Organization 2015: World Health Statistics*: *http://www.who.int/gho/publications/world_health_statistics/2016/EN_WHS2016_AnnexB.pdf?ua=1*

Wood, Allen, *Kant's Ethical Thought* (Cambridge: Cambridge University Press, 1999)

World Bank, 'Poverty Overview' World Bank IBRD+IDA: *http://www.worldbank.org/en/topic/poverty/overview*, last updated 11 April 2018

Wraight, Christopher, *The Ethics of Trade and Aid: development, charity or waste?* (London: Continuum Press, 2011)

Žižek, Slavoj, 'In the Wake of the Paris Attacks the West Must Embrace Its Radical Western Roots' *In These Times*, 16 November 2015: *http://inthesetimes.com/article/18605/breaking-the-taboos-in-the-wake-of-paris-attacks-the-left-must-embrace-its*

Žižek, Slavoj, *Less than Nothing: Hegel and the Shadow of Dialectical Materialism* (London and New York: Verso Press, 2012

Žižek, Slavoj, 'Liberal Multiculturalism Masks an Old Barbarism With A Human Face', *The Guardian*. 3 October 2010: *https://www.theguardian.com/commentisfree/2010/oct/03/immigration-policy-roma-rightwing-europe*

Žižek, Slavoj, *The Parallax View* (Boston: MIT Press, 2006)

Cases Cited

AME v The Netherlands (Application no. 51428/10)

AS v Switzerland (Application no. 39350/13)

Aziz v Cyprus (Application no. 69949/01)

Choc v Hudbay Minerals Inc., 2013 ONSC 1414

Citizens United v Federal Election Commission, No. 08-205, 558 U.S. 310 (2010)

DH and Others v Czech Republic (No. 57325/00)

Government of the Republic of South Africa and Others v Grootboom and Others (CCT11/00) [2000] ZACC 19; 2001 (1) SA 46; 2000 (11) BCLR 1169

Hirst v United Kingdom (Application no. 74025/01)

Lovelace v Canada, Communication No. 24/1977: Canada 30/07/81, UN Doc. CCPR/C/13/D/24/1977

Ontario (Attorney General) v Fraser, 2011 SCC 20

Richardson v Ramirez, 418 U.S. 24

Riza and Others v Bulgaria (nos 48555/10 and 48377/10)

Soobramoney v Minister of Health (Kwazulu-Natal) (CCT32/97) [1997] ZACC 17; 1998 (1) SA 765 (CC); 1997 (12) BCLR 1696 (27 November 1997)

Index

H

K

L

M

N

O

P

R